T. 50

TOUGHEST, MEANEST, SCARIEST

HARD-MEN

IN HURLING HISTORY

BY EDDIE RYAN

HERO BOOKS

PUBLISHED BY HERO BOOKS
LUCAN
CO. DUBLIN
IRELAND

Hero Books is an imprint of Umbrella Publishing

First Published 2023

A CIP record for this book is available from the British Library

ISBN 9781910827703

Cover design and formatting: jessica@viitaladesign.com
Photographs: Sportsfile

DEDICATION

To my inspirational partners-in-crime
Mary O'Shaughnessy Ryan & Freddie the 'Great'!

INTRODUCTION

*'THE TRUE SOLDIER FIGHTS NOT BECAUSE HE
HATES WHAT IS IN FRONT OF HIM, BUT BECAUSE HE
LOVES WHAT IS BEHIND HIM'*

– G.K. CHESTERTON

THEY WERE the 'Most Wanted'.

Fifty of the 'toughest', 'meanest', 'scariest' warriors ever assembled on a hurling field. A rare breed of men that had their county's colours coursing through their veins. Men whose deeds and misdeeds have left their fingerprints all over the history of the Liam MacCarthy Cup.

An elite band of warriors who never took a backward step, or ever bent their knee on the field of battle. They walked the line and took it to the very edge and sometimes beyond...

They were the sniping assassins who picked defender's pockets. They were merciless defenders, who placed a bounty on your head, then hunted you down to collect their blood money.

The men profiled in this book are no angels. They also, most certainly, are not demons. They were men who went to war with their hearts on their sleeves, their noble legacy forged in blood, sweat, and no little tears.

Wherever their county needed battles to be fought and conflicts to be won, these men of selfless courage helped turn the tide. Men who faced huge physical and mental battles, and even their own demons from within to answer their county's call.

Whatever sacrifices were asked, they delivered in spades. For the pride of their families and the honour of the parish. For the love of the GAA, and their unbridled passion for their county's crest.

They took the hits and returned them with interest, knowing no fear and willing to risk all consequences. They were the front-line soldiers, the first responders. The men who dared to venture... where angels fear to tread.

It was a responsibility they never took lightly, a cross they were willing to carry right to the very end. Even when all hope was lost, they were a shining light that raged against the swirling inevitability of defeat. They never gave up, as true warriors never do. When the end arrived, they all went out upon their shields.

The exchange between Colonel Nathan R. Jessup (Jack Nicholson), and Lt Daniel Kaffee (Tom Cruise), in the movie *A Few Good Men* provides a startling insight into the mind of a highly trained US marine. It is, in essence, the story of every man-of-war, and of the GAA's 'Most Wanted'.

Jessup pulls no punches as he takes us deep into the psyche of a fighting machine, and even deeper into the darkness of war.

'Son, we live in a world that has walls, and those walls have to be guarded by men with guns. Who's gonna do it? You? You, Lieutenant Weinberg? I have a greater responsibility than you can possibly fathom. You don't want the truth because deep down in places you don't talk about at parties, you want me on that wall

– you need me on that wall.

'We use words like "honour", "code", "loyalty". We use these words as the backbone of a life spent defending something. You use them as a punch line.

'I have neither the time nor the inclination to explain myself to a man who rises and sleeps under the blanket of the very freedom that I provide and then questions the manner in which I provide it.'

The players featured within these pages were the ones their county needed guarding the wall against enemy attackers. Men who used the words 'honour', 'code' and 'loyalty' not as a punchline, but as an ethos by which they lived and died during their magnificent careers.

It gives me great pleasure to introduce these remarkable men, whose incredible exploits have helped shape the course of hurling history.

The '50 Toughest, Meanest, Scariest, Hard-Men' in hurling history.

Eddie Ryan
September 2023

ACKNOWLEDGEMENTS

My thanks to my publisher, Liam Hayes, and all the hard-working team at Hero Books. Liam has set such a standard in the world of GAA, and journalism and publishing, it is an incredible honour to be able to collaborate on a subject so close to his heart.

To my wife, Mary, an amazing soul mate, thanks for all your hard work and endless support. Always smiling, always full of bright and breezy energy, your companionship is a gift that keeps on giving.

To my late mother, Mrs Dorcas Ryan, your love and courage, and incredible sacrifice is a debt that can never be repaid.

Thanks also to all the Cardiac Critical Care Unit and the Cystic Fibrosis teams at Limerick and Nenagh Hospitals, for their outstanding professionalism and loving care. Special thanks to my heart surgeon Dr Kiernan and Jacinta Glasgow, my nurse of 'endless patience' and excellence.

My thanks to *Ireland's Own* and my monthly editor, Shea Tomkins. Shea is a true sports fanatic and an incredible editor for the publication. To Sean Nolan and all the rest of the *Ireland's*

Own crew. It is a rare privilege to write for what is truly an Irish institution.

My thanks also to Mary's mum and dad, Val and Susan, who taught being parents was tough going – until their daughter landed them with the son-in-law from hell!

Thanks also to Anna Louise O'Shaughnessy – 'a true book lover.' Thanks to Mannie and Ruth, for all the craic and great days out. Special thanks also to my good friends, Oliver and Shelley, Lauren and Cathal, and to John Savage my manager!

Last, but not least, many thanks to all the good people of Roscrea… The town I loved so well.

Eddie Ryan
September 2023

CONTENTS

INTRODUCTION

PHOTOS AND TOP 50 LIST

OLLIE BAKER

(Height 6' 3", Weight 15 St)

Decade... 1990s/2000s

(Position... Midfield)

CHIEF CHARACTERISTIC... BAKER WHO TURNED UP
THE HEAT IN THE OPPOSITION KITCHEN

TOP ACCOMPLICES... COLIN LYNCH, ANTHONY DALY,
FERGAL HEGARTY, BRIAN LOHAN

OLLIE BAKER

*'I HAD A BACK-UP PLAN IN MY MIND. I THOUGHT THAT IF I
GOT AS FAR AS MATT THE THRESHER'S IN BIRDHILL, I'D
HANG ON INSIDE THERE AND LISTEN TO THE MATCH ON THE
RADIO AND SURELY SOMEONE COMING HOME FROM THE
MATCH WOULD GIVE ME A LIFT BACK TO BAREFIELD.'*

– OLLIE BAKER

'**B**US gone!

'I was thinking that they couldn't be gone too long, so the next stop was down in Clarecastle. The uncle drove me to Clarecastle, but they were gone from there too.

'The uncle then tore down the road to Newmarket... GONE! The last stop they had in the county was in Bunratty. My uncle was saying, "I've to go back to my mother's mass!" He dropped me to Bunratty. Bus gone from there too.

'There was my starting place gone.

'Everything... GONE!'

It was the one and only time he let the 'Banner' down, and it looked like his Clare career had hit the rocks... just as it was about to get started!

As auditions for a treasured slot on intercounty panels go, it's fair to say events couldn't have transpired much worse than they did for Ollie Baker. It would be his first full start for the county, and things certainly didn't go to plan.

**HARD
MAN
RATINGS**

TOUGHEST:
9.3/10

MEANEST:
8.5/10

SCARIEST:
9.4/10

HARDEST:
19.5/20

☠

TOTAL
HARD MAN

46.7/50

His grandmother's funeral was on the morning of the league fixture against Laois in Portlaoise, and Ollie, naturally enough, had mixed emotions. Having worked so hard to get his opportunity, it certainly looked like he had tossed it away as the events of a tumultuous day started to overtake him.

Ollie would go on to have much better days, but as he revealed long after his career had ended, it very nearly all went pear-shaped.

'This game sticks in my memory because my grandmother (Maureen Baker) passed away on the Thursday beforehand.

'The team had been named at training on the Thursday night and I was picked to start. I had come on in two games against Galway and Limerick, before Christmas. It was my first year on the panel and this was my first opportunity to get a starting jersey.

'These were the days before mobile phones. You generally found out you were named in the starting 15 when it came out in *The Clare Champion* on Thursday.

'Ger (Loughnane) and Mike (McNamara) came to the removal and shook hands with everyone. They presumed that when I wasn't there five minutes before the bus was leaving on the Sunday, that I wasn't going to turn up at all.

'At home, my father had said, "What are you doing hanging around here? Will you go away and play a game of hurling. There's nothing you can do here anyway. So go on away".

'My timekeeping, generally, is 'five minutes late'. So, my uncle Noel dropped me to the West County Hotel.'

The alarm bells were ringing for Ollie as his 'Banner' audition had gone badly awry. He was convinced Ger Loughnane and Mike 'Mac' would take a very dim view of his 'no show' at the various pick-up points for the senior side. Having secured a spot on the team, he was hoping to nail down a position for the championship and the Laois game would have provided him with the perfect dress rehearsal. Intercounty careers can be decided on the tightest of margins and as Ollie revealed, his window of opportunity was by now... diminishing fast.

'After being told to go to the match by my father, I knew I wasn't going to be welcome at home either. So that's why I had my thumb out, beside Bunratty Castle.

'It was getting tight enough at that stage. I had to make up my mind as to whether I was going to continue on. There were 20-minute intervals between every lift. I had a back-up plan in my mind. I thought that if I got as far as Matt the Thresher's in Birdhill, I'd hang on inside there and listen to the match on the radio, and surely someone coming home from the match would give me a lift back to Barefield.

'I had all that in my mind and the next thing, a car passed by. They jammed the brakes and reversed back. It was John Casey from Fanore. He was going to the match himself so I said, "That's great". The car was full but I was bundled into the back of it.

'There were a few questions about why I was late, and I was trying to explain myself. I hadn't known it but the team was stopping at The Racket Hall in Roscrea. I saw the bus as we were passing and I said, "I'll be grand here". John jammed again and I got out.'

{ ALL'S WELL THAT ENDS WELL }

'The players and management were coming out to the bus. Loughnane heard the story of how I got there and he said that he couldn't leave me off after that.

'As it turned out, I scored four points from midfield and a sideline cut. The next time I scored a point from a line-ball was in the All-Ireland final. I had a really good game and, in my own mind, I felt completely at home at that level.'

Baker's breathless dash had certainly been worth it – as he added an extra dimension to a Clare side built in the likeness of their manager.

Ollie and his midfield partner, Colin Lynch, who arrived in 1997, were just the pair of snarling enforcers, that Ger Loughnane was looking for. He loved a player with a bit of 'dog' in him, and Baker and Lynch were the pair of menacing Rottweillers they needed to patrol that crucial area of the battlefield.

Ollie Baker brought huge physicality to the middle sector the Banner had often struggled in. It also helped that Baker was a sublime stickman, whose party piece included sending sideline cuts sailing over the black spot. After Ollie's dream debut, Liam MacCarthy was locked and loaded for a civic reception in Ennis.

The hurling gods work in mysterious ways and Ollie's early misadventures were the only bump on the road in a glorious career as he went the extra mile to secure the Banner's rightful place in the history books.

A BAKER'S LIFE

OLIVER BAKER was born on July 14, 1974. He made his debut for the Banner in the 1994-95 National League fixture against Laois, scoring five points as Clare recorded a resounding victory by 1-17 to 0-5.

In a career that lasted almost a decade, he amassed a total of 1-18 from the middle of the park. After helping the Banner to a first All-Ireland in 81 years, he was also honoured with his first-ever All Star award. He won a further Celtic Cross in 1997 as Clare defeated old rivals Tipperary in both the Munster and All-Ireland Finals. He won three Munster titles, two All-Irelands, and two All Star awards during his senior career.

He played his club hurling with St Joseph's Doora-Barefield. Having negotiated the minefield of the Clare Championship – which included losing two championship deciders to Clarecastle, Baker won his first county senior championship medal in 1998 following a defeat of Kilmaley.

St Joseph's advanced to the Munster final, defeating Tipperary's, Toomevara. He later added an All-Ireland Club Championship medal to round off a memorable season. During his career with the club he won three Clare titles and two Munster medals, to add to his All-Ireland crown. He has also managed Offaly and Kilmacud Crokes and was a selector with Westmeath, Clare, and Antrim.

PHIL BENNIS

(Height 5' 9", Weight 14.5 St)

Decade... 1960s/1970s

(Position... Centre-Back)

CHIEF CHARACTERISTIC... LEADER OF
THE NOTORIOUS BENNIS GANG

TOP ACCOMPLICES... RICHIE BENNIS, EAMONN CREGAN, NED REA,
LIAM O'DONOGHUE, JIM O'BRIEN, SEAN FOLEY

PHIL BENNIS

'HE ROARED... "HEYYY RICHARD... RICHARD! IT'S TIME TO START
TAKING A FEW OF THESE F****** OUT!"'
– JOHN CALLANAN

BAND *of Brothers*, the Emmy Award-winning mini-series charts the fortunes of E Company
(Easy Company), 2nd Battalion, 506th Parachute Infantry
Regiment of the 101st Airborne Division, from jump training
in the United States through its participation in major actions in
Europe, up until Japan's capitulation and the end of World War II.

It was created by Steven Spielberg and Tom
Hanks, who also executively produced the show.
The pair had collaborated on the 1998 World
War II film *Saving Private Ryan*. The series is
based on Stephen E. Ambrose's 1992 non-fiction
book of the same name. The title of the book and
series comes from the St Crispin's Day Speech in
William Shakespeare's play *Henry V*, delivered by
King Henry before the Battle of Agincourt.

Ambrose cleverly intertwines the Bard of
Ayrshire's exquisite prose from the speech on
his book's first page; this passage is spoken by
Carwood Lipton in the epic, and tension-fuelled

**HARD
MAN
RATINGS**

TOUGHEST:
9.6/10

MEANEST:
9.3/10

SCARIEST:
9.2/10

HARDEST:
19.6/20

☠

TOTAL
HARD MAN

47.7/50

series finale. The stirring speech formed the title of the series which portrays all the bloodshed, hopelessness, and the savagery of modern warfare. It also elicits the finest of human traits… friendship, honour, sacrifice, and the bond that binds men eternally together – on the blood-soaked fields of war.

The Bennis 'Band of Brothers' were bound together by family plasma, and their DNA coded in 'Treaty' green and white. Back in 1966, at a time when Geoff Hurst's hat-trick ensured that 'Football would be coming home' for the first and only time, Patrickswell had six Bennis brothers playing. They would have numbered a 'Magnificent 7, had Seán not created a political storm, when he married into the other side of the parish and hurled for Ballybrown!

The 'Well were barely out of the womb when the Bennis boys were growing up. Richie Bennis asserted that its history, 'could have been kept on the back of a fag packet'.

The Bennis Brigade would ensure that the club's historians kept their pencils sharpened, winning two successive county titles in jig-time.

John Callanan, one of Clare's finest, takes us down memory lane in his autobiography from the 'Legends Series' with a story that features Phil as one of the central characters.

'Limerick were in their pomp as All-Ireland champions. Out of courtesy, we formed a guard of honour for Eamon Grimes and clapped Limerick out onto the field.'

The pleasantries, however, ended there. Shannonside derbies demand a certain level of intensity… and acrimony, as John revealed.

'The whole idea was to get stuck into them from the first

whistle. We did that. Then 10 minutes into the second-half, Vincent Loftus was sent off for a pull on Ned Rea. Gus Lohan was playing full-forward and he was brought down from the other end of the field to go full-back.

'As he was coming down, Ned Rea walked up along the sideline on the stand side with a cut on the head, but with the first aid men gathering around it looked much worse than it actually was.

'When he saw Rea passing by and saw the blood, Phil Bennis started hitting the ground with the flat of the hurley behind my heels. Phil was no shrinking violet.

'He roared… 'HEYYY RICHARD… RICHARD!

'It's time to start taking a few of these f****** out!'

'It was bravado after seeing their man bloodied and being helped off the field. The big row that threatened never happened though, but it was very tough.

'After he had been sent off by John Moloney, Loftus stood behind the goal and even intervened in the game on one occasion. In a moment of danger, he came back onto the field – it was his instinctive reaction. In the words of the referee afterwards he, 'Stopped the ball with his hurley from entering the Clare net'.

'In the dressing-room afterwards, Vincent was bending down, taking off his boots and I said, "Lofty, what happened… what happened?"

It was at this stage we were reminded about why we all love the Munster Senior Hurling Championship so much… as Callanan continues.

'It was my innocence of youth. And he looked up at me. "If he moved again, I would have hit him again". All is fair in love and war… and all that!'

Phil was honoured by a Mayoral reception from Cllr Sean Lynch in 2018. Lynch paid tribute to a herculean son of Limerick at a special ceremony at City Hall. Friends and dignitaries gathered to remember Phil's starring role in both the 'Well and Limerick's revival of fortunes, and the enduring legacy he left for future stars of the ilk of 2021 Hurler of the Year, and another proud son of Patrickswell, Cian Lynch.

'He brought a real air of respectability back to the game. He infused his team with purpose and real belief. A touch of steel as a player, who could be ruthless in management at times, making big calls for the better of the team,' Cllr Lynch added.

It was a fair summation of Phil's stellar career. Phil was one of the pillars that Limerick hurling history will forever lean upon.

A stir of echoes from the blood-soaked fields of battle bids him a fond farewell. A tribe, a brotherhood, bonded by blood and driven by a love so deep it is the very stuff the Limerick hurling universe is proudly built upon.

On the eve of the Battle of Agincourt, which fell on Saint Crispin's Day, Henry V urges his men, who were vastly outnumbered by the French, to imagine the glory and immortality that will be theirs… if they are victorious.

When Limerick called out in their darkest hurling hours, Phil Bennis and his band of Patrickswell brothers valiantly carried their camáns into battle and fought to the bitter end.

William Shakespeare's epic words pay homage to their memory.

But we in it shall be remembered
We few, we happy few, we band of brothers;
For he today that sheds his blood with me
Shall be my brother.

THE BROTHERHOOD

PHIL BENNIS was born near Limerick city in the heartland village of Patrickswell. Bennis played his club hurling with his local team. He was part of a famous generation of the club's underage hurlers who would rewrite parish history. After some successes at the schoolboy grades, Phil and his brothers would form the backbone of a golden crop, who would become one of the dominant forces in Limerick club hurling.

Patrickswell would enjoy tangible success when winning a host of coveted Limerick championship titles throughout the 1960s and 1970s. The profile of the club ensured Phil and his brother Richie would go on to become major components in the Limerick intercounty set-up, as they blazed a trail that would ultimately end up in All-Ireland glory.

Phil Bennis won a National League medal with Limerick in 1971. Limerick was a model of consistency in that period reaching five consecutive league finals.

They would lose out in four of them, but Phil did taste success winning the 1973 senior Munster title. He later won his first and only All-Ireland medal following a hard-fought victory over Kilkenny in the final.

At managerial level, he managed his native county for two separate spells in the late 1980s and early 1990s, winning the National League title in 1992.

DIARMAID BYRNES

(Height 6' 3", Weight 14.5 St)

Decade... 2010s/2020s

(Position... Wing-Back)

CHIEF CHARACTERISTIC... AIR TRAFFIC
CONTROL SHANNON REGION

TOP ACCOMPLICES... DECLAN HANNON, BARRY NASH, SEAN FINN,
NICKY QUAID, DAN MORRISSEY, WILL O'DONOGHUE

DIARMAID BYRNES

'MY PRIORITY IS THE TEAM, THE MAN IN FRONT OF ME, THE MAN BESIDE ME... AND LOOKING AFTER THE GROUP ALWAYS.'

– DIARMAID BYRNES

TUS GAELIC GROUNDS MAY 28, 2023.

Limerick's bid for hurling immortality was on life support. The second-half had ebbed and flowed – but Cork had stayed in the fight. This was not supposed to be the way it ended.

A beautiful sunny afternoon on Ennis Road was no place for Limerick to die. Yet death became them. A late penalty award hinted at an olive branch from the sporting gods.

John Kiely knew it was time to send for his most trusted soldier. Patrickwell's, Diarmaid Byrnes was the king of the long-range frees and just about everything else. The Banshees of Limerick hurling past whispered tales of never-ending sorrow as Byrnes lifted cleanly and sent a missile that would resonate across the corridors of time...

The book *Unlimited Heartbreak* chronicles the Treaty story as viewed through the lens of a hundred former players. The book is a candid, warts-and-all look inside the victories, defeats,

HARD MAN RATINGS

TOUGHEST:
9.5/10

MEANEST:
9.8/10

SCARIEST:
9.9/10

HARDEST:
19.8/20

☠

TOTAL HARD MAN

49.0/50

controversies, rows, and hard luck stories of a proud hurling county.

In September 1940, Limerick were crowned All-Ireland champions for the third time in six years. The Limerick minor team also collected national honours. The hurling world belonged to Limerick – so what happened next, would defy all logic or explanation. Limerick hurling would descend into eternal darkness, with just a solitary Liam MacCarthy win in 1973. Against all hope and reason, the Treaty never gave up believing.

He is, in many ways, the eye of the storm.

A towering, brooding figure, as tenacious a fighter as the Treaty has unleashed across the hurling landscape.

Here is a warrior who would unleash the thunder – driving the winds of change which would stiffen as they echoed across the Shannon. Slowly, but surely, Limerick would rise. The hurling world kept on turning – oblivious to the gathering squall...

JUNE 4, 2017, SEMPLE STADIUM THURLES.

Half-time couldn't come soon enough.

'Rock me, Mama, like a wagon wheel...'

Nathan Carter belted out over the PA, as the announcer put out an SOS for a missing wedding ring. At the interval in Thurles, the wedding ring wasn't the only thing missing.

Thankfully, nobody was touting the notion that this was a Munster Championship clash between warring neighbours. Challenge matches packed more of a punch than what resembled an afternoon bowls session between two octogenarians.

Newly installed Limerick hurling manager, John Kiely had gambled on youth; it was, at best, a spectacular misjudgment.

The game had never really got going – nor had Limerick. Kiely's 'bright young things,' had reinforced that old linear assertion that you cannot win anything with kids.

They say the scoreboard never lies, but this was a four-point hammering. Clare won while almost dozing off at the wheel. Limp and lifeless, Limerick hobbled out of the championship for the second season running. Shannonside derbies were renowned for their fire and fury, yet, there was little to stir the passions on or off the pitch.

Debutant, Kyle Hayes' late goal glossed over the proverbial damp squib. Barry Nash, Richie English, Tom Morrissey and Aaron Gillane all entered the fray – joining the callow on-field crew that contained Cian Lynch and Sean Finn.

It was cloudy as evening beckoned in the Field Of Legends. The mood among the Limerick faithful was sombre; it felt like they had mistakenly stumbled in on a wake. Chastened they scurried away, for fear of being identified as supporting a lost cause.

A few hastily discarded programmes flapped in the wind as an overweight cat chased a chip bag down Jimmy Doyle Road. Even the ginger feline appeared to have more heart for the battle than the timid Treaty men.

Diarmaid Byrnes did not play that evening, as he had sustained a knee injury that would keep him out of the championship. Byrnes was far from a household name in his own native county – a footnote from the previous train wreck of a season.

{ ESCAPING THE GHOSTS OF LIMERICK PAST }

Diarmaid Byrnes slipped away into the gathering gloom. In keeping with the order of the day, the cat gave up the ghost, spooked by another low rumble from the heavens.

Empires, however, can rise from humble origins. Forged from unbridled youth and flashes of untapped potential, the expected requiem for Limerick hurling would never arrive.

Byrnes and Limerick rehabilitated for the 2018 Championship with little fanfare. While not pulling up any trees, the Treaty finished third in the Munster round-robin and advanced in the All-Ireland series against Kilkenny.

Cork, the Munster champions, awaited in the penultimate stage and the 'Vegas Line' pointed to the Rebels advancing to the decider. Freed from the shackles of injury, Byrnes was giving a season-long masterclass in defending. Patrickwell's talisman was also chipping in with some outrageous points from play and placed balls. Limerick stuttered near the finish line but eventually prevailed – grateful for keeper Nick Quaid's miracle save.

Liberated at last, there was no stopping the monster.

Limerick laid waste to every hurling stronghold in Ireland, with a staggering run of five winning All-Irelands in six seasons.

Cork would remain central to the Limerick narrative, however, and when the sides clashed again, the Treaty's bid for four titles in-a-row was met with furious Rebel resistance.

TUS GAELIC GROUNDS MAY 28, 2023.

Nicky Quaid's miracle save seemed a lifetime away now as Diarmaid Byrnes stood over the ball. This was it, history in his hands. An eerie calm fell over the packed Gaelic Grounds. The gravity of the moment was incalculable, the tension unbearable.

Byrnes was ready. When you gaze into the eye of a stone-cold killer, you will only witness the darkness. Patrickswell's finest squeezed the trigger.

The only ones dying that day would hail from Cork...

Rebel goalkeeper, Patrick Collins hardly moved as the net danced. The ghosts and devils retreated back to their bastions of despair. By the time Collins retrieved the sliotar from the back of the goal, Diarmaid Byrnes was already back in position.

Ready to unleash the eye of the storm...

▸──→ IN A LIFETIME ←──◂

DIARMAID BYRNES was born in his native club's village of Patrickswell. He played at all levels and grades underage before graduating from the senior team. He won a Limerick Hurling Championship medal after scoring a half dozen points from centre-back in Patrickswell's 1-26 to 1-7 defeat of Ballybrown in the final in October 2016. Byrnes added a second title against Na Piarsaigh in October 2019.

Byrnes was at his brilliant best as the club added to its haul of 19 championships, cementing their position as market leaders within the county's senior hurling ranks.

He joined the Limerick under-21 hurling team, making his first appearance on June 4, 2014. In his second term in the grade, Byrnes won a Munster Championship title after a 0-22 to 0-19 win over Clare in the final. He later collected an All-Ireland medal as Limerick defeated Wexford in the All-Ireland final. He was also voted onto the Bord Gáis Energy Team of the Year.

He made his senior debut in February 2016 against Wexford in the National League. His first championship appearance arrived in a 3-12 to 1-16 defeat by Tipperary in Munster.

He has won a total of five All-Irelands, five Munster titles, and three National League titles. He was voted Hurler of the Year in 2022, and has won three All Star awards.

KIERAN CAREY

(Height 6' 0", Weight 14 St)

Decade... 1950s/1960s

(Position... Corner-Back)

CHIEF CHARACTERISTIC... GUARDIAN OF THE GATES OF HELL

TOP ACCOMPLICES... LEN GAYNOR, TONY WALL, MICHAEL MAHER,
JOHN DOYLE, JIMMY DOYLE, JOHN O'DONOHUE

KIERAN CAREY

'HE WILL LIVE LONG IN THE MEMORY AFTER THE REST OF US HAVE GONE.'

– JOHN COSTIGAN

WHILE repairing the embankment of the River Ribble in Cuerdale, near Preston in England, a group of workmen dug up a lead box. Inside was one of the biggest hoards of Viking treasure ever found; more than 8,600 items were documented, including silver coins, various bits of jewellery, and silver ingots.

When members of the Tipperary hurling selection panel travelled more in hope then expectation to a lowly 'Gold Watch Tournament' in the late 50s, they were to breathe life into an old truism... You can discover gold in the most unlikeliest of places.

The journey they undertook on a balmy summer's evening required a leap of faith. The 'ugly-duckling' of GAA competitions, the dreaded Gold Watch tournament, rarely yielded any hurling nuggets. The travelling party's excavations, however, would unearth one of the most significant finds in Tipperary hurling's

HARD MAN RATINGS

TOUGHEST:
9.4/10

MEANEST:
9.1/10

SCARIEST:
9.5/10

HARDEST:
19.5/20

☠

TOTAL HARD MAN

47.5/50

glittering history and the player who would provide the final piece of the Premier County jigsaw.

The raw uncut diamond would add the final coat of polish to one of the greatest defensive units in GAA history, and prove that Hell… ain't a bad place to be.

To opposition forces, he was the 'Beast'. Tales of his fearsome deeds were drenched in blood, sweat and tears. In hurling circles, he was the ultimate 'Urban Legend'.

The Reverend Billy Graham famously once said, 'Courage is contagious. When a brave man takes a stand, the spines of others are often stiffened'.

Those were lines he could well have penned about the man from Knock; the mere whisper of his name was enough to rally the troops, and send icy shivers down the enemies' spine.

For Kieran Carey, however, hell was never a bad place to be. Those who came bearing brimstone left with barely a whimper. Size nor strength, nor reputation, cowed him.

When the air raid sirens sounded, he hurled with a cold fury, a low humming engine.

He was a quiet, efficient dealer in realism.

He feasted gleefully on the bones of seasoned veterans, or new recruits, with the same regal impunity. Drenched in courage, blue and gold coursed proudly through his noble veins.

If AI (Artificial Intelligence), could be measured in hurling terms, Carey was fitted with the perfect defender's prototype. He thrived on pain and revelled in physical contact.

His hurling was neat and tidy, and extremely nuanced. He spurned the spectacular for safety first, providing an early warning system whenever the Premier goal was under threat. His instincts seemed to house a very sophisticated high-end, inner GPRS system, that acted as an extra safety valve in the Hell's Kitchen pressure cooker.

He seemed at times to shape-shift and morph into another version of himself. There was nowhere to run, nowhere to hide as Carey came calling.

For all his physical prowess, and amid all the chaos and the anarchy, he played on autopilot which housed a chillingly controlled, cruising speed.

Carey's spectacular rise from a bit-part player in a low-key hurling tournament, to hurling's most prestigious inner circle, provided the most compelling of storylines. With a dash of devilry thrown into the heady mix… for good measure, he enthralled and bewitched hurling fans, for well over a decade.

Like compatriot John Doyle, he left the stage on his shield, after an agonising All-Ireland final defeat to a defiant Black and Amber in 1967.

{ FAREWELL TO THE ULTIMATE WARRIOR }

John Costigan, who took over his position at corner-back, paid tribute to him as a player of outstanding quality and character.

'There is great sadness at the death of one of the most revered players of his generation,' he commented. 'He will live long in the memory after a lot of us have gone.'

Kieran Carey had played against many of the hurling greats, including Christy Ring (Cork), Paddy Barry (Cork), Hopper McGrath (Wexford) and Jimmy Smyth (Clare). It's fair to say he left an indelible impression on all who encountered him.

His devil-may-care approach to lofty reputations ensured many left with their tails firmly between their legs.

The cult that grew around Hell's Kitchen was ably assisted by Kieran Carey's refusal to compromise. He was happy to put his head where many would refrain from putting a hurley.

He was a 'cult' hero to the Tipperary public and was undoubtedly one of the most under-rated hurlers of his generation. In the pantheon of the hardest, most unyielding hurlers of all time, Carey surely stands alone.

Colleague and fellow Tipperary soldier-at-arms John Doyle lamented that Carey never got the recognition he deserved, as he witnessed his cherished teammate's, unwavering dedication to the Tiobraid Árann cause. There was no doubting, however, the esteem his daring exploits were held by both his peers, and the adoring Tipperary public.

Carey, truly, was that rare diamond. Discovered in relative obscurity, his service to Tipperary hurling will never be truly measured. Selflessly, he patrolled the lines, along with Maher and Doyle, doing the dirty, unheralded work in hurling's 'graveyard shift'.

Rarely have three defenders received more column inches than Tipperary's terrific trio.

Hell's Kitchen was quite simply 'Box-Office'. The Hollywood triple act, who always had the most engaging storylines, who revelled in their notoriety.

Kieran, John Doyle and Mick Maher always had a warm welcome for their opponents…

Welcome to Hell!

His persona, and his legendary hurling exploits, were best

captured by former Tipperary chairman, Costigan's powerful and stirring graveside oration. It was a moving and poignant tribute, for Kieran's family, friends, and legion of admirers around the country.

'And today, when the final whistle for Kieran has blown, and he stands at last at God's final throne, may the great referee when he calls his name, say, you played like a man, you played the game. And as we say farewell to Kieran Carey, I pray that the green sod of his beloved Knock, rest lightly on brave and noble remains.'

»———→ TO HELL AND BACK ←———«

KIERAN WON a Laois Senior Hurling Championship medal in 1952 with Kyle, the famous O'Moore County side located near Ballaghmore on the Laois-Tipperary border. The Carey brothers formed the spine of a talented side and he was fortunate to share a special moment, when winning his first major honour - alongside his brothers Mick and Tommy.

Kieran moved from his native Knock to the town of Roscrea and represented the emerging town side in the early 1950s. He was instrumental in helping them claim the Dan Breen Cup, and win a first-ever Tipperary Senior Hurling Championship in 1968.

Roscrea then won the first-ever All-Ireland club final after they defeated Offaly's St Rynagh's in 1971. On June 1, 1958, Carey made his senior Tipperary championship debut in a 2-10 to 1-5 Munster quarter-final defeat of Limerick. He won his first Munster medal following a 4-12 to 1-5 trouncing of reigning champions Waterford. It would turn out to be the first of a magnificent seven winners medals in the province for Carey.

Five All-Ireland and five National League titles would follow, as Carey became a vital cog in the Premier's mean machine of serial winners. For all the glory, it was his membership of the most feared backline in hurling history which he will be most remembered for.

TOM CHEASTY

(Height 5' 8", Weight 13.5 St)

Decade... 1950s/1960s

(Position... Centre-Forward)

CHIEF CHARACTERISTIC... APTLY TITLED
'THE IRON MAN' A MANTLE HE WORE EASILY!

TOP ACCOMPLICES... SEAMUS POWER, PHIL GRIMES,
JACKIE CONDON, FRANKIE WALSH, JOHN KIELY

TOM CHEASTY

'HAPPILY ENOUGH, HURLING SEEMS TO SACRIFICE NOTHING OF ITS
SKILL ON THE ALTAR OF SPEED. I SHALL NEVER FORGET SOME OF THE
INCREDIBLE FORWARDS I AND 74,000 OTHERS SAW ON SUNDAY AND
ONE MAN STANDS IN MY MEMORY, TOM CHEASTY.'

– KENNETH WOLSTENHOLME

THE Boulevard of Broken Dreams?

The massed ranks of Deise supporters put their heads in their hands… again! Just like in '57 The Cats had pounced late in the day with lethal intention – were Waterford to be denied yet again? A day of pulsating action had one final twist left.

Trailing by three points, Waterford's Seamus Power gathered a miscued line ball… and let fly.

There was a deflection and the ball squirmed past Ollie Walsh's despairing clutches in the Kilkenny goal. Kenneth Wolstenholme, the celebrated BBC soccer commentator exhaled, along with 74,000 other patrons in Croke Park. A sharp blast of referee Fitzgerald's whistle ended 60 minutes+ of unrelenting drama as the 1959 All-Ireland final ended in a breathtaking draw.

Having delivered one of the greatest All-

**HARD
MAN
RATINGS**

TOUGHEST:
9.3/10

MEANEST:
9.1/10

SCARIEST:
9.7/10

HARDEST:
19.5/20

☠

TOTAL
HARD MAN

47.6/50

Irelands in living memory two years previously, Waterford and Kilkenny would head to the well one more time.

Wolstenholme, whose off-the-cuff commentary in the closing moments of the 1966 World Cup final at Wembley Stadium had included 14 words that became among the most famous ever uttered in a live commentary, was a gifted practitioner of the art of sports broadcasting.

With England edging West Germany 3–2, a small pitch invasion of enthusiastic fans took place during injury time, just as Geoff Hurst scored to put England 4–2 ahead. The events prompted Wolstenholme to say: *'Some people are on the pitch… they think it's all over… it is now!'*

The man who would go on to be involved in some of the biggest broadcasts in sporting history could barely comprehend the wonder he had just witnessed. He had been covering the final for the BBC *Sportsnight* highlights show. It was his first visit to Croke Park and he was more than a little impressed with the fare on show… and one man in particular!

'I'm still raving to my friends about Sunday's final between Kilkenny and Waterford, and since that excerpt was shown on BBC television on Wednesday. Yet remember, I am a self-confessed soccer maniac. I still think soccer is the finest game in the world but, now, hurling is pretty strong around second place.

'Happily enough, hurling seems to sacrifice nothing of its skill on the altar of speed. I shall never forget some of the incredible forwards I and 74,000 others saw on Sunday and one man stands in my memory, Tom Cheasty.

'That time in the second-half when he caught the ball, swerved around an opponent, tipped the ball onto his hurley, started to run, dropped the ball... but regained it, then burst between two men and shot a point, will forever remain as one of my finest sporting memories.'

One among many memories the irrepressible Cheasty would leave. The legend dubbed the 'Iron Man' certainly lived up to that billing on the pitch. In an era where forwards were 'Fair Game', Cheasty embraced and relished the trench warfare with defenders. Scores normally were earned rather than taken, with defenders extracting their pound of meat, and Cheasty paying them back with a chilling level of interest.

The 1957 All-Ireland final was the first-ever championship meeting between Waterford and Kilkenny. The Cats sprung an early surprise, parading behind the 'Artane' with a convoy of 16 men. The tall six-foot-plus stranger certainly did not look out of place as he marched behind his Kilkenny comrades, which included future GAA President, Paddy Buggy.

Eagle-eyed supporters sensed the whiff of a diabolical conspiracy but the identity of the Kilkenny 16th man soon put those particular conspiracy theories firmly to bed.

The Rank Movie Organisation had requested permission for British actor John Gregson to march in the parade as part of the movie *Rooney*. The motion picture also featured Barry Fitzgerald, and was about a Dublin dustman who leads his native county to an All-Ireland decider.

Waterford and Kilkenny players each received five pounds for their part in the 'drama,' which certainly added to the pageantry of an enthralling occasion.

When Tom Cheasty put Waterford six points to the good with just 14 minutes remaining, a second-ever Liam MacCarthy success looked like a distinct possibility. Whatever the occasion, whatever the era, Kilkenny's DNA defies any reasonable logic. Up to 1957, they had won over fifty percent of their All-Ireland finals by a single point. They duly rallied with team captain Michael Kelly pointing from the shadow of the Cusack – to break Deise hearts.

{ A SUIR THING }

One of the greatest All-Irelands of all time ended Kilkenny 4-10 (22 points), Waterford 3-12 (21 points). It was a bitter pill to digest for the warrior spirit of Tom Cheasty and his crestfallen teammates.

Two years later, with both sides at the peak of their undoubted powers, they set off on an inevitable collision course in September. The Deise dispatched champions Tipperary with a stunning nine-goal blast and The Cats, not to be outdone, hit Laois with an eight-goal salvo, to ready the stage.

Tom Cheasty was at his imperious best, contributing crucial scores at critical junctures. Kilkenny, as ever, located green flags when required to press three clear with the time expiring, before Seamus Power's divine intervention.

While a certain BBC commentator waxed lyrical – the two sides lined up again a month later.

The day dawned bright, balmy, and breezy as the Deise struggled to find any early fluency. A trademark Cheasty goal on 20 minutes put daylight between the sides at the break.

A youthful Eddie Keher entered the fray in the second period, but the Deise kept a firm grip on proceedings, with captain

Frankie Walsh's accuracy keeping the scoreboard operator up to his work. 1959 proved to be the high watermark for Waterford and Cheasty, as they were foiled by The Cats in the 1963 final. A man who soldiered with Cheasty, Jim Irish summed up his incredible contribution to the Waterford cause.

'The greatest centre-forward I ever played with or saw in Waterford.'

Move over... Geoff Hurst!

DEISE DAYS

TOM CHEASTY was born on February 4, 1934 in Knockaderry near Ballyduff. Cheasty started his club hurling with the local Ballyduff Lower club, winning a junior county medal in 1961. The club then merged with Portlaw GAA in the latter part of the 1960s.

He won one county medal with Ballyduff Lower/Portlaw in 1970. Ballyduff and Portlaw then separated in 1971, with Cheasty electing to line out with Portlaw, where he won four more county championships - the last coming in 1977, at the age of 43.

He arrived at the senior inter-county ranks at a pivotal time in the Deise's history, making his senior debut in the 1954-55 National League. Cheasty went on to play a major part for Waterford in what was to be one of the most successful periods in their history, winning one All-Ireland medal and three Munster medals.

Cheasty starred for Munster on the inter-provincial team on a number of occasions throughout his career, winning three Railway Cup medals in 1958, 1960, and 1961. He was still going strong on the club scene when winning a junior county medal with his native club Ballyduff Lower in 1983, a few months shy of his 50th birthday.

Cheasty retired from inter-county hurling after sustaining an injury during the course of a 1967 championship clash with Cork.

TOM CONDON

(Height 5' 11", Weight 14.5 St)

Decade... 2000s/2010s/2020s

(Position... Corner-Back)

CHIEF CHARACTERISTIC... ENSURING LIMERICK
HURLING LIVED HAPPY EVER AFTER

TOP ACCOMPLICES... SEAMUS HICKEY, DIARMUID BYRNES, RICHIE
MCCARTHY, PAUL BROWNE, GAVIN O'MAHONY, NICKY QUAID

TOM CONDON

*'NEXT THING WE SEE THE WHITE HELMET OVER ON THE FAR SIDELINE.
WE TURNED TO ONE ANOTHER AND SAID, "IT'S CONDON!" IT WAS JUST
MAJESTIC. TOM CATCHING THAT BALL AND THE REFEREE BLOWING THE
FINAL WHISTLE. TYPICAL OF TOM, HE HAD TO LEVEL THE GALWAY LAD
IN FRONT OF HIM ON THE POINT THE WHISTLE WAS BLOWN.'*

– RICHARD WALL

THE man that grasped the future…

There is a painting that is simply entitled *The Shot*. It captures the scene as Ireland's Christy O'Connor Jnr played one of the greatest shots in Ryder Cup history. O'Connor was in the twilight of his career – with many within the European camp questioning his late inclusion in the 1989 rendition of golf's Intercontinental 'Clash of the Titans.'

On the 18th hole of his singles joust with Fred Couples, both players needed one hell of an iron to strike the telling blow in an absorbing contest that saw them locked together coming down the last.

His captain, Tony Jacklin urged one final effort. 'One more good swing for Ireland. You get anywhere on the green and you're going to put huge pressure on him.'

O'Connor selected a two-iron and from approximately 229 yards landed it on the green to

**HARD
MAN
RATINGS**

TOUGHEST:
9.3/10

MEANEST:
9.1/10

SCARIEST:
9.7/10

HARDEST:
19.5/20
☠

TOTAL
HARD MAN

47.6/50

within four feet from the pin. The rest is history – as Europe held on to one of the most sought-after prizes in golf.

The image of O'Connor in the moment of his triumph, having secured his precious point from Couples, tells a story of a man that had journeyed many miles in the search for salvation.

After being passed over for selection and failing to win a single point on his only appearance in the competition, redemption day had finally arrived for the Knocknacarra native, who had always lived in the shadow of his illustrious uncle, Christy Snr.

With his arms outstretched, putter and cap in his left hand, and his head tilted back towards The Belfry heavens, O'Connor finally escaped – and was now no longer a hostage to history.

Sunday, August 19, 2018. Shortly after 5 pm.

A moment arrived ending one of the most torrid journeys ever endured in the history of a proud hurling nation. 'The 'Catch' would end 45 years of unrelenting pain, and finally close the 'Doomsday Book' on Limerick's heartbreak. In those final heart-stopping moments, one of the county's finest had slipped unnoticed into the cauldron of the 2018 All-Ireland final. The last play of the final was about to be enacted.

Every man, woman, and child with green and white etched across their hearts could barely bear to watch.

As the ball entered the danger zone, the alarm bells were belting out across the sea of green-clad supporters. Many hands reached and clawed, fighting frantically for the precious sliotar.

He knew he was near his journey's end.

It was time to usher in a new generation. He had hurled his heart out in Limerick's darkest hours. Now it was time to take the 'Treaty' back to where they belonged. As the ball dropped –

the moment appeared suspended in an eternal second.

Tom Condon kept his eyes trained firmly on the ball. He had been preparing all his life for this. He took flight, suspended half-way between heaven and hell. Tom Condon and Limerick were seconds out from immortality...

Tom Condon's iconic 'Catch' seemed a lifetime away in Chicago. A career with the Treaty appeared dead in the water for a man who had caught the eye in the 2004 Limerick junior hurling final.

Condon had worked hard to get his senior call-up, a 2009 All-Ireland intermediate victory had showcased his abilities even further. He hadn't looked out of place beside Limerick legend, Ciaran Carey. A cull by then manager, Justin McCarthy saw a mass exodus from the squad and Tom walked in solidarity with his teammates.

Condon was a rugged campaigner and left his calling card early, and often. After that, no further introductions were required as Tom's reputation preceded him! He was making eye-catching progress, seemingly unhampered by his club's lowly intermediate status. Then all hell broke loose as McCarthy axed 12 high-profile characters from the panel.

A Munster title in 2013, a first in 17 years, saw Tom return in the green and white, but the Treaty crucially failed to build upon that monumental moment. It took the arrival of John Kiely in 2017 to breathe new life into the Treaty cause.

The anatomy of one of the most important moments in the Shannonsiders' proud history was stranger than fiction. If it was part of the grand design, then Tom Condon would definitely have questioned the merits of the program.

{ THE CATCH }

TOM WAS warming the bench as the 2018 All-Ireland final hurtled towards its end-game. A red card incurred against Clare in the Munster Championship had seen him plummet down the pecking order. It appeared time had run out for Tom and it looked odds-on he would play no meaningful part in one of the greatest days in Limerick hurling history.

Then Mike Casey sustained an injury around the hour mark. John Kiely motioned to Tom Condon and Richie McCarthy to warm up. It would be McCarthy who would get the nod, and Tom returned to his seat with the prospects of joining the party looking distinctly remote.

Fate works in mysterious ways, however, and when McCarthy limped off in the 71st minute, Tom Condon was about to produce a cameo for the ages. His chairman at Knocknaderry, Richard Wall described hurling's version of the famous 'Shot'.

'Next thing we see the white helmet over on the far sideline. We turned to one another and said, "It's Condon!" It was just majestic. Tom catching that ball and the referee (blowing the final whistle).

'Typical of Tom, he had to level the Galway lad in front of him on the point the whistle was blown. It was huge.'

Out of the posse numbering around 12 players, Tom Condon had rather fittingly emerged with the ball. The iconic catch could well be the subject of another sporting masterpiece. After an epic journey from the junior ranks to the highest echelons of Irish sport, Tom Condon had swooped to conquer. He was the man that finally ensured Limerick would grasp the future…

➤ TREATY TIMES ◄

TOM CONDON was born on November 9,1987. The right corner-back played his club hurling with intermediate side Knockaderry. Having participated in the club from an early age, he duly progressed to the senior ranks.

Condon first appeared in the famous Treaty colours as a member of the minor team during the 2005 Munster Championship, when he was positioned at left corner-back in a 2-14 to 1-6 defeat of Tipperary. Limerick faced Cork in the decider and suffered a 2-18 to 1-12 defeat in the Munster final. Limerick qualified for the All-Ireland final on September 11 though the backdoor, but were thwarted again, this time by Galway.

Condon also played with the Limerick under-21 team, as part of the panel for the 2007 Munster Championship. He also played the following season at full-back in Limerick's 1-13 to 0-15 defeat by Tipperary in the Munster Championship semi-final.

He lined out with the Limerick Intermediate team in successive seasons in 2007 and 2008.

On 8 February 2009, Condon made his first appearance for the Limerick senior team in a 3-13 to 1-18 defeat of Clare in the National League. He has won three Munster titles, two All-Irelands, and one National League during his career.

JOHN CONNOLLY

(Height 6' 2", Weight 15 St)

Decade... 1960s/1970s/1980s
(Position... Midfield/Full-Forward)

CHIEF CHARACTERISTIC... ENSURED THE MEN FROM
THE WEST WERE ALWAYS AWAKE

TOP ACCOMPLICES... P.J. MOLLOY, SEAN SILKE, PASCAL RYAN,
BERNIE FORDE, NIALL MCINERNEY

JOHN CONNOLLY

> *'THERE WAS A FAMILY OUT IN THE MIDDLE OF NOWHERE WITH THE BONFIRE...*
> *THE FATHER, MOTHER, GRANDMOTHER, GRANDFATHER, AND ALL OF THE KIDS*
> *ON THEIR OWN... NOBODY AROUND THEM. JUST ON THEIR OWN WANTING TO BE*
> *HERE TO SHOW THE TEAM, THE BONFIRE LIT AS WE DROVE PAST.'*
>
> ## – JOHN CONNOLLY

INTO the West…

The young man peered across the shimmering expanse of the Corrib. He buttoned his coat as a sharp blast of wind billowed off the lake. This is the heart of the County of Tribes. A couple of gulls screeched overhead as they reached landfall. They paused for a moment, before veering away – wings flapping furiously.

The first canal on the island of Ireland was cut in the 12th century. Known as the Friar's Cut, it allowed boats to pass from the lough to the sea at Galway. The parish extends from Lough Corrib across to Merlin Park by the old Galway-Dublin Road. If you listen closely during the month of July, you can almost hear a low rumble of the thunder of hooves from Ballybrit, where the annual Galway Races are held.

The man had a face that was wise beyond his years, and hardy handsome. He could feel their

HARD MAN RATINGS	
TOUGHEST:	9.7/10
MEANEST:	9.0/10
SCARIEST:	9.2/10
HARDEST:	19.9/20
☠	
TOTAL HARD MAN	**47.8/50**

despair, their longing. It lingered in the fields, on the boats, in every nook and cranny. It was time to put an end to this malignant cycle of endless suffering.

When John Connolly was even younger – a wee 'bairn' – he dreamed many things. Now the man who was crowned Connacht Junior Welterweight Champion... was finally about to land the knockout blow for Galway hurling.

Galway hurling fans were a bit like a bunch of desperadoes waiting for a train... called Liam MacCarthy! The Highwaymen's classic rendition of the famous ballad that was written by Guy Clark, tells the tale of a boy who admires and looks up to an old man. However, as the little boy watched the man grow *older*, he found him becoming just like every other older man he knew.

All through the song, he compared himself and the man to desperados waiting for a train – something that may seem to be exciting and treacherous, yet in the end, peters out to an empty, soulless, conclusion.

Every man, woman, and child, and even the odd dog, had grown weary as the maroon and white express rattled along a never-ending set of tracks – with no final destination in sight.

The hunt for an elusive All-Ireland hurling title had taken over half a century. This statistic was hard to digest when you consider the Tribesmen in the guise of Mellick, had contested the first-ever All-Ireland final.

Galway won their first All-Ireland in 1923, defeating Limerick, but lost another four in the 20s. The suffering continued unabated with no further appearances on the biggest stage in the 1930s or 40s, before they lost a run of finals in the 50s.

In 1975 they lost out to Kilkenny but returned in '79, when

The Cats kept their claws firmly embedded in the maroon and white. John Connolly summed up the mood in the camp and within the stricken county.

'If you think about '79 for Galway players, supporters, and hurling people... we lost the Railway Cup, we lost the National League final, the All-Ireland final, and lost the Oireachtas final.

'For a county and players that were starving for success to lose them all, to lose so much, so often...'

For John Connolly and Galway hurling this was without doubt the lowest ebb... but incredibly one year later, it would also be the turning of the tide.

Galway lived in a curious world where they entered the All-Ireland stage at the penultimate round, which on paper looked like a hell of a deal!

John, however, played only 26 championship games for Galway in a senior career that started in 1967, and finished in 1981.

Four of those were All-Ireland finals, and he was adamant when speaking after it all, that the Tribe were hamstrung by not being properly road-tested to embrace the rigours of Liam MacCarthy.

'The biggest regret I have is that the system was terrible when I played. For many years we played one match... an All-Ireland semi-final and that was it for the year. It was always around the time of the Galway Races at the end of July, so we were training all summer and we couldn't even get challenge matches because all the other teams were playing their provincial championships.

'So, we would go into the All-Ireland semi-final against a team who was up to the speed of the All-Ireland Championship, having come through Munster or Leinster.

'They would have their team settled after three or four matches.

They would know where they were going and there we were…
the first day… Croke Park, live on television, thrown in at the
deep end and we just wouldn't be ready for it most times. How
could we be?

'Most times, it was one game and we were out of it again for
another 12 months. How could we develop or get stronger? It
was nearly impossible.'

{ A GALWAY HURLING FAMILY }

John was the eldest sibling of the famous Connolly clan from
Castlegar. He played his first senior game against Clare in 1968.
The maestro was a calm reassuring presence in midfield, and later
on the front line at full-forward. John was a strapping specimen
and he had a hefty frame – which made him impossible to knock
off the ball.

The 1980 All-Ireland semi-final against Cork was one of John's
most imperious displays for the Tribe. Lining out in midfield, as
Galway's captain, he was partnered by Carnmore's Sean Murphy
and they were pitted against Cork captain, Gerald McCarthy,
and his partner Pat Hegarty.

It would be Galway's day, as John led them to the decider which
was the proverbial bookend, against Shannonsiders, Limerick.
Lightning duly struck twice as the tribesmen emulated the class
of 1923 and inflicted another defeat on Limerick.

The teak-tough Connolly was a beacon of hope during the
wilderness years for Galway hurling. Connolly, the warrior
supreme kept the 'West Awake,' all the way from the shores of
the mighty Corrib to the steps of the Hogan Stand.

OF TRIBES
AND MEN

HE WAS born in Leitir Móir, Galway, and Connolly's first taste of competitive action was at school in St Mary's College, Galway. He played minor hurling with the county after turning 16, and later joined the under-21 side.

In the 1967 championship, he pulled on the maroon jersey for his first start with the senior side, and he remained a fixture with the Tribesmen for 14 years. He was an All-Ireland runner-up on three different occasions before Galway got that particular monkey off their backs, when capturing Liam MacCarthy in 1980.

He was a standout performer for the Connacht inter-provincial team, which was the Galway senior team under a different banner, winning the Railway Cup in 1980.

He hurled for Castlegar helping the side to an All-Ireland title, and six county titles. He won two All Stars and announced his retirement from the county game, following the conclusion of the 1981 championship.

He was the eldest of the famous Connolly clan, which comprised Pádraic, Joe, Michael, Tom, Gerry, and Murt, who all played with distinction for club and county.

He has also served as a coach, and selector with the county senior team.

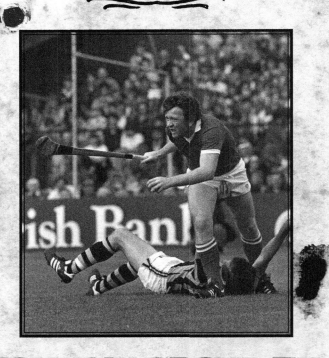

JOHNNY CROWLEY

(Height 6' 0", Weight 14.5 St)

Decade... 1970s/1980s

(Position... Centre-Back)

CHIEF CHARACTERISTIC... TERMINATION OF
TENANCIES CROKE PARK GOALMOUTH

TOP ACCOMPLICES... MARTIN O'DOHERTY, BRIAN MURPHY, PAT
McDONNELL, MARTIN COLEMAN, TOM CASHMAN, DERMOT MACCURTAIN

JOHNNY CROWLEY

'WHEN THEY GOT THE GOAL TO GO FOUR POINTS AHEAD, I THOUGHT WE WERE BEATEN - I THINK WE ALL DID. ONE OF THEIR PLAYERS RUNNING OUT GAVE ME A SHOULDER AND SAID, "YE'RE IN TROUBLE NOW!"... AND WE WERE A BIT DEFLATED, BUT WITHIN TWO MINUTES, THE WHOLE THING HAD CHANGED AGAIN AND THAT PLAYER GOT A BELT IN RETURN.'

– JOHNNY CROWLEY

MALCOLM Thorpe Fleming Churchill – nicknamed 'Fighting Jack Churchill' and 'Mad Jack' fought in the Second World War with a longbow, a basket-hilted Scottish broadsword, and a bagpipe.

While many correctly perused about 'Mad Jack's state of sanity, this unique warrior got on with doing what he did best – winning battles!

Churchill was second in command of No. 3 Commando in Operation Archery during a daring raid on the German garrison at Vågsøy, Norway, on December 27, 1941. As the ramps were lowered on the first landing craft, he sprang into action – playing *March of the Cameron Men* on his bagpipes, before throwing a grenade and charging like a demented lunatic into battle.

For his actions at Dunkirk and Vågsøy, Churchill received the first of his many decorations for bravery, the Military Cross.

HARD MAN RATINGS

TOUGHEST:
9.6/10

MEANEST:
9.2/10

SCARIEST:
9.2/10

HARDEST:
19.6/20
☠

TOTAL HARD MAN
47.6/50

It is important to note at this juncture that Mad Jack come through the war unscathed – and lived to the ripe old age of 89!

You don't have to be crazy to play inter-county hurling at the highest level but, just like Mad Jack, a raw mixture of a little insanity and a whole lot of courage goes a long way.

Johnny Crowley was one of Cork's most decorated soldiers, with his Tour of Duty beginning in 1976 and ending in 1987. He was a soldier that fought with incredible courage and a never-say-die attitude to lead his beloved Cork to spectacular glory.

His underage exploits had preceded him with the talented Bishopstown youngster winning both hurling and football All-Ireland minor titles in 1974. He also collected an under-21 All-Ireland hurling medal in 1976.

Six years had elapsed since Liam MacCarthy had visited the banks of the Lee, and many felt the Rebels had gone a little too soft. The natives were grumbling and getting restless; since winning their first All-Ireland in 1890, the cupboard had rarely been bare.

Johnny had just turned 20 – but was already a superb reader of the algorithms of the ancient game. He had a real feel for defending and was just the enforcer that Cork had been crying out for in those wilderness years.

Johnny made his senior championship debut with Cork on June 13, 1976 in the defeat of old rivals Tipperary. Like all good Cork teams, success breeds success, and for the Rebels a win over the Premier had the potential to spawn a thousand fathers.

He later collected his very first Munster medal as Cork torched a feeble Limerick effort by seven points before a gleeful local audience at the newly-opened Páirc Uí Chaoimh.

Wexford made a fast start in the All-Ireland final on September

5, 1976, blazing into an eight-point lead, but the margin had shrunk ominously to just two, with about 10 minutes remaining. Cork scrambled a goal from the boot of team captain Ray Cummins to prevail, 2–21 to 4–11.

It was a case of deja vu the following season as the two protagonists locked horns with Wexford seeking some atonement for the previous season's reversal. Martin Coleman between the Cork sticks would prove to be the hero as he saved a goal-bound effort from the Slaneysiders' Christy Keogh to heap even more misery upon the Leinster kingpins.

Johnny was by now a commanding presence at the heart of the Cork backline as the Rebels notched a third Munster title in-a -row, but had to dig deep against an obdurate Clare challenge. Kilkenny stood in the way of the first three on the spin in over two decades, but a Jimmy Barry Murphy goal paved the way for a notable success.

Cork sailed through the by-now-still waters of Munster the following season, with the whiff of rebellion long gone from their chastened opponents.

A 2–15 to 0–9 hiding of Limerick gave the county a record-equalling fifth consecutive provincial title. Galway then produced one of the hijacks of the hurling century to send the Blood and Bandages crashing out of the championship at the penultimate stage.

When Limerick surprisingly denied Cork in the 1980 Munster final the feel-good factor began dissipating in the Cork heartlands. The following season produced little, but in 1982, Johnny and company rampaged through Munster, to inevitably face Kilkenny in the All-Ireland decider.

The Cats not only served up Cork on a platter, but they also followed up in the 1983 final to inflict defeat on the double on a shell-shocked opponent.

{ BACK UP ON THE HORSE }

Cork again reigned supreme in Munster the following year beating Tipperary in the decider. Johnny recalls it turned out to be a battle, in more ways than one!

'When they got the goal to go four points ahead, I thought we were beaten – I think we all did. One of their players running out gave me a shoulder and said, "Ye're in trouble now!" … and we were a bit deflated, but within two minutes, the whole thing had changed again and that player got a belt in return.'

The Rebels were now on the verge of a different kind of history as they qualified for the centenary All-Ireland final against Offaly in Thurles. With a third defeat in quick succession unthinkable, Johnny recalls the heat was on.

'It was the centenary final, and we had lost the two prior to it. The losses to Kilkenny in 1982 and '83 were very disappointing. We had chances in both, but we didn't take them and that's sport. After that, there were a lot of people questioning us and a few fellas retired as well, so the pressure was on. The media were wondering if it was the end for the team.'

Johnny and Cork answered their critics in some style. He was voted Man of the Match as the Faithful were overpowered in the Thurles sunshine. At the conclusion of his Rebel Tour of Duty the defensive colossus laid down his Broadsword, leaving with full military honours in 1987.

THE ROAD
TO REBELLION

JOHNNY CROWLEY was born on February 21, 1956 in Enniskean, County Cork, and first teamed up on the inter-county scene at the age of 18 as a dual player with the Cork minor teams. He later graduated to the Cork under-21 hurling team, making his senior debut during the 1976 championship.

Crowley enjoyed well over a decade of unparalleled success with the Rebels – winning five All-Ireland senior titles. Cork was a commanding presence in Munster, and he collected nine Munster medals. He also won a National League medal with the Leesiders and was an All-Ireland runner-up on two occasions.

Crowley also lined out with Munster in the inter-provincial series, but the province never won the Railway Cup title during his tenure with them. At club level, he enjoyed a lengthy career with Bishopstown. He played both hurling and football with the club in a career that only yielded a city Junior Hurling Championship medal in 1977.

He won the Man of the Match award in the 1984 Centenary All-Ireland final against Offaly, which was held in Thurles. He was later voted on to the All Star selection for the only time in his career

PJ CUDDY

(Height 6' 0", Weight 14.5 St)

Decade... 1980s/1990s

(Position... Full-Forward)

CHIEF CHARACTERISTIC... THE NOTORIOUS HEAD OF THE CUDDY
CLAN WANTED FOR CRIMES AGAINST HURLING'S NOBILITY

TOP ACCOMPLICES... MICHEAL 'MAGGIE' WALSH, EUGENE FENNELLY,
PAT CRITCHLEY, MARTIN CUDDY, CHRISTY JONES, PAT CLEARY

PJ CUDDY

'WE WERE TRAINING FOR THE ALL IRELAND CLUB THAT TIME UNDER
LIGHTS OF CARS AND FLASH LAMPS, AND I CAN REMEMBER SADIE
DELANEY GIVING US SOUP AND SANDWICHES IN THE HALL IN CAMROSS.'
– PJ CUDDY

I'*VE Had) The Time of my Life.*
Ninety-nine years, 195 days. He had lived a remarkable life. The last ever Laois man to lift the All-Ireland hurling trophy passed away in 1977. The final link with a remarkable day for Laois hurling had been broken.

When Jack Carroll led Laois (Ballygeehan) to beat Cork, (Redmonds) on the score of 6-2 to 4-1 in the final, played at Croke Park on October 24, 1915, it was supposed to herald the start of an incredible voyage. Instead, Laois would toil valiantly for many decades in the shadows of Kilkenny, Wexford, and even Offaly in the province, and apart from a couple of collector's items, including the tasty scraps of Dublin in 2019 and Offaly in 2015, they had to be content with scrambling around looking for morsels of comfort.

As they prepared to meet Wexford in the 1985 Leinster Championship semi-final, expectations were pretty much on the floor. Laois had lost

**HARD
MAN
RATINGS**
TOUGHEST:
9.1/10

MEANEST:
9.3/10

SCARIEST:
9.0/10

HARDEST:
19.2/20
☠
TOTAL
HARD MAN
46.6/50

their previous 10 championship clashes with Wexford and their last victory over the Slaney men had arrived 44 years previously!

They had, however, scalped Wexford twice in the league, including a relegation play-off that sent them down to Division 2. Those victories certainly eliminated the 'fear factor' but clashes with Wexford in the championship were a totally different beast.

For all the statistical and historical gloom, Laois were a talented outfit whose half-back line of Christy Jones, Joe Dollard and John Taylor were a formidable line, and Micheal 'Maggie' Walsh was touted as a certain All Star. Eugene Fennelly was a model of consistency on the frees, and they possessed an inspirational captain, Pat Critchley.

The brothers Cuddy, meanwhile, were renowned for representing the heart and soul of the Laois DNA, doughty warriors, who had little respect for lofty reputations.

A fully paid-up member of the Camross Cuddy Clan, PJ was a bustling goal-getting full forward, who frightened the life out of No. 3s up and down the country. Cuddy like his brothers was a man you wanted to go into battle with, and in his day, was simply unstoppable.

Laois, however, got off to a very slow start and were a tad fortunate only to be in arrears by a single score, albeit a goal, 1-3 to 0-3 down after 15 minutes.

The triumvirate of Jones, Dollard, and Taylor was described by the *Irish Independent* as 'splendid throughout' and helped steady the ship after a ropey first quarter.

Eugene Fennelly's precision from placed-balls kept the scoreboard ticking over, as Laois remained embedded in the contest at the interval.

The Laois policy of bombarding the Wexford full-back line with missiles paid a rich dividend before half-time as PJ's sibling, Martin caught one with snow on it and dispatched it to the net, to leave the protagonists dead-locked at the break.

Things got better after the break as the O'Moore men powered on, leading by six. Wexford replied and Martin Fitzhenry, Billy Byrne and George O'Connor had them back within one point with time almost up.

PJ Cuddy had been his usual combative self and while Wexford had done a decent job in keeping him shackled, it was a case of 'cometh the hour- cometh the man'.

Cuddy had made a career out of winning the 'dirty ball' and managed to win a ferocious duel for possession to draw a late free from an exhausted Wexford rearguard. 'Dead Eye Dick' Fennelly ensured the transgression was penalised, and buoyant Laois were heading for the Leinster final.

{ REDEMPTION AND REGRETS }

Decades of disappointment and near misses in the championship were swept aside in a frenzy of excitement as Laois bravely resisted the anticipated Wexford comeback, reported the *Leinster Express*, capturing the mood in the county the following week.

The Faithful represented a serious outfit and were seeking a second Liam MacCarthy Cup after their maiden win in 1981. Laois had fallen to the Faithful that year courtesy of a controversial goal – that PJ Cuddy remembers well.

'We were a bit naive too. When Offaly scored the goal through the side-netting in the game in 1981, we didn't kick up enough of a fuss about it.

'And late in that game, I can still see John Delaney coming up the field with the ball. The ref was probably trying to keep it a draw and he gave a free against him. But Paddy Kirwan drove the free over the bar from his own half.'

It rained goals in the Leinster final, but sadly they were all at the O'Moore County end, as Offaly ran riot raising five green flags. While it was a day when Laois never really got motoring, Martin Cuddy remembers the decade's adventures fondly.

'That was just a brilliant time, absolutely brilliant. We took some great scalps… Tipperary, Kilkenny. The league quarter-final when we were nine points down against Tipp. The huge crowd in Borris-in-Ossory when we beat Cork in the league.

'We took them all in the Centenary year – Kilkenny, Limerick, Galway. We got a run going, got some great scores and late winning points. We had a fierce following at the time.

'Everyone was behind us and Laois teams never had hype like it.

'Maybe we weren't experienced enough but Offaly and Kilkenny were going on to win All-Irelands those years. We weren't far off.'

PJ Cuddy hurled in a different, yet no less competitive era. He recalled training for a club All-Ireland before the advent of proper floodlights.

'We were training for the All-Ireland club that time under lights of cars and flash lamps, and I can remember Sadie Delaney giving us soup and sandwiches in the hall in Camross.'

PJ Cuddy was part of an incredible Laois hurling journey, breathing new life into the hurling revolution, began by people like Jack Carroll.

When they look back at those heady days of the 80s, long-suffering Laois fans could well recall the words of Jennifer Cairns's hit song.

(I've Had) The Time of my Life.

THE KING FROM CAMROSS

PJ CUDDY played hurling with his local club Camross. He won his first Laois Senior Championship medal with Camross in 1976. Further success was just around the corner as the Laois kingpins then secured a famous Leinster Senior Club Championship title with a victory over James Stephens (Kilkenny). The journey continued as they subsequently beat Ballycran (Down) in the All-Ireland semi-final, but they were denied the national crown by Cork's, Glen Rovers.

PJ Cuddy was part of a Camross side that at one stage included seven siblings, and collected 12 Laois titles. Two decades on from their Leinster title, Camross and PJ won another - when they defeated Dublin's O'Tooles in the decider. They advanced to the All-Ireland Club final where they were defeated by Galway's, Athenry.

He captained the Laois under-21 side that reached the Leinster final, but subsequently missed the final through suspension.

The following season, Cuddy was promoted to the senior team, making his debut in a National League defeat to Clare at Portlaoise. Laois were promoted to Division 1 in 1981, and qualified for the quarter-final against mighty Tipperary. Two goals from Cuddy secured a famous victory. He won the Railway Cup with Leinster in 1988.

FRANK CUMMINS

(Height 6' 0", Weight 15 St)

Decade... 1960s/1970s/1980s

(Position... Midfield)

CHIEF CHARACTERISTIC... ON AND OFF FIELD DEMOLITIONS

TOP ACCOMPLICES... GER FENNELLY, DICK O'HARA, BILLY
FITZPATRICK, LIAM FENNELLY, RICHIE POWER SNR

FRANK CUMMINS

*'FRANK WAS ONE OF BEST, IF NOT THE BEST,
KILKENNY PLAYER I'VE EVER SEEN.'*
– BRIAN MURPHY

CROKE *Park, Dublin, 1982.*
The shadow of the Hogan Stand.

Tim Crowley was virtually indestructible. So, what happened next was a bolt from the blue, or should we say black and amber?

When Frank Cummins shouldered Crowley in the 1982 All-Ireland final, all bets were off as to what the likeliest outcome would be.

As Crowley reflected from a prostrate position on what had just transpired, Cummins had left Kilkenny's calling card. Crowley and Cork were shaken… and badly stirred!

The day went badly pear-shaped for the Rebels after that. Things normally went sideways for Cork after a collision with Frank Cummins. The Cats midfielder would play in four All-Ireland finals against the Leesiders, and lap up the cream on each and every occasion.

Ten previously, he had rampaged through the startled Cork defence and leathered a missile

**HARD
MAN
RATINGS**
TOUGHEST:
10/10

MEANEST:
9.0/10

SCARIEST:
9.5/10

HARDEST:
20/20

💀

TOTAL
HARD MAN
48.5/50

past the astounded Paddy Barry; the goal was just the spark the very 'flat' Cats needed, and set them on their way to an eight-point triumph.

Things always tended to go bottom-up for your ambitions when Frank came to town!

While Cummins had decided to seek out a new vocation, unfortunately for his opponents, he was still fully committed to his career in inter-county hurling. Cummins had decided to leave his post as a Garda and found his true vocation as a demolition expert!

This was an area of expertise that most people that knew him intimately, or even on a casual basis, felt he would truly excel!

Demolition became a way of life for the former Belcamp College graduate; he was a midfielder that was wrought from iron. A hard-bitten, sledgehammer-swinging, bruiser.

It was apparent from his fledging days at Belcamp that Frank was quite simply a force of nature. The college were a decent football outfit and in 1965 he contested the All-Ireland football championship final with his school. His speed and power were already evident as he kicked four points that day, as the contest finished all square against Derry outfit, St Columb's. Frank would be absent for the replay with a broken ankle and was sorely missed as Belcamp lost.

His performances with the hurling team against the likes of mighty Kilkenny kingpins, St Kieran's College among others, put him firmly on the radar of the Kilkenny management teams.

Legendary Cats' boss Monsignor Tommy Maher recalled the first time he encountered the 'Marathon Man' at a colleges fixture in Kilkenny, as Frank's tour-de-force almost sank the Mighty 'Saints'.

'The first day I saw him playing with Belcamp College against St Kieran's College I knew I was looking at a special player.

'He was big and strong even then, and in the inter-county senior game that same strength was an invaluable asset.'

While Frank was in the fray, Kilkenny always prospered. He was the foundation the Kilkenny dynasty was perched upon. He won a magnificent seven Celtic Crosses from midfield, the only hurler to collect seven of his medals in the same position.

The man that featured in an eye-watering 16 Leinster senior finals was inducted into the GAA's Hall of Fame along with Kerry's Jack O'Shea, and the Offaly duo of Matt Connor, and Pádraig Horan. He did not look out of place in such exalted company, with the Fab Four having a combined haul of 18 All-Ireland senior medals and 14 All Star awards. They likely hired a removals van to ferry all the gold and silver to GAA Headquarters.

{ SAVING THE BEST UNTIL LAST }

'Late in his career, he won the Texaco Player of the Year Award (1983). That was some achievement in itself. It proved that right to the finish, Frank was the best,' as Kilkenny trainer- coach, Pat Henderson related in tribute to one of Kilkenny hurling's finest.

'He was truly one of the greats in hurling,' Henderson continued, from a vantage point few had witnessed. He had been a teammate for five of those All-Ireland victories.

'For anyone to win so much and play so consistently well for so long, just had to be special.'

In a county with no shortage of All-Ireland medals, he strode like a giant in very exalted shoes. His incredible winning streak equalled the 70-year-old record of a player winning his seventh medal on the field of play. This put him in the same bracket as fellow Kilkenny legends, the great Jack Rochford of Threecastles, and another iconic figure in the shape of Sim Walton of Tullaroan. That former quintet of Cats' giants was completed by Mooncoin pair, Dick Doyle and Dick Walsh.

'The lads won the league,' he explained when he broke the bad news about his retirement.

'They looked good when winning it and the team was beginning to take on a new shape. I was delighted with the way they played in the conclusion of the league, and I felt the time was right to go. It was a tough decision to make, but I had to make it someday.'

That was the calibre of the man. It was never about Frank Cummins, just always, always about his beloved Kilkenny. He had waited until he felt the time was right and the crown would rest easily on younger heads.

The harsh reality for Kilkenny was, as well-intentioned as Frank's actions were, he was quite simply irreplaceable. It was little coincidence that when Frank retired in 1983, Kilkenny hurling fell on hard times. He left a yawning chasm as wide as the banks of the Nore.

The Kilkenny side who had become accustomed to their 'Marathon Man' running the show from 'lár na páirc' found it hard to come to adjust to a life without Frank's super-charged engine.

The Demolition Man who always left a trail of destruction in his wake…

▶——→ LET'S BE FRANK ←——◀

FRANK CUMMINS was born on November 9, 1947, in Knocktopher, County Kilkenny, Frank first hurled with Belcamp College, and later represented Kilkenny at minor and under-21 level.

He first donned the famous black and amber when he made his senior debut in the 1966 Oireachtas Cup. At club level, he lined out with the club that would become Ballyhale Shamrocks. He later moved to Cork where he joined Blackrock, winning his first senior county title in 1971, before later adding his first Munster Club and All-Ireland titles.

Blackrock and Cummins repeated the dose the following season, as Blackrock emerged as one of the most formidable sides in the country. In all, his haul included a staggering six Cork county titles, five Munster Club, and three All-Ireland crowns.

Over the course of his Kilkenny career, he won eight All-Ireland medals, nine Leinster medals and three National League medals. He was also an All-Ireland runner-up on three occasions.

At inter-provincial level, Cummins won six Railway Cup medals. He made almost 50 appearances for Kilkenny, collecting four All Star awards as well as Texaco Hurler of the Year in 1983.

ANTHONY DALY
(Height 6' 0", Weight 14.5 St))

Decade... 1980s/1990s/2000s
(Position... Wing-Back)

CHIEF CHARACTERISTIC... HEAD OF THE GAA TROPHY
LOST AND FOUND DEPARTMENT

TOP ACCOMPLICES... DAVY FITZGERALD, BRIAN LOHAN, SEANIE
MCMAHON, FRANK LOHAN, OLLIE BAKER, LIAM DOYLE

ANTHONY DALY

'WE TRAINED LIKE SAVAGES IN THE LEAD-UP TO THAT CORK GAME. AT ONE STAGE, WE DID 20 NIGHTS OUT OF 22. WHEN WE MET CORK AGAIN, WE WERE LIKE WILD ANIMALS. AS I WAS LEADING THE LADS OUT THE TUNNEL, I NEARLY MOWED DOWN JIMMY BARRY-MURPHY AND DR CON MURPHY. "GET OUT OF MY F***ING WAY," I ROARED AT THEM. THEY DID. SO DID CORK.'

– ANTHONY DALY

O N Wednesday, November 24, 1971, a man who was named Daniel Cooper boarded a Northwest Airlines, Flight 305 from Portland, Oregon to Seattle, Washington, after purchasing a one-way ticket.

Cooper was described as being in his mid-40s, dressed in a business suit, brown shoes, and wearing a white shirt, with a black tie. Opening a cheap attaché case, Cooper called a hostess and showed her a glimpse of a bag containing a mass of wires and red-coloured sticks. Cooper then told her to remember every word he was saying.

'I want $200,000 by 5pm in cash exclusively in $20 bills, put in a knapsack. I want two back parachutes and two front parachutes.'

When the flight landed in Seattle, he exchanged the flight's 36 passengers for the money and parachutes. Cooper kept several crew members and ordered them to set a course for Mexico City.

HARD MAN RATINGS

TOUGHEST:
9.7/10

MEANEST:
8.9/10

SCARIEST:
9.1/10

HARDEST:
19.4/20

TOTAL
HARD MAN

47.1/50

Just after 8pm at a location somewhere between Seattle and Reno, Nevada, David Cooper jumped from the rear door of the plane with two of the parachutes and the money.

He duly vanished and was never sighted again.

After one of the biggest manhunts in FBI history no trace of David Cooper was ever discovered. His real identity and fate remain a mystery today.

Maybe they should have called Anthony Daly...

'There has been a missing person in Clare for 81 long years... well today that person has been found alive and well, and that person's name is Liam MacCarthy.'

September 3, 1995, Croke Park, Dublin.

Having successfully closed one of the most enduring 'Cold Cases' in hurling history, life would never be the same again along the Wild Atlantic-Way. The famine was over, and as Anthony Daly reminded the faithful, they loved their traditional music in Clare, and their hurling too!

Anthony Daly was a hurling life in two parts. The inspirational warrior captain of Ger Loughnane's 'history boys', and his equally fiery incarnation as a manager.

Let's face facts here, if Ger Loughnane chose him as his captain, it's fair to assume a career in the priesthood did not await Clarecastle's finest.

Daly and Loughnane had a colourful relationship over the years. Anthony was not a puppet or a 'yes man', but he always respected rank. When questioned on his relationship with Loughnane, Dalo summed it up as only Anthony can, describing the relationship as, 'A bit like Collins said to Dev... Loughnane will always be my general'.

While they fought like tigers, the dynamic duo always put the Banner cause front and centre. Nothing was allowed to get in the way of business, and with Loughnane, and Daly, driving the Banner chariot, that business involved winning. Nobody could read a room quite like Dalo, and after the high of throttling the Premier County in 1997, there were whispers that Loughnane might call it a day. Dalo sought his general out and received firm assurances that Loughnane was going nowhere.

After an indifferent league campaign, Clare somehow qualified for the semi-final against Cork. It turned out to be a testing day at the office for the Banner as the Rebels put them to the sword. The sides would duel again later in the season in the Munster semi-final, and as Dalo would later reveal, Clare was chomping at the bit for an opportunity to put Cork back on their arses.

'Cork had to play Limerick in a Munster quarter-final but we knew it would be Cork that we'd be facing. We felt aggrieved. We had a point to prove. And that mentality set the tone for our summer.

'We trained like savages in the lead-up to that Cork game. At one stage, we did 20 nights out of 22. When we met Cork again, we were like wild animals. As I was leading the lads out the tunnel, I nearly mowed down Jimmy Barry-Murphy and Dr Con Murphy. "Get out of my f***ing way", I roared at them. They did. So did Cork.'

While ultimately the Banner never added to their haul of All-Irelands, they left a footprint on the GAA landscape that will never be erased. The sights, the sounds, of those indefatigable warriors thundering on to Croke Park, or Semple Stadium, would put the hairs standing on the back of anyone's neck.

{ A CAPITOL APPOINTMENT }

When Dalo took over the Dublin hurling team, on November 24, 2008, the only thing anybody could have been certain of was that sparks were about to fly. Dublin had a tendency to blow hot and cold, which used to drive Daly bonkers. After a particularly chastening defeat against Kilkenny 'Dalo' duly lost the plot.

'Conor McCormack and Ryan O'Dwyer were already in the showers by the time we got to the dressing-rooms, so I told them to come straight back out... "Get out. Now".

'IS EVERYTHING FUCKING OK NOW? I roared, as I swung the stick on the table with the force of an executioner. Bottles of water and hurleys, and the table itself which crumpled on its fold-up legs, were the victims. Everyone was in shock. Paul Ryan nearly recoiled three feet.

'To go out and do what we did against Kilkenny was just unbelievable. Give me days like last year's All-Ireland semi-final against Cork any time. I cried for nearly two days with the pain of not being in that final. It took me a month to get over it, but by God, give me the pain, but don't give me the shame. The absolute shame in all of us facing our families that evening was just heart-breaking.'

Anthony Daly's infectious touch was just what the doctor ordered for Dublin as they won their first National Hurling League final in 65 years. Dalo also managed Dublin to finally hunt down the Leinster hurling title against Galway, their first title in 52 years.

None of these successes came as a particular surprise from a man with a background in locating missing trophies!

DALO DAYS

ANTHONY DALY was born on October 22, 1969. The left wing-back is a native of Clarecastle, County Clare. Like many future Banner hurling stars, he was part of the production line at St Flannan's College.

He took the traditional route to the top, lining out with both the Clare minor and under-21 sides. Daly made his senior debut during the 1989–90 National League campaign.

He quickly emerged as a natural leader, powering the Banner to a memorable All-Ireland breakthrough in 1995. He also captained the 1997 Liam MacCarthy-winning side and collected three Munster medals.

He won five Clare championship medals with Clarecastle and he also picked up a Munster Club medal. Daly announced his retirement from inter-county hurling on February 21, 2002. He also garnered a very impressive haul of three All Star awards.

Upon retirement, Daly sign-posted his ability in management as he coached Clarecastle, Kilmoyley, and Kilmihil to club titles in their respective counties. While his time with his native county was unsuccessful, his six-year stint as Dublin manager bore real fruit as they won the Leinster title and reached an All-Ireland semi-final, narrowly losing to Cork.

JJ DELANEY

(Height 5' 11", Weight 14 St)

Decade... 2000s/2010s

(Position... Wing-Back/Full-Back)

CHIEF CHARACTERISTIC... SWIFT
APPREHENSION OF CAT BURGLARS

TOP ACCOMPLICES... JACKIE TYRRELL, MICHAEL KAVANAGH, TOMMY
WALSH, PADRAIG WALSH, PAUL MURPHY

JJ
DELANEY

*'WHEN JJ WAS INJURED FOR THE 2006 ALL-IRELAND FINAL,
AND WE WEREN'T GOING TO BE ABLE TO PLAY HIM, I SAID AT
THE TIME THAT I HAD NEVER SEEN A BETTER DEFENDER. I
HAVEN'T SEEN ANYTHING TO CHANGE MY MIND SINCE.'*

– BRIAN CODY

THE Vikings were a terrifying band of cold-blooded warriors who set sail from Scandinavia, initially raiding northern parts of Europe. To the Vikings, honour and glory in battle was the only thing that really mattered.

Warriors who died with courage in battle were bestowed with immortality in Viking heaven, which was called Valhalla.

The Vikings didn't have uniforms and supplied their own fighting attire. The warrior would always be buried with his most sacred possessions... his spear, sword or axe.

'Berserkers' were the most feared of all Viking warriors.

They fought without armour in a trance-like state. The mantra of all Vikings and indeed every warrior, is to die well, with great fortitude. For Viking warriors to end well was the most important thing of all.

If ever a GAA career ended well, there were few better than the one scripted by Kilkenny's Viking

**HARD
MAN
RATINGS**
TOUGHEST:
9.6/10

MEANEST:
9.5/10

SCARIEST:
9.3/10

HARDEST:
19.9/20

☠

**TOTAL
HARD MAN
48.3/50**

warrior, the majestic JJ Delaney.

His legendary hook on Seamus Callanan in the 2014 All-Ireland final replay set the tone for one of his finest-ever displays for the black and amber.

In a game that was always going to be enacted out upon a knife-edge, the crucial intervention ensured the perfect ending, to the perfect inter-county career.

The announcement of his retirement caught everybody by surprise, including his manager, the great Brian Cody.

'JJ rang me a couple of days before, so I was aware of it. But yeah, I was surprised a bit. But not massively either. You never know what players will decide. He was on top of his game, that's the way he decided it, and that's it.

'But I think everybody feels there is more in JJ. But again, that's only for JJ to decide.'

Cody could make some case for the defence with The Cats over the years but asserted that Delaney was quite simply in a league of his own.

And he finished, not just as a nine-time All-Ireland winner, but still the best defender in the game.

'When JJ was injured for the 2006 All-Ireland final, and we weren't going to be able to play him, I said at the time that I had never seen a better defender. I haven't seen anything to change my mind since.'

Delaney emerged from the unfashionable Fenians club from Johnstown, which is situated close to the Tipperary border. The club has produced some fine hurlers, including the likes of Pat and Ger Henderson, Pat Delaney, Nicky Orr, and Billy Fitzpatrick.

While not a tall man, there were few better under the dropping ball. Despite giving away many inches to towering forwards, the Fenians' star always had the uncanny knack of lording the skies and winning his aerial duels. Waterford legend Dan Shanahan recounted what a nightmare assignment marking Delaney always turned out to be.

'His timing was unreal in the air. If he didn't catch it, you could be guaranteed you wouldn't catch it either …and I knew all about it.'

JJ revealed his technique for catching the ball that stymied some of the greatest attacking talents in the small ball game. 'I never really caught the ball in front of my face. I used to catch it at the back of my head, let the ball pass my opponent because you have the ball falling into your hand, rather than hitting your hand.

'All you've to do is clear the path.

'You win that ball in the air, it's demoralising for your opponent. You can dictate where play is going to go as well. It's a real individual battle, whoever wants it more…'

His interventions normally terminated opposition attacks. Nobody seemed to want it more than Delaney. His quiet power was very understated. He seemed stapled to the earth and immovable in a physical confrontation. He thrived in Nowlan Park under Brian Cody's 'no rules' training games.

He was totally unfazed by size or stature. 'The bigger they are, the harder they fall' was the Fenian magician's match-day mantra.

Like all great defenders, he had his fair share of scuffles over the seasons. One was a high-profile skirmish with Tipperary's Lar Corbett, in which the Premier man's ribs were fractured. JJ protested his innocence and claimed the Tipperary man struck first.

'What you don't see is, Lar hits me under the chin before that camera goes on,' said Delaney on the *GAA Hour Live* All-Ireland final preview at the Liberty Hall in Dublin.

To which host Colm Parkinson playfully interjects. 'Yeah, but JJ, you have to understand that his helmet is harder than your fist'.

{ THE QUIET MAN }

Delaney was immeasurably relaxed on game-day, his demeanour seemed totally unprepared for the carnage that lay ahead. Brian Cody must have been perplexed by Delaney's nonchalant approach to the inter-county scene, but he quickly realised he had little cause to worry, as he revealed in JJ's tribute show.

'He'd sit down, look through the programme while everyone else would be out pucking or walking around. Then, when everyone else was half-togged out, he might start getting changed.

'He wasn't a massive talker, but whenever he did speak, it was worth hearing. I suppose because he was hugely concentrated on his own performance – and that stood to him. He was always preparing, and that's the most important thing for every player, that you're ready to go yourself…'

Delaney's versatility was a major plus during the Cody era, and while perennial question marks linger around the deployment of wing-backs at No. 3, he was an outlier who purred like a Rolls Royce at the anchor position.

JJ Delaney was always ready to go. Better than that, he knew when it was the best time to leave the stage. Like a true Viking, the ending was just as important as the titanic journey that preceded it. The Fenians' legend's spectacular, yet unexpected exit, guaranteed his legendary career would end well.

And that above all else… it's what great warriors aspire to do.

A CAT WITH NINE LIVES

JJ DELANEY was born in Waterford in 1982 and is a native of Johnstown. He first played competitive hurling at Coláiste Mhuire. He played minor and under-21 for The Cats, in what was a rare barren spell at underage level for Kilkenny.

Delaney's uncles, Billy Fitzpatrick and Pat Delaney won a total of nine All-Ireland medals between them, between 1969 and 1983, while his father, Shem Delaney, was also a panellist for Kilkenny.

He made his senior debut during the 2001 championship. He was comfortable in all roles within the Kilkenny rearguard, but Brian Cody favoured him at wing-back. The man that tasted little success at minor or under-21 level certainly banished those demons at senior level.

He won nine All-Ireland medals, 11 Leinster, and eight National League medals on the field of play. He represented his province Leinster on a number of occasions and won two Railway Cup medals.

Delaney made 66 championship appearances and announced his retirement from inter-county hurling on December 5, 2014.

At the conclusion of an epic career, he had seven All Star awards, while he also made a clean sweep of all the top individual awards, winning the All Star, Texaco, and GPA Hurler of the Year.

TONY DORAN

(Height 6' 0", Weight 15 St)

Decade... 1960s/1970s/1980s

(Position... Full-Forward)

CHIEF CHARACTERISTIC... FARMER WHO PUT
FULL-BACKS OUT TO PASTURE

TOP ACCOMPLICES... JACK BERRY, PAUL LYNCH, DAVE BERNIE, JIMMY
O'BRIEN, PHIL WILSON, JOHN QUIGLEY

TONY DORAN

'TONY WAS SUCH A WARRIOR. I WISH WE COULD FIND A TONY DORAN NOW. SOMEBODY SAID THAT TONY WOULD CATCH THE BALL WITH THESE BIG HANDS THAT HE HAD AND IF THERE WAS TIME, HE'D ACTUALLY SHOW IT TO HIS OPPONENT BEFORE HE BURIED IT."

– BILLY ROCHE

HOLDING 'The 'Dead Mans's Hand'…

Jack McCall swung through the saloon doors of the Nuttal & Mann's Saloon in Deadwood in Dakota Territory. James Butler Hickok (better known as 'Wild Bill' Hickok), never looked up from the poker table where he was holding a five-card draw hand.

McCall had played poker with Hickock the night previously and lost a considerable sum of money. Hickok had generously offered McCall money to buy breakfast, and advised him not to play again until he could cover his losses. McCall accepted the money, but he reportedly felt insulted, vowing a chilling revenge.

The following day on August 2, 1876, at another poker game, Hickok who always sat facing the door, arrived late and asked to change seats – an offer that was refused by the other players.

HARD
MAN
RATINGS
TOUGHEST:
9.7/10

MEANEST:
8.9/10

SCARIEST:
9.5/10

HARDEST:
20/20
☠

TOTAL
HARD MAN
48.1/50

A drunken McCall entered the saloon ordering a drink from the bar. He then moved a few steps behind Hickok and shot him in the back of the head with a single-action .45-calibre revolver, shouting… 'Damn you! Take that!'

Hickok died instantly.

According to a publication by Western historian Carl W Breihan, the cards that the deceased was holding were retrieved by a man called Neil Christy, who then passed them on to his son. The son, in turn, revealed the composition of the hand to Mr Breihan.

'The ace of diamonds with a heel mark on it; the ace of clubs; the two black eights, clubs, and spades, and the queen of hearts… with a small drop of Hickok's blood on it.'

The infamous cards Hickok had in his possession were christened the 'Dead Man's Hand' and would be forever associated with ill fortune, and one of the most notorious killings in the history of the 'Wild West…

At half-time in the 1968 All-Ireland hurling final, Wexford appeared to be holding The Dead Mans's Hand. Their worried supporters congregated in little knots at the interval, holding crisis meetings in every available nook and cranny of the vast cavernous bowl.

In the opening period, a buoyant blue and gold had refused to blink and had amassed an eight-point lead. Powered by Mick Roche's tour de force, they appeared to be holding all the aces at the interval.

The young man was a wild-looking warrior. A mop of fiery red hair and a hard-boned chiselled look. He looked older than his tender years, with a countenance that wore the hurling world upon his brow – his eyes blazing with raw intention.

His dreams in the witching hours had whispered great stories of 'Model Men' from days of Yore… Paddy Kehoe, Nicky and Bobby Rackard, to name a few. The road to Hurling's 'Oz' was paved with many bumps and potholes, but here was a young lion that would never lack for courage.

When Tony Doran was switched from his half-forward position to full-forward, it appeared a bold, but foolish move. The 22-year-old looked like a sacrificial offering, but soon it would be the Premier County's much-vaunted defence that would become lambs to the slaughter. Doran was a tall man at just over six foot, but he appeared to grow a few inches in that second period. The ball appeared to be a magnet to his bucket-sized hands.

Time and again he rose, he fetched, he turned, and he scored! If he didn't score, he generated enough mayhem to allow somebody else to burgle the Tipperary bank.

At every juncture, Doran's high-wire fielding delivered or created a lodgement in the Wexford account. Tipperary tried to claw their way back into the contest, but Doran's long shadow appeared to block out the sky, as he trampled all over a perplexed Tipperary rearguard. He plundered 2-1 and also nourished the rest of a ravenous Model pack. Wexford squeezed ahead, 5-8 to 3-12 at the final bell. It was an astonishing turnaround as the 'Yellow Bellies' turned the tables on their arch adversaries.

{ HOLDING BACK THE YEARS }

Doran had arrived on the big stage, and there the big man stayed for nearly two decades.

Brian Cody had seen a few real soldiers in his time and his estimation of Tony Doran summed up the view from the top cat who had been mauled more than a few times by the Buffers Alley hitman.

'The heart of a lion and the strength of an Ox,' he concluded, having locked horns with the red-haired Boolavogue destroyer on many painful occasions. Kilkenny mainly held the whip hand – with Doran at times waging a solo war on The Cats and the other imperial hurling forces.

Wexford and their wily warrior came close to a further Celtic Cross in 1970, but a deluge of Cork goals wrestled the precious silverware from their despairing fingertips.

Kilkenny's stranglehold on Leinster for five successive seasons at the dawn of the 70s ensured a five in-a-row of the unwanted variety for the frustrated Model County.

Twice they came agonizingly close to breaking the vicious cycle. In 1972, they brought The Cats to a replay and, two years later, when they lost only by a solitary point.

Finally, in 1976, they escaped The Cat's claustrophobic clutches when stunning the seemingly invincible six in-a-row seeking champs.

Cork awaited in the decider and duly engineered the mother-of-all smash 'n' grab raids to pilfer Liam MacCarthy. This time it was Wexford squandering an eight-point lead as the Cork men swooped late to deny them in a breathless finish.

It was a case of deja-vu the following season as the Leesiders found another devastating finishing kick to prevail by three points.

In an era when first Tipperary, then Kilkenny and Cork, were all at various stages at the peak of their powers, the luckless Buffers Alley titan always appeared to be holding a hand of 'Aces and Eights'.

Yet, he still found a way to prevail as he garnered All-Ireland club and county titles, and National League and Railway Cup medals, plus Leinster crowns a plenty.

Unbreakable, unstoppable, the magnificent Tony Doran always managed to come up smelling of roses… while holding The Dead Man's Hand.

»——→ A MODEL LIFE ←——«

ANTHONY 'TONY' Doran was born in April 1946. A native of Boolavogue, he first arrived on the inter-county scene at the age of 17 when featuring with the Wexford minor team, and subsequently graduated to the under-21 side.

He joined the senior panel during the 1964–65 National League. Doran played a key part for the team over the next two decades, winning one All-Ireland medal, four Leinsters and two National League medals.

He won his sole All-Ireland medal in 1968 against a fancied Tipperary side. He was also an All-Ireland runner-up on three occasions with the 'Yellow Bellies'.

At club level with Buffers Alley he won 12 county senior medals, three Leinster titles, and one All-Ireland title. He also won an All-Ireland Sevens title. As part of the Leinster inter-provincial team Doran won a total of seven Railway Cup medals.

Tony Doran was a prolific scorer and amassed a career tally of 41 goals and 57 points, making him Wexford's second-highest championship scorer. In total, he made 40 championship appearances with Wexford, averaging over a goal a game. He announced his retirement from the game at the conclusion of the 1984 championship.

He was chosen as full-forward on the All-Ireland club hurling silver jubilee team, and in the same position on a specially-chosen 'Greatest Ever' Wexford side in 2002.

JOHN DOYLE

(Height 6' 1", Weight 14.5 St)

Decade... 1940s/1950s/1960s

(Position... Corner-Back)

CHIEF CHARACTERISTIC... BORDER PATROL INTER-COUNTY UNIT

TOP ACCOMPLICES... TONY WALL, JOHN O'DONOHUE,
KIERAN CAREY, MICHAEL MAHER, JIMMY DOYLE

JOHN DOYLE

He was an integral part of the GAA's 'Most, *Most* Wanted'. History recorded them as one of the most unforgiving backlines in the annals of the ancient game.

John Doyle, however, despite all his physical prowess, could whip up a hurling storm of beguiling beauty. He was a master of the defensive craft, who was also blessed with a concert pianist's lightness of touch. From his position deep within the bowels of the Tipperary dungeons, forwards were held hostages to his hurling masterpieces, as he cast a dizzying spell of brilliance and brutality, leaving them bewitched and thoroughly bewildered.

Doyle's directness on the pitch was matched by a raw and searching honesty off it.

Looking back over his career, he pulled no punches in his searing assessment of those heady days of Hell's Kitchen generated heat, and added a degree of balance to a narrative that often portrayed the celebrated Premier crew on a very

HARD MAN RATINGS

TOUGHEST:
9.8/10

MEANEST:
9.4/10

SCARIEST:
9.7/10

HARDEST:
19.7/20

☠

TOTAL HARD MAN

48.6/50

unflattering canvas.

'I'll put it this way, we got as much punishment as we were supposed to have handed out,' said Doyle. 'I can assure you of that.

'I'd have to say about myself, I never hit a fella with a hurley in my life. If I had, that would have been the day I'd have had to give up. Oh, I hit them with my body alright. But with a hurley… no. And I stand over that.

'It was a lot more physical then. But nobody hurt anybody. And there was no big need for frees. Fellas didn't lie down for the sake of lying down. They didn't want to give you the saying that a fella knocked them down.

'I never cared about anybody, physically or otherwise, but I would beat them with my strength and my hurling ability.'

Hurling ability was certainly something the man titled 'The Legend' had coursing through his veins during his storied career.

Born on February 12, 1930, John was a member of the Tipperary senior panel while still a minor in 1948. He wore the famous blue and gold for the first time when lining out as a substitute in the 1947/1948 National League final defeat to Cork.

His first championship outing was in an unfamiliar role at corner-back in the 1949 Munster Championship replay victory over Cork. It would usher in a memorable era in Tipperary hurling, which would see them win three Liam MacCarthy Cups when completing three in-row from 1949 to 1951.

John Doyle would go on to become an ever-present for his native county. He was never dropped, or taken off injured, since his 1949 championship debut. Inevitably, John's hurling career would be forever viewed through tinted glass, as his association with fellow enforcers, Carey and Maher, was akin to being a member of the 'James Gang' in hurling's Wild West. The imposing Doyle enjoyed the notoriety, and like the rest of 'Hell's Kitchen' often traded on its fearsome currency. Michael Maher remembers John as a man who always give his opponent exact directions as to the whereabouts of the Tipperary goalmouth.

'They were all well aware too that they had the reputation they had and they played up to it, especially Doyle.

'At the start of a match, when the corner-forward came in on him, he'd say something like, "Do you see that line, little boy? If you know what's good for you, then you won't dream of going in past it".'

John was born into an era when the ancient game was at its most lawless and forwards were an unprotected species. Everyone and everything was fair-game, in a world that was light years away from the peering camera angles and the relentless trial by jury on social media.

Wexford's Ned Wheeler stepped into the 'Kitchen' in the 1962 All-Ireland final. Weighing in at a strapping 6'3" in height and weighing 15 stone, he appeared to possess the perfect profile for waging war against Doyle and company.

Wheeler was a midfielder by trade; like many before him, he discovered that a full-forward's role should have carried a government health warning, as he received a proper 'Premier' welcome, from the infamous trio. He explained that rather challenging scenario as he ruefully reflected on a tough day at the office.

'I found it the very same as putting a man into a pram. I was not built for it at all, I just didn't have the natural game to be a full-forward. I had a few good games alright, but in the '62 All-Ireland final I should have played much smarter.

'The rules of that era allowed full-back lines to be ferociously tough, and John Doyle, Michael Maher and Kieran Carey were certainly that. Many of the great forwards of the current game would have found it a lot more difficult were they hurling back then because it was a much more physical game.

'The forwards of that era had to be very robust themselves to cope. Take Christy Ring for example. He was built like a tank, and so was someone like Nicky Rackard. They were hard, brawny tough men, but they had to be to counteract the likes of John Doyle and the rest.'

Doyle's illustrious career was also beautifully captured by Paddy Downey, writing in *The Irish Times* in the 1960s.

It is a quality of style that is intrinsically a part of the man; the rugged power, the sweeping stroke, the touch of dare-devilry, perhaps; and certainly the cold courage.

Speaking to *The Sunday Tribune* columnist Enda McEvoy on the occasion of his 75th birthday in 2005, the Premier icon was asked how he would like his career to be remembered, he said, 'As far as the GAA is concerned, I hope club and county will always remember me as giving 100 percent'.

It was a sentiment that those lucky enough to have seen him in the flesh would surely echo.

A HURLING LIFE LESS
⟶ ORDINARY ⟵

JOHN DOYLE and Tipperary painted the 50s and 60s Blue and Gold. They won a plethora of national titles including the National League 1950, 1952, 1954, 1955 and 1957. The Premier pillaged those five NHL titles and four All-Ireland titles between 1959 and 1965. The Celtic Crosses were piled up for John Doyle and company, and following the 1965 All-Ireland victory he equalled Christy Ring's record of eight All-Ireland medals on the field of play.

When Tipperary qualified to play Kilkenny in the 1967 All-Ireland final, John was presented with the chance to become the first ever-player to win an unprecedented nine All-Ireland's on the field of play. Kilkenny had other ideas and were in a typically defiant mood to deny the Holycross man and put an end to their bitter rivals' recent dominance.

After the defeat, a crestfallen John Doyle called time on his inter-county career, and wrote the final chapter in one of hurling's most gripping storylines.

During his outrageously successful career, he garnered six Railway Cup medals along with Munster and six Oireachtas Cup medals. He also won the Texaco Hurler of the Year award in 1964. Rubber-stamping his place among the pantheon of greats, he was named at left corner-back on the GAA Hurling Team of the Century in 1984 and the GAA Hurling Team of the Millennium in 2000.

MICHAEL DUIGNAN

(Height 6' 0", Weight 15 St)

Decade... 1980s/1990s/2000s

(Position... Wing-Forward)

CHIEF CHARACTERISTIC... LOCKING CROKE PARK EXIT DOORS

TOP ACCOMPLICES... JOHNNY DOOLEY, DAITHÍ REGAN, JOE DOOLEY,
JOHN TROY, JOHNNY PILKINGTON

MICHAEL DUIGNAN

'EDDIE TROTTED BACK INTO THE CORNER, EFFING AND BLINDING AT NOT HAVING BEEN AWARDED A FREE. "THAT'S IT, EDDIE", I SAID. "YOU KEEP SOLOING OUT WITH THEM AND I'LL KEEP TAPPING THEM OVER THE BAR, YOU F***ING EEJIT."'

– MICHAEL DUIGNAN

YOU could feel it in the bricks and mortar. Growing up on the aptly named Cuba Avenue, Banagher in the 60s, you would nearly have expected to shoot the breeze with Fidel Castro, but Micheal Duignan certainly didn't lack revolutionary inspiration.

He lived next door to legendary Tipperary and Galway netminder, Tony Reddin who nourished him on a steady diet of all things iománaíochta, while granting him a 'golden ticket' to his very own version of the GAA Museum.

These were not just any old trinkets from the ancient game, featuring a camán from Christy Ring. Apparently, Ring had fired it at Reddin one day and Tony doing what goalkeepers do best… took it into his possession!

A couple of doors down were two bona fide rebels in the shape of the Fogarty brothers, who blazed a trail all the way to Liam MacCarthy

HARD MAN RATINGS

TOUGHEST:
9.3/10

MEANEST:
9.1/10

SCARIEST:
9.0/10

HARDEST:
19.6/20
☠

TOTAL HARD MAN
47.0/50

in the 80s. The area was thickly populated by a formidable array of Offaly players both past and present, including Shane McGuckian, who would man the corner-back berth on the 1994 All-Ireland winning side.

In Michael Duignan's searingly honest memoir of his hurling career and family ties, it is not hard to gain a sneaking affection for the St Rynagh's Goliath. He is the kind of fella you would love to go for a pint with, always entertaining and self-deprecating, a thoroughly decent sort. If empty platitudes and bull**** were your things though, then the former Offaly midfielder and forward was never going to be your cup of tea.

Duignan was on board as the Faithful's 'next generation' hurled up a storm and joined the pantheon of Offaly legends. Some forwards are not known for their durability, tending to be fast and light.

Built like a tank, skilful and quick off the mark, once Duignan built up a head of steam, he was more like an old-style hurling forward – barrelling and bulldozing all before him.

{ CHILDREN OF THE REVOLUTION }

The Faithful loved nothing more than putting one over on hurling's 'High Society,' and the upper-class didn't get much more toffee-nosed than Kilkenny. The two sides from different *sides* of the hurling tracks got to know each other very well during Micheal's stellar career.

In his book, he recalls an encounter with the 'Cats' in the 1995 Leinster final, where there was skin and fur flying!

'The match started a few minutes late but the weather didn't bother us. In fact, I felt it was a positive because we had more skilful hurlers and, in those conditions, your control comes under closer scrutiny. As it was, we walked on water.

'My outlook when it came to playing Kilkenny was that they would have to be matched physically in the first 20 minutes and then let the hurling look after itself. We weren't too worried about the scoreboard early on.

'If you went out trying to simply out-hurl them from the off you were on a loser straightaway. They'd just walk all over you. You had to meet them head-on in the physical battle and then see who blinks first thereafter.

'Some of the hurling in that first-half was savage. The hits, the hooking, the blocking. I scored the first point after a couple of minutes, which was equalised by PJ Delaney. That was the only point they scored from play all day. Eddie O'Connor was marking me and started very well, bursting out with possession several times.

'Make no mistake about it, they were well up for it, too, and Eddie was their lightning rod. At one stage, as he launched a kicked clearance, Johnny Pilkington came in and buried him. No free was given and the ball worked its way back down to Billy Dooley. He picked me out and I whipped over another point.

'Eddie trotted back into the corner, effing and blinding at not having been awarded a free.

"That's it, Eddie", I said. "You keep soloing out with them and I'll keep tapping them over the bar, you f***ing eejit."

'And, with that, he went absolutely ballistic.

'Chances to goad Eddie should never be passed up. I was switched to full-forward in a swap with Pat O'Connor and him and Eddie took lumps out of each other, and both got booked. Elsewhere, another Kilkenny player pulled a dirty stroke on Johnny Dooley, jabbing the hurley into his face and breaking his nose.

'Johnny was a pure hurler and didn't get involved in that stuff usually, but when the next ball broke between them, he lashed straight across him and shattered his hurley in the process. No quarter was asked or given. Every ball was contested furiously.

'Looking at the likes of Daithí Regan diving headlong to block players down, you couldn't but feed off it.'

Micheal and Offaly lived through extraordinary times.

All-Irelands won and lost in the blink of an eye. It was a wildly thrilling voyage that rattled through the decade at breakneck speed. The wins in 1994 and '98 were sandwiched between that late loss against the Banner in '95, as Liam MacCarthy was a late cancellation for a night in Dooley's Hotel, Birr.

Offaly appeared to have regenerated in the mould of a *Doctor Who* towards the start of the new Millennium. They reached the All-Ireland final in 2000, but Kilkenny put them to the sword in the decider.

Micheal recalled the aftermath and the realisation that the magic... was all, but gone. 'We were sore losers but that night was the exception. Nobody articulated it, but we knew that this was the end of the road for us.'

Micheal Duignan stayed on the road to the journey's end. That glorious, faithful generation, that answered the County's call to arms.

The Children of the Revolution...

A FAITHFUL SERVANT

DUIGNAN WAS a member of the St Rynagh's club from an early age and played in all grades in juvenile and underage levels. He graduated to the senior set-up aged just 16.

He appeared in his first county final on October 19, 1986, scoring a point from play as St Rynagh's suffered a narrow four-point reversal. Duignan lined out in a second successive senior final on September 27, 1987, and secured his first championship medal after the 0-11 to 0-09 defeat of Seir Kieran. In total, he appeared in 10 championship finals, winning four.

He played for the Offaly minor team, winning an All-Ireland final in 1986. And he lined out in three successive Leinster Under-21 finals, securing a winner's medal in 1989. He made his debut for the senior team in October 1987, when he lined out at left corner-forward in a 3-11 to 0-11 defeat of Laois.

In 1988, Duignan won his first of five Leinster Championship medals in a 3-12 to 1-14 defeat of Wexford. In 1991, he and Offaly claimed their very first league title after a 2-6 to 0-10 defeat of Wexford.

He won his first Celtic Cross in 1994 and won a further All-Ireland in 1998, and his first All Star award.

PETE FINNERTY

(Height 6' 1", Weight 14 St)

Decade... 1980s/1990s

(Position... Wing-Back)

CHIEF CHARACTERISTIC... OFFERING 'GOOGLE TRANSLATE'
TO UNCULTURED TIPPERARY FORWARDS

TOP ACCOMPLICES... TONY KEADY, GERRY MCINERNEY, STEVE
MAHON, BRENDAN LYNSKEY, OLLIE KILKENNY, SYLVIE LINNANE

PETE FINNERTY

'THE GREAT THING WAS, NOBODY EVER TOLD JOHN
LEAHY I DIDN'T HAVE A SISTER. NOWADAYS HE MIGHT
HAVE BEEN ABLE TO GOOGLE IT AND FIND OUT'
– PETE FINNERTY

THEY were Galway Hurling's Holy Trinity... Finnerty, Keady, and McInerney. A mythical trio of the finest tribal warriors. Pete Finnerty had a dream as a young man as he once revealed. He was inspired by the heroes of the past to become the legend of the future.

'In Mullagh National School, we had a picture on the wall... Carroll's All-Stars. How ironic a cigarette company sponsored the first All-Stars in '71! I remember John Connolly and I can still picture him to this day.

'I remember looking at that poster and wondering what would it take to get one of those bronze statues. It was something that people aspired to, although I wouldn't judge a player by how many All Stars he had. I'd judge him by his performances... the player he was, and his character.'

John Connolly was the 'alpha' that Finnerty aspired to be. Pete speaks about the impressive

HARD MAN RATINGS

TOUGHEST:
9.4/10

MEANEST:
9.5/10

SCARIEST:
9.3/10

HARDEST:
19.3/20

☠

TOTAL HARD MAN

47.5/50

Leitir Móir, native, in almost reverential tones. 'Without a doubt. I still look up to him today. Look at the man, look at the physique of him, look at the way he carries himself, look at the way he represented the county and Galway hurling… the way his family have.

'They are just incredible people. So, he is an incredible man. Absolutely.'

Pete certainly chose his role model well as Connolly was emblematic of the Westerners' hurling evolution and revolution, when they ended a bitter harvest of suffering that had lasted aeons.

'Iggy' Clarke was another of Galway's 'Dogs of War', whom Pete was inspired to emulate. When Iggy visited his school after a rare National League title, Pete displayed the kind of quick thinking that could have secured a spot on a reality business show, *The Dragons Den*.

'In '75, when they won their first league, he brought the cup to the national school and I got to see it that time. Then, one day, Brendan Hobbins, a neighbour of his, got a broken hurley of Iggy's and I remember bartering for it with a box of crayons and a few shillings.

'When I got the hurl, I thought it could nearly hurl by itself. Iggy would have been another huge inspiration.'

Pete Finnerty was determined to emulate his heroes. It was clear from an early stage that his style of defending did not include the taking of hostages. Ballinasloe Secondary School won three All-Ireland Vocational Schools titles, with Finnerty's imposing presence proving central to the Galway school's success.

His hurling exploits in secondary school saw him become an automatic selection on the Galway minor hurling team, who lost out to Tipperary in the All-Ireland final of 1982. Finnerty and Galway quickly atoned for that defeat, with the under-21 team subsequently winning an All-Ireland medal with the side in 1983.

Tipperary would be a central theme in the Mullagh man's career, and those early underage duels would be replicated with ferocious intensity at senior level, during the 80s and 90s.

{ THE TRIP TO TIPP }

Wherever they turned, the maroon and white always seemed to bump into the Premier County. The sides clashed in the 1987 All-Ireland semi-final, with Pete and Galway needing little motivation to take down their pompous neighbours.

'I remember Richie Stakelum made a statement that 'the famine is over'. And it was the greatest motivational speech you could ever give to us. And there was a feeling that Tipp were going to steamroll everyone and take their divine right at the top of the table.'

Galway would prevail but, inevitably, the pair returned for the 1988 All-Ireland final. Galway had beaten Offaly at the penultimate stage, with Finnerty revealing an exchange between Galway great Brendan Lynskey and Offaly substitute Michael Duignan. Duignan stretched out his hand to the Galway man as the raw 18-year-old nervously entered the fray. Lynskey glared at him and offered a greeting through gritted teeth.

'A mhaicin, what are you doing here? The minor match is over!'

Pete would invariably lock horns with Tipp's John Leahy and the Mullinahone Maestro had a penchant for in-game conversation.

'I said on the radio that someone should have told John (Leahy) that I didn't have a sister. John would be saying things and I'd be saying things. It went on wholesale.'

Galway had the edge in those years as they saw off the Premier in the 1988 decider, but relations were deteriorating as time progressed and Tipperary would reassert their stranglehold of previous decades by the end of the 90s.

The 1989 All-Ireland semi-final was fuelled by 'The Tony Keady' affair', as the Galway man had been suspended for playing in the US. Pete was his usual pillar of strength, as he tried to rally the Tribe in a year where the fates had appeared to conspire against them.

'If Keady had broken his thumb or broken his collarbone and was out for the year, we probably would have won the three in-a-row. A lot of the bitterness came off the field.'

The game was a nasty encounter with a real sense of malice permeating the city air.

John Leahy pulled right across the body of Pete early in the game. It would have felled many a man, but the Goliath that was Pete Finnerty was not for turning back. He shrugged off the incident and provided insight into the mindset of trench warriors at the highest level.

'There was nothing about it early in the game. Leahy was laying down a marker against me. I wouldn't lay down for Leahy, no matter what. So, I just went straight out through the tackle.'

Taking the hits and giving them. The lion-hearted Pete Finnerty was the complete hurling defender. The man who had aspired to be his hero, John Connolly, carved out a tribal legacy all of his own.

A QUEST IN
THE WEST

THE MAN from Mullagh lined out for the club made famous by the great Galway and Tipperary net-minder, Tony Reddin. His time with the south-eastern club yielded little in the way of success as they struggled to emerge from the shadows of neighbouring giants, Loughrea and Portumna.

Pete pulled on the famous maroon and white for Galway in 1983. He made his senior debut in a National League game and had cemented his place in the side by the time the 1985 championship got underway. Galway reached the All-Ireland final that season, but they were undone by Offaly in a close-run affair - eventually, losing out by two points. Despite the setback, Pete was the recipient of an All Star at the end of the season.

In 1986, Galway reached yet another All-Ireland final, however, they were again defeated, by serial Liam MacCarthy winners, Cork. A second All Star followed in 1987, and the Tribesmen qualified for their third All-Ireland final appearance in-a-row, as they faced Kilkenny. It was a case of third time lucky for Pete Finnerty, as Galway emerged with the victory. He had by now established himself as the top wing back in the country, as Galway crossed swords with neighbouring giants Tipperary in the 1988 All-Ireland final.

Pete gained a second Celtic Cross and put the cherry on top with a very impressive fourth All Star on the trot.

AARON GILLANE

(Height 6' 0", Weight 14 St)

Decade... 2010s/2020s

(Position... Corner-Forward)

CHIEF CHARACTERISTIC... A FORWARD WHO TAKES NO PRISONERS

TOP ACCOMPLICES... GEARÓID HEGARTY, CIAN LYNCH, TOM
MORRISSEY, WILL O'DONOGHUE, SEAMUS FLANAGAN, PETER CASEY

AARON GILLANE

'IT WAS A SMALL BIT WILD, A BIT STUPID. THAT'S NOT MAKING ANY EXCUSES, I LOST THE HEAD THERE FOR A FEW MINUTES. I WAS VERY LUCKY TO STAY ON THE FIELD AND I WAS THANKFUL FOR THAT.'

– AARON GILLANE

YOU have got to pick a pocket or two… You could picture him on the streets of Victorian London. Lurking in some back-alley, waiting to prey on some poor unsuspecting soul. He is after all, the master of his craft.

Whether they seek him here, or seek him there, he always manages to melt back into the shadows leaving his victims to count a rather heavy cost.

Jack Dawkins was better known as the Artful Dodger, a character in Charles Dickens' 1838 novel *Oliver Twist*. The hero, or should we say villain, is a pickpocket and so labelled for his skill and cunning in that noblest of occupations

The Dodger leads a gang of child criminals on the rat-infested streets of London, under the tutelage of an elderly master of the art named Fagin. The infamous 'Artful Dodger' has passed into legend and is the byword for describing a person with skilful deception.

It might be a stretch to cast Limerick's

HARD MAN RATINGS

TOUGHEST:
9.1/10

MEANEST:
9.6/10

SCARIEST:
9.5/10

HARDEST:
19.0/20

☠

TOTAL HARD MAN

47.2/50

headmaster and manager, John Kiely, as the conniving Fagin, but one of the central characters in his all-conquering side hosts a CV that might well land him a role in the production!

You have to scratch a living on the inter-county scene and it certainly helps if you can pick a pocket or two!

It was one of the first interviews the Treaty's Artful Dodger had given, and Aaron Gillane, the spring-heeled, elusive Patrickswell forward had just stitched seven points in the All-Ireland under 21 final. Kilkenny had chased him in and out of shadows, only to go back to the dressing-room and find the Cross Of Cashel Trophy had been removed from right under their noses.

Smiling broadly, Gillane naturally enough was rather pleased with what had been a profitable day on the 'street'. The genie had certainly tumbled out of the bottle and the hunt would soon be on for Limerick's Dodger.

'We're finished our underage career now, we've been playing together since we were under-14. We're going try to kick on and make the senior panel again. You never know, you might see a few of us on the senior panel next year, that's the plan anyway.

'There's game plans and all that, but once you go out on the field, it's all instinct. You're training all year, all you're doing is hurling training. You go out on the field and let the hurling do the talking.'

Aaron Gillane certainly turned out to be a man of his word. He is the central cog in a formidable Limerick green machine. The smiling assassin Gillane would go on to terrorise even the most seasoned county defenders and anybody looking for trouble had arrived at the right place. He readily admits that sometimes he is a little eager to engage the close attention of his intimidators.

{ I FOUGHT THE LAW }

His mantra could well have been mined from the 1987 Brian De Palma gangster movie, *The Untouchables* where the old Bible adage of 'An Eye for an Eye' most definitely held sway.

'He sends one of yours to the hospital, you send one of his to the morgue.'

Sometimes the 2022 Hurler of the Year nominee crosses the line, putting himself and his teammates firmly behind the eight ball. Getting up close and personal with Cathal Barrett wouldn't be everyone's cup of tea, but the Patrickswell firebrand kept yanking the Premier man's chains, before lashing out and nearly decapatating the Holycross hardman.

Referee Paudie O'Dwyer took a long hard look at the incident and brandished a yellow. Aaron Gillane heaved a huge sigh of relief as he somehow avoided suspension.

'I knew myself it wasn't acceptable, especially with what was on the line. We were going for three Munsters in-a-row. I had to say *Cop on, don't be the person to make Limerick lose out on such an unbelievable achievement… to keep the head, keep the cool. Take whatever you're given and use your brain.*

'It was a small bit wild, a bit stupid. That's not making any excuses, I lost my head there for a few minutes. I was very lucky to stay on the field and I was thankful for that. It would be embarrassing to be sent off. More that you let down the team, which is more important than any individual. You don't want to be letting down the team, to be that person that did something stupid to cost the team winning a match or in that instance winning a Munster final. So, I'd definitely take learnings from it.'

Aaron Gillane truly is no-nonsense personified. Whatever way the posse seeks to apprehend him, he has too many guns at his disposal. The Patrickswell sharpshooter possesses a turn of foot-like greased lightning and an even faster-hurling brain.

Gillane is a throwback to an age when forwards were the ones who set the rules of engagement. When you think you are holding his hurley, it's likely he is holding yours. He has reimagined every trick in the book of Dark Hurling Arts. By hook or by crook, he is happy to live and die by the sword.

An inter-county forward's lot is supposed to be difficult, but Gillane makes the fine art of scoring look ridiculously easy. He is the Rolls Royce version of a county hurler's engine. He glides, he purrs, and then he blows you out of the water, before darting back into the shadows to leave your team ruefully counting the cost. Just when you think you have him, he is already disappearing around the next corner.

Aaron Gillane is the original three-card-trick. The three-card Monte is an example of a classic 'short con' where the dealers employ sleight of hand, and misdirection to prevent the victim locating the target card.

The elusive Gillane has been the target card for a few years. Hiding in plain sight and then by some magical sleight of hand, he isn't there.

'You got to pick a pocket or two…'

THE LIFE
OF A
GUNSLINGER

AARON GILLANE was born in 1996 and is a product of the Ardscoil Rís production line in Limerick. He was part of the college's 2014, Harty Cup side that defeated Scoil na Trionóide from Doon by 2-13 to 0-4 in the final.

As part of the Mary Immaculate College senior hurling team, in 2017 he won a Fitzgibbon Cup medal as Mary I duly retained the trophy following a 3-24 to 1-19 defeat of Carlow Institute of Technology in the final.

At club level, he hurled without much success in the underage ranks. In 2016, he scored seven points in the Limerick senior final as Patrickswell claimed their first championship in 13 years.

Gillane was first selected for the Limerick Minor panel in 2014. They reached the All-Ireland, but he did not feature on the matchday squad. He made his debut with the Limerick under-21 team in June 2016. In September 2017, Gillane was the chief marksman with seven points in Limerick's 0-17 to 0-11, defeat of Kilkenny in the All-Ireland final. He was also the championship's overall top scorer with 0-44.

At senior level he won the All-Ireland Championship in 2018, 2020, 2021, 2022 and 2023. He has won five Munster Championships and two National Hurling Leagues, along with two Limerick County titles, and collected three All Stars.

JIM GREENE
(Height 6' 0", Weight 14.5 St)

Decade... 1960s/1970s/1980s
(Position... Centre-Back/Full-Forward)

CHIEF CHARACTERISTIC... SHINING LIGHT
IN A DECADE TO FORGET FOR THE DEISE

TOP ACCOMPLICES... PAT MCGRATH, PAT O'GRADY, JOHN GALVAN,
MARTIN GEARY, MOSSIE WHELAN, SEAMUS HANNON

JIM GREENE

*IT WAS A RICH AND VARIED Q&A ON THE MOUNT SION
WEBSITE, BUT IT WAS QUESTION 25 THAT
PERHAPS PROVED TO BE THE MOST REVEALING.
Q.25. IF YOU COULD GO BACK IN TIME, WHERE WOULD YOU GO?
JIM GREENE: ANCIENT IRELAND
TO CHALLENGE CÚCHULLAIN AND WIN!!*

IF any man could have locked horns with one of Irish mythology's greatest warriors, it had to be Waterford's Jim Greene. A man who spent a decade in the backline and then upped sticks, and pitched his tent in the forwards for another decade, had to be a very special kind of player.

Jim Greene would have been happy to throw on a Waterford shirt to go to Mass! As long as he was part of the Deise line-up, no job was too big or too small for the iconic Mount Sion Mauler.

Jim was pitched in at the deep end when he made his Waterford debut against a couple of 70s legends, in the shape of Jimmy Doyle and Francis Loughnane. It was in an era when men were men, as teammate Pat McGrath revealed.

'In my time, there was a lot more hitting, to be honest about it. You had to sort a few fellas out at times. If someone hit you, that's it, you get him back. That was in the 70s. When the ball was up

**HARD
MAN
RATINGS**

TOUGHEST:
9.3/10

MEANEST:
9.0/10

SCARIEST:
9.0/10

HARDEST:
19.6/20

☠

TOTAL
HARD MAN

46.9/50

the field and a fella gave you a dunt, you gave it back to him.

'You couldn't take it. You had to give it back to him.

'That's the way it was, if you didn't stand up a fella had you in his pocket… you know what I mean… you had to stand up and be counted.'

Times were hard on and off the pitch – as Waterford performed an off-broadway version of the iconic Munster Hurling Championship. They kept plugging away, but an elusive title was always a bridge too far for an eternally frustrated Noreside outfit.

They took some serious scalps along the way, and there were times when they had their pockets picked late on – as was the case in 1969 when a Richie Bennis-inspired Limerick caught them at the death.

It might have helped the Waterford cause if Cork had been expelled from Munster – on the basis that they were playing way above the other county's pay grade. Any assessment of the Deise's annual credentials were always tempered by glancing through a Cork lens.

The Leesiders housed an all-singing, all-dancing, All Star ensemble, which put any prospect of a Munster title very firmly in the 'not a snowball's chance in hell variety'! The original 'dog's dinner was all that was on offer in the southern province, with many counties vying for scraps off the Rebel table, as Jim Greene lamented.

'In my time, we didn't win anything really. We won half a league one time coming out of the second division, that was about the size of it. We had some great days in Munster, we got to Munster finals, got destroyed in the two of them… but the semi-finals were memorable.

'Cork were the dogs in those days, Cork were huge. They had a super team; they had about 20 All Stars... they had All Stars that were subs on the team! We were never really good enough.

'We never came out of Munster, sure. We never played Kilkenny in the championship. We never got to test ourselves any further than Munster. That was as far as we went.'

There was, however, for Jim and Waterford the very odd rose lurking among the thorns.

'We beat Cork in 1974 in the Munster Championship which was huge. I was centre-back in those days. That was one of the best, that day we beat Cork in Walsh Park.

'We had no chance. Seamus Power was our selector at the time. There was no such thing as managers and trainers. Seamus, who was on the 1959 team, he was our motivator and by Jesus, he had us up for it that day.'

{ BACK TO THE FUTURE }

One of the great myths of inter-county fare today is the notion that players from the 60s, 70s and 80s, never really trained, or cared as much as the modern-day player. Players from those eras did not have access to Strength & Conditioning coaches and hi-tech, highly monitored environments, but the crucial point was they trained at the optimal level of those times.

The game produced fast and skilful players, and with access to today's dazzling array of tools they could possibly have produced players of a similar ilk.

It was a point Jim reflected on. 'Nowadays, it's different. You'd be going to a gym. My name is Jim... that's the closest I got to a gym!

'Coaches were for travelling on! It was a different world completely. The game was different as well… much tougher, much harder, much more physical. Today, the game is much faster. It's played at a different pace and it's played in a different way as well.

'We were serious about our game. We did our three or four nights a week but after the match it would be common to celebrate, even if you were beaten. It was more acceptable in those days.

'It was an amateur sport played by amateurs and lived accordingly. We gave it our best shot. It's nearly professional now. Chaps have to watch the colour of their pee! Everything is monitored. A totally different approach to it.

'Our love of the game wasn't any less than fellas' love of the game today. If that's what was there in our day, that's what we would have done. We were all terrible serious men and loved our county.

'We would give second to nobody, the same as the lads today.'

The redoubtable Jim Greene would never give second to nobody… including Cúchullain!

GREENE VALLEYS
AND PEAKS

JIM GREENE was born in 1950 and played his club hurling with the local club Mount Sion.

The Waterford giants were mainly a hurling club – but have won five Waterford senior football titles – albeit the last one arriving in as far back as 1961.

Greene would go on to enjoy great success with Mount Sion. Despite Ballygunner's recent dominance, Mount Sion sits comfortably ahead on the Roll of Honour list as Waterford's most successful hurling outfit. As in the case of the football side, the club had not enjoyed too much recent success, with its last title arriving in 2006. Jim Greene won a total of eight Waterford senior medals with Mount Sion and was part of the side that won a historic Munster club title back in 1981.

He joined the Waterford senior panel in 1968, after serving his apprenticeship with both the minor and under-21 panels. He was a powerful, physical presence in a number of positions, as Waterford reached a handful of Munster finals.

Despite many near misses, the converted back would never win any Munster medals or grace Croke Park on All-Ireland day. He was, however, one of the finest players of his era.

He was rewarded with an All Star award selection in 1982, at left-corner forward, with Kilkenny's Christy Heffernan, securing Jim's more natural berth in the centre.

MARTIN HANAMY
(Height 5' 10", Weight 14 St

Decade... 1980s/1990s
(Position... Corner-Back)

CHIEF CHARACTERISTIC... TIMBER TESTING AND
TIMBER RELATED PRODUCTS SALESMAN

TOP ACCOMPLICES... BRIAN WHELAHAN, KEVIN KINAHAN, HUBERT
RIGNEY, BARRY WHELAHAN, KEVIN MARTIN, MICHEAL DUIGNAN

MARTIN HANAMY

'THE TOUGHER THEY WERE THE MORE I LIKED THEM. I USED TO ENJOY THE CLASHING AND THE PULLING. THAT'S WHY I DON'T LIKE THE MODERN GAME THAT MUCH... IT'S ALL POKING AND TIPPING. I DON'T KNOW WHEN I LAST SAW A BROKEN HURL.'

- MARTIN HANAMY

THE MAN WHO WOULD BE KING...

The Hittites were a fearsome warrior race that rose to power during the Bronze Age – 3300 BC to 1200 BC. They were the first army to have three occupants in a chariot, one a shield-bearer guarding and the other two soldiers, who were armed with a spear and a bow-and-arrow respectively.

This innovation proved to be a game-changer on the battlefield, as they overpowered their Egyptian enemies at the Battle of Kadesh. The future king of the Hittites was required to have proven his prowess on the battlefield with great feats and deeds of courage.

St Rynagh's Martin Hanamy was always destined to lead the Faithful.

From an early age his prowess on the battlefield singled him out as a brave and mighty warrior. When the stars aligned for Offaly hurling in 1994 – the time for coronation had arrived.

HARD MAN RATINGS

TOUGHEST:
9.7/10

MEANEST:
9.2/10

SCARIEST:
9.5/10

HARDEST:
19.3/20

💀

TOTAL HARD MAN

47.7/50

THE MAN WHO WOULD BE KING…

Applications for a career in Offaly's hurling defensive ranks were thin on the ground in the late 80s and 90s. There was a 'NO VACANCIES' sign for any of the defensive berths as the Faithful County boasted their very own elite band of Charioteers!

Brian 'Syd' Whelahan, Offaly's only 'Millennium Man' was untouchable at wing-back and a variety of other positions. Kevin Kinahan defiantly anchored the 'Mean Machine' at full-back. Martin Hanamy's clubmate, Hubert Rigney was a 'shoot-em-up style' of centre-back. The growling, prowling Martin Hanamy's enduring defensive excellence, ensured applications for a corner-back berth were always going to be kept at a premium.

Martin's menacing and marauding presence guaranteed forwards tended to avoid his corner… like the plague!

Hanamy was a man who was renowned for introducing plenty of 'bite' into proceedings, and enjoyed the concept of in-your-face warfare which was up close and personal.

'The tougher they were, the more I liked them. I used to enjoy the clashing and the pulling.

'That's why I don't like the modern game that much… it's all poking and tipping. I don't know when I last saw a broken hurl.'

After a few near misses, Martin and Offaly seemed ideally placed to build on the 'Class of 85' Liam MacCarthy win, but they were beaten by Kilkenny in 1993 amid some controversy, and Martin alluded to this in a subsequent interview.

The Faithful's latest golden generation was finding out that rewriting the history books nearly always involved a few blood-stained chapters!

'John Power made a big fall and got a penalty, which DJ Carey goaled. Pat Delaney was refereeing at the time, it was a bad decision. We were looking good until then.'

In 1994, Offaly were back and hell-bent on revenge. The teams had a healthy dislike for each other, with Offaly feeling the Cat's favourite tag largely undeserved.'You could beat Kilkenny two years running, and still be underdogs the next year if they showed some form in the league. You'd say to yourself... *We beat these hoors 10 points last year and they're favourites again.'*

Such is an underdog's lot but, undeterred, Offaly prevailed in the Leinster semi-final to set up a date with Wexford in the decider, which they won without being fully extended.

After accounting for the perennially dangerous 'Galwegians' in the All-Ireland semi-final, Martin was inching ever closer to the Holy Grail. Limerick awaited at GAA headquarters and the mood in the Faithful camp was a relaxed one, as the mercurial Johnny Pilkinton revealed when chatting with RTÉ's Ger Canning.

When Canning enquired of Johnny in the build-up, asking him, 'What will it mean to Offaly, Johnny?' the gifted Birr man needed no probing.

'A lot of drinking Ger!'

Marin narrowly missed out on an All-Ireland minor win in 1986 as he was overage for the grade, but was re-united with players of the calibre of John Troy, Brian Whelahan, Johnny Dooley and Adrian Cahill at senior level. There was a growing realisation that Offaly were on the cusp of a second wave of hurling greatness.

{ THE FIVE-MINUTE FINAL }

The final would turn out to be one of the most extraordinary in living memory as Limerick looked to have both hands on Liam MacCarthy. The 'five-minute final' as it came to be known, would see the Faithful get up off the canvas and deliver a devastating knock-out to the Munster champions – with the Dooley brothers, Joe, Johnny, and Billy, scoring an eye-watering combined total of 2-11.

The incredible scoring burst from the Seir Kieran trio was no surprise to Martin Hanamy; they had notched the exact same total against St Rynagh's in the 1988 Offaly final. The quiet man of Offaly hurling, as ever, did his real talking on the pitch. Time and time again, Martin Hanamy rallied his troops as Offaly's famed rearguard eventually stemmed the tide.

The valiant Treaty challenge finally ran out of gas – with the Faithful scorching past the startled Shannonsiders. Offaly's second generation had come of age and Hanamy had steered the Faithful chariot safely home.

Battered and bruised, the rock that the team leaned most heavily upon sported a heavily bandaged and bloodied forehead as he hoisted the precious silverware.

Martin sold his soul to the Faithful, when he began his affiliation with the senior team in 1987. Thirteen seasons, two All-Irelands, and eight different managers later, his fantastic voyage came to an end. In that period, he missed a single championship match, a first-round tie against Meath.

Offaly manager Pat Fleury, whom a teenage Hanamy succeeded, and who went on to become his manager, paid a glowing tribute to Hanamy's career.

'Martin has been a magnificent corner-back. Certainly, one of the greatest backs that I have ever had the privilege of seeing. It's going to be strange looking at an Offaly team without him.'

Fleury also paid tribute to the man's unwavering level of consistency. 'He had one bad match in 13 years... how many players can say that?'

THE MAN WHO WOULD BE KING!

A FATEFUL VOYAGE

MARTIN HANAMY hurled with St Ryangh's senior team in the mid-1980s. The famous club derives its name from the sister clubs that encompass Cloghan and Banagher, in County Offaly. The St Rynagh's Hurling Club is based in Banagher and wears blue and gold jerseys.

Hanamy won his first Offaly hurling championship title in 1987. He would go on to captain the club as St Rynagh's enjoyed a sustained period of success, when winning four Offaly senior titles.

He was selected for the Offaly minor and under-21 hurling sides, before migrating to the senior ranks, making his first appearance at senior level for Offaly during 1986-87 National League.

From 1988 to 1990 the Faithful were top dogs in Leinster but were unable to pass the penultimate test - missing out on three consecutive All-Ireland finals, including to an unfancied Antrim, who were later trounced by Tipperary.

In 1991, Hanamy captured a National League title, making history with Offaly's first ever league win. Three years later in 1994, he was captain of Offaly, and he won his fourth Leinster title.

They finally made it to an All-Ireland final and made no mistake beating Limerick, after trailing by five points late on. Hanamy won his second All-Ireland medal in 1998. A model of consistency, he won three All Star awards.

DECLAN HANNON

(Height 6' 2", Weight 14.5 St)

Decade... 2010s/2020s

(Position... Centre-Back)

CHIEF CHARACTERISTIC... CHIEF EXECUTIVE, ALL-IRELAND
WINNING SPEECHES DEPARTMENT

TOP ACCOMPLICES... DIARMUID BYRNES, SEAN FINN,
NICKY QUAID, KYLE HAYES, CIAN LYNCH

DECLAN HANNON

MAHALANGUR *Himal sub-range, Himalayan Mountains, 1978.*

Reinhold Messner savoured the view from the summit. His breath came in short-sharp rasps. He gazed across the blue, snow-capped peaks and undulating valleys that were dotted along the Chinese and Nepalese borders.

Reinhold Messner and his partner in crime, Peter Habeler, had just completed the first ascent of Everest without supplemental oxygen. Widely acknowledged as the greatest mountaineer in the world, he was used to clocking up firsts.

He was the first climber to ascend all 14 peaks over 8,000 metres (26,000 ft) above sea level – achieving the feat without the aid of supplementary oxygen. The intrepid Messner was also the first man to cross Antarctica and Greenland, with neither snowmobiles nor dog sleds. He then trekked across the treacherous scorched earth of the Gobi Desert on foot.

HARD MAN RATINGS

TOUGHEST:
9.5/10

MEANEST:
9.3/10

SCARIEST:
9.2/10

HARDEST:
19.4/20

TOTAL HARD MAN

47.4/50

The words of the Marvin Gaye and Tammy Tyrrell smash-hit readily applied the perfect summation of Reinhold Messner's astonishing feats.

Ain't no mountain high enough...

Declan Hannon savoured the view from the summit. His breath came in short-sharp-bursts.

Even Reinhold Messner hadn't managed to ascend one of the highest peaks in Irish sport on four different occasions. He smiled as he looked across at his partner-in-crime, Cian Lynch, gazing out at the sea of expectant, smiling, Limerick faces. It had been an incredible journey.

As they raised the sacred chalice into the Dublin sky, Hannon and the Treaty's ambitions knew no limits.

Ain't no mountain high enough...

Eamon Cregan cast his hawk-eye over proceedings. Cregan resembles the Treaty's version of the venerable Jabba The Hut – it feels like he has lived 600 lifetimes. He is Limerick's Yoda, a wise, thoughtful man, a captivating creature. When Eamon Cregan speaks, he always holds the world in the palm of his hand.

He has the countenance of an old sailer – a look that transcends time. Every second of his journey, every drop of salt water, seems etched upon his brow. Cregan has been around the block several times – you simply cannot kid a kidder!

Hannon's coach at Mary Immaculate could smell a hurler a mile away. He knew he was looking in the mirror, and the reflection he saw was Adare's Declan Hannon. Cregan's career arc had taken the scenic route from left-corner forward to centre-back. He indicated that Hannon's conversion into an All-Ireland winning No.6 was not as hopeful a punt as many of the Treaty faithful felt.

'He's comfortable anywhere because he has that ability, good first touch, and strikes well off the left and the right.'

Declan Hannon had certainly got everybody's attention in Páirc Uí Chaoimh. Adare had just exited the Munster Club Championship to a powerful Newtownshandrum outfit, but the performance of a 16-year-old kid gave the flagging Treaty supporters a real shot-in-the-arm.

While the side that lived in the shadow of lofty neighbours Patrickswell had been outfoxed by a slicker Cork unit – losing by three points, 1-17 to 1-14 – incredibly, all but one of Adare's scores came from one player, Declan Hannon.

The gangly kid migrated to the Limerick senior side, making his inter-county bow in a National League tie against Antrim. Hannon was selected as a right-wing forward for the 2010 encounter. Fast forward three seasons later... and he was being deployed at full-forward in the Munster final against Cork.

When John Kiely took charge in 2017, he decided it was time to switch up and shuffle his pack. Hannon was promoted to captain and surprisingly relocated to centre-back. It was an experiment that didn't bear any spectacular dividends initially, but Kiely persisted, ignoring the urge to redeploy Hannon on the front line.

It turned out to be a masterstroke as Limerick and Declan Hannon were about to get up close and personal ... with Liam MacCarthy!

On August 19, 2018, Hannon scored two points from play and powered the Shannonsiders to the Holy Grail of their first All-Ireland title in 45 years – after a 3-16 to 2-18 defeat of Galway in the final.

Hannon had revelled in his newfound role and brought his trusty scoring irons with him.

Limerick and Declan Hannon had arrived – and in some style. Kiely's addition of Hannon to the half-line was the component that ring-fenced the Limerick rearguard.

As Limerick's relentless juggernaut hoovered up further titles in 2020, 2021, 2022 and 2023, Hannon and his marauding trench warriors released the Treaty version of 'shock and awe,'on the bemused hurling fraternity.

{ STEERING THE TREATY SHIP }

After a brief respite in 2019, when Kilkenny swooped late to steal the champion's thunder, not even hurling's high-kings could decipher the riddle of the heavy-hitting Limerick half-back line.

Hannon's incredible strength allied with his supreme athleticism had added another steely layer of protection. On song, he makes that formidable unit hum. He is a superior defensive barrier – the 'Factor 50' of one of the most potent backlines in the annals of the ancient game of hurling.

Hannon steers the Treaty ship with the minimum of fuss. In 2021, he emulated Christy Ring as the only other hurler to lift Liam MacCarthy three times, while joining another exclusive club. Along with Micheal Maher of 'Hell's Kitchen' fame, he has also captained three All-Ireland-winning teams in four years.

Hannon is not a man to be too weighed down by history and when queried about his fantastic feats, he refused to get carried away with all the bells and whistles.

'Not really,' he said, when asked did he think much about

taking the Cloyne master's record.

'I'm not lying, but I haven't really thought about that at all. For players, there's always something else coming around the corner.'

You can bet that Declan Hannon, and Limerick, are already thinking about scaling many more peaks in their incredible climbs.

For the man who has travelled to one of the most rarified peaks in Irish sporting history, the relentless desire to scale even greater heights still burns brightly.

Ain't no mountain high enough…

»———→ THE ←———«
CAPTAIN'S TALE

DECLAN HANNON was born on November 25, 1992. Hannon attended Scoil Naomh Iosaf, Boy School, situated in his local village of Adare. Hurling is in the family bloodlines and his granduncle, Pat Stakelum captained rivals Tipperary to the All-Ireland title in 1949.

Hannon shot to fame as a hurler with Ardscoil Rís in Limerick. He scored three points from play when Ardscoil Rís defeated Thurles CBS in the final of the Harty Cup final in 2010.

He was again at centre-back as Ardscoil Rís retained the Harty Cup title after a 3-19 to 0-3 defeat of Cork's CBS Charleville.

He was part of the Mary Immaculate College senior team and won a Fitzgibbon Cup medal in 2016.

He first represented the Adare senior side when he was 16. He was part of the side that defeated Na Piarsaigh the final of the Limerick Senior Championship. He has won three Limerick Senior Football titles and one Senior Hurling County medal.

He is the only man to captain a side to four All-Ireland titles: 2018, 2020, 2021, 2022, and has also won six Munster Senior Championships. He holds three National Leagues: 2019 (c), 2020 (c), and Division Two in 2011. Hannon has won three All Star Awards: 2018, 2021, and 2022.

CHRISTY HEFFERNAN
(Height 6' 2", Weight 14.5 St)

Decade... 1980s/1990s
(Position... Centre-Forward)

CHIEF CHARACTERISTIC... ALWAYS TOOK THE ONLY ROAD THAT
MATTERS TO FULL-FORWARDS... ROUTE ONE

TOP ACCOMPLICES... FRANK CUMMINS, JOE HENNESSY, BILLY
FITZPATRICK, LIAM FENNELLY

CHRISTY HEFFERNAN

'I WAS A LOT MORE WARY IN 1992 AND 1993. THE FEAR OF LOSING WAS PLAYING ON MY MIND. I HAD LOST TWO ALL-IRELAND FINALS IN 1987 AND 1991, AND I DIDN'T WANT TO LOSE ANOTHER ONE.'
– CHRISTY HEFFERNAN

MILO of Croton, one of ancient Greece's most famous wrestling champions, had a rather unusual training routine. When Millo went for his morning run in downtown Athens, he always liked to bring along a companion… with a difference!

After consuming 40 pounds of meat and bread daily, Milo was a man who believed in the merits of a hearty breakfast, before he set off for his daily run. If running a mile with a fully grown ox on your back is your thing, then Milo was your kind of Greek grappler!

Milo, whom one online source rather unkindly labelled the inventor of progressive strength training, is credited with saving the life of a very famous philosopher, namely Pythagoras. Such was our intrepid ox-carrying wrestler's strength, legend informs us that he held the roof of a collapsing temple as the philosopher ran to safety.

While many students would have preferred

HARD MAN RATINGS

TOUGHEST:
9.5/10

MEANEST:
8.5/10

SCARIEST:
9.1/10

HARDEST:
19.7/20

☠

TOTAL HARD MAN

46.8/50

if Milo might have demurred, and left our mathematically challenged philosopher to deal with the consequences alone, Milo's heroic efforts did not extract any particular fortune from the gods.

He reportedly died in mysterious circumstances when becoming stuck in a tree he was trying to tear apart, and getting devoured by wolves!

Christy Heffernan was a man you could certainly envisage carrying an ox or two on his broad shoulders. The towering Glenmore giant was a scrapper who always ensured the walls of Kilkenny's castle never caved in.

Heffernan played in six All-Ireland senior finals for Kilkenny between 1982 and 1993, with an impressive strike rate, winning four of them. Christy was a full-forward who always went for the jugular and if green flags were your thing, Christy was the man to provide them. He signposted that rather precious ability in his very first tilt at Liam MacCarthy. In what amounted to a dream All-Ireland final debut in 1982, he stitched two goals inside a minute to help Kilkenny trample all over a bewildered Cork side. Kilkenny repeated the dose the following season, with Christy's considerable presence very much to the fore.

Kilkenny, like most Cats, were the ultimate big-game hunters, a side that could kill you in many varied and imaginative ways. They always had the hurling side of matters sorted, as any child wielding a camán in the Marble County was always guaranteed to have been genetically challenged in a hurling direction.

Heffernan posed a different type of challenge as he appeared to have everything bar a self-levelling construction laser in his toolbox! He was like some futuristic cyber-cop, he could transform himself into whatever shape the contest evolved into. Christy was born for the coalface and loved to get himself down and dirty in the trenches, yet, he was deceptively fast, and skilful and housed the stony gaze of an executioner's-eye.

He was a cult figure with the Cat's loyal followers who appreciated his bamboozling, all-action presence, far more than the opposition!

All-Ireland finals were no less intense in those days, but the preparation was light years away from the spreadsheet laboratory-fuelled machine of the modern game.

Christy, having tasted victory in his two visits to the 'big show', duly digested defeat in his next to sorties to Jones' Road, in 1987 and 1991. Having played under two different managers (Pat Henderson and Ollie Walsh), he recalled a more laid-back approach to one of the biggest days in the Irish sporting calendar.

'I played under two different managers in All-Ireland finals, and both men used to stress the importance of getting a good night's sleep before the game. If that meant having a few pints, well so be it. As long as you slept well, that was the main thing,' Christy recalled.

'We didn't take things as seriously as teams do now, but it didn't seem to do us any harm. Before we'd leave our hotel on the morning of the game to head for Croke Park, we had a puck around in the car park or maybe in the nearest open park. That wouldn't happen now.'

{ THE CALM BEFORE THE STORM }

The routine rarely varied for Christy as the years rolled by and almost a decade later, he also revealed a similar modus operandi.

'It was important to have a routine. I think it was a big help to us that we were able to sleep in our own beds the night before. We used to get the train from Kilkenny on the Sunday morning and spend a few hours in a hotel before the game.

'After the All-Ireland final, we would go back to the hotel where we would spend the night. A banquet for the two teams was held in The Burlington Hotel every year on the Monday and we would then travel back to Kilkenny by train. And win, lose, or draw, there would be a parade around the town that night. It was the same routine every year that I played.'

Christy would have happier memories of his next two visits to Croker, adding another pair of Celtic Crosses to his ever-expanding collection.

'No matter how many All-Ireland finals you play in, the nerves are always there. I was less nervous for my first final than I was for my last two. That's because I didn't know what to expect.

'I was a lot more wary in 1992 and 1993. The fear of losing was playing on my mind. I had lost two All-Ireland finals in 1987 and 1991, and I didn't want to lose another one.

'Pat (Henderson) and (Ollie Walsh) were completely different. Whereas Pat was a bit of taskmaster, Ollie was more relaxed. He had a way about him and that seeped through to the players. But both men were very good at getting us prepared and into the right frame of mind coming up to the All-Ireland.'

We can only surmise if both men extolled the virtues of a hearty breakfast, minus the ox-carrying part!

A LIFE AT
THE COALFACE

CHRISTY HEFFERNAN was born on December 26, 1957. A native of Glenmore, he was a late arrival to the inter-county scene and first arrived aged 22, when he first linked up with the Kilkenny senior team.

Despite the disadvantage of not having played at underage level for his county, he would go on to become one of their most celebrated full-forwards of all time.

He made his first senior appearance during the 1981 championship, and throughout his career Heffernan made a total of 32 championship appearances. He retired from county hurling at the conclusion of the 1993 championship.

Heffernan played his club hurling with his local side, Glenmore. He had a very successful spell with the side, who won four Kilkenny Senior Championships, two Leinster titles and an All-Ireland Club title.

Heffernan played in a total of six All-Ireland finals, winning four medals. He also amassed seven Leinster titles, and four National Hurling Leagues, and won a solitary All Star award.

He was a regular member of the Leinster inter-provincial team, winning the title in 1989.

He was a talented footballer and captained the Glenmore football team to victory in the 1989 county final. He gave a superb individual display on the day, winning Man of the Match, and contributing five points from midfield.

GEARÓID HEGARTY

(Height 6' 4", Weight 15 St)

Decade... 2010s/2020s

(Position... Wing-Forward)

CHIEF CHARACTERISTIC... LIMERICK SEARCH AND
RESCUE LIAM MACCARTHY DIVISION

TOP ACCOMPLICES... CIAN LYNCH, TOM MORRISSEY, WILL
O'DONOGHUE, SEAMUS FLANAGAN, PETER CASEY, AARON GILLANE

GEARÓID HEGARTY

*'DEFINITELY, TALKING FROM MY OWN SENSE, SURE IT WAS STUPID, I
WAS EMBARRASSED. IT'S A HORRIBLE FEELING, I NEVER GOT SENT OFF
BEFORE… A STRAIGHT RED, DEFINITELY NOT WITH LIMERICK ANYWAY.'*
– GEARÓID HEGARTY

'**H***ERE it is, Merry Christmas everybody having fun…'*
A street sleeper folded his tattered jacket and
carefully prepared his bed of cardboard. An old hand at the game
of sleeping rough, he went through the motions, before wearily
slumping in the doorway. He fumbled in his pockets, producing
a brown longneck, taking a swig, before pulling his hat over his
ears against the icy chill.

A couple of old ladies shuffled past wearing
face masks and arguing about the merits of
'Social Distancing.' The Pandemic was the only
show in town.

He was homeless in the city that housed a
million – a man encased in an invisible world.

Grafton Street, the hub and the heartbeat of
December festive shopping days, was muted, and
deathly still.

If you had a copy of *A Christmas Carol* to hand
– Dickens' opening salvo readily sprung to mind.

'Nothing stirred not even a mouse.'

**HARD
MAN
RATINGS**
TOUGHEST:
9.2/10
MEANEST:
9.4/10
SCARIEST:
9.6/10
HARDEST:
19.0/20
💀
TOTAL
HARD MAN
47.2/50

Up on the Jones' Road, an All-Ireland hurling final with a difference was petering to an inevitable conclusion. A couple of lone voices echoed around the vast and virtually empty cavernous spaces around Croke Park. The contest had all the urgency of a Sunday afternoon puck around.

The sights, the sounds, and the colours of an All-Ireland Sunday were strangely absent. The last time the showpiece was played under the Holly Boughs was way back in 1924.

The air was punctuated by the odd staccato blasts of urgency from the respective sidelines and the dull thud of the sliotar off the flying ash. Even the seagulls had stayed away en masse; Croke Park often laid on a feast for our feathered friends – but in the absence of any food-laden patrons this was definitely one All-Ireland they would be giving a swerve.

Everything seemed to have been dialled down to zero – if an All-Ireland couldn't warm your soul, you were already halfway to Hell.

Mr Spock played with underscored brilliance by Leonard Nimoy in the Gene Roddenberry classic sci-fi drama, *Star Trek* would possibly have said, 'Fascinating' before elaborating a little further.

'This is life Jim… but not as we know it.'

In a dreadfully anti-climatic, low-key affair – there was one shining light. Croker had a rarefied atmosphere on the day; it had been a struggle for the players to embrace the unrelenting emptiness of the occasion.

He had a quiet steely gaze.

You got the impression, if you started digging you would never get to the bottom of his furious, raging, spirit. He duly shot the lights out with a magnificent seven from play, from all angles and areas of the Jones' Road terrain.

Nothing seemed to dim his fire or quell his determined, quiet fury. He tore into every play as if it was his last. Then again, Gearóid Hegarty had always hurled like there was no tomorrow...

Christy Ring famously once said, 'Cork hurlers are like mushrooms... they spring up overnight'. The assembled faithful in the Gaelic Grounds hardly noticed the lanky frame of Hegarty entering the fray at half-time, in March 2016. Seánie O'Brien had been relieved of his duties at the interval, in a 6-29 to 1-12 defeat of Laois. The game resulted in a routine win for the Treaty, with most oblivious to the low-key entry of a future Limerick 'Hall of Famer.'

The Hegarty revolution was of the slow-burning variety.

He hailed from a small unfashionable city club, and had looked half-decent as footballer for the Limerick senior side. He seemed a little too long and gangly at times as he struggled with the transition from the big ball game.

His touch gave a decent impression of a cat chasing a marble. There were stages in games where he cut a frustrated figure – but the Treaty fans loved the way he always emptied the tank.

A couple of 'so-so' seasons would pass in the hothouse of inter-county hurling before Gearóid Hegarty and Limerick would give the mushrooms a run for their money...

The Treaty duly crept up on their unsuspecting enemies, as if they had been sprung from John Kiely's Trojan Horse, ransacking the hurling aristocracy. Hegarty led the charge as winning no longer became a privilege, but instead became a way of life.

Like all great soldiers of war, Gearóid Hegarty rarely entertains the clarion call of retreat.

He is 'Public Enemy No.1' and a prized trophy for fired-up opposition forces.

A wild swing in a fraught National League encounter with Galway earned him a straight red card and it was one he truly regretted.

{ LAW AND DISORDER }

'Definitely, talking from my own sense, sure it was stupid' said Hegarty. 'I was embarrassed. It's a horrible feeling, I never got sent off before… a straight red, definitely not with Limerick anyway.'

'Everyone that's after coming in to watch the game, my family, it's just awkward… you don't even want to go home and look them in the eye after doing something so stupid…'

The Homeless man tossed and turned a little, before curling up in his corner. Nothing stirred in the capital city – not even a mouse.

Up on the Jones' Road, the 2020 All-Ireland final was in the can. Limerick's Hegarty had just given a performance for the ages. The Waterford team appeared to adhere to social distancing protocols while marking the St Patrick's clubman.

The former footballer had displayed a velvet touch. He stickwork and striking belonging in another galaxy. He had, like his teammates, crossed a great divide in a very short space of time.

Hurling's eternal bridesmaids had shed their oily skin. The hurling world would never be the same again. Most significantly, the group had backed up their maiden All-Ireland triumph of

2018. The message to the hurling superpowers was crystal clear. This was now Limerick's world – the others merely existed in it.

As the great pointy-eared one would have said, 'It's life Jim … but not as we know it'.

THE WORLD ACCORDING TO 'HEGO'

HEGARTY WAS born on August 10, 1994. His father, Ger Hegarty played in the 1994 All-Ireland with the Treaty, as they lost out to a late surge from Offaly.

Hegarty hurled with Castletroy College and was in the forward division on the first college team to play in the Harty Cup. He studied at the University of Limerick and quickly became a regular fixture on the senior hurling team. On February 24, 2018, he won the prestigious Fitzgibbon Cup, following UL's 2-21 to 2-15 defeat of Dublin City University in the final. He was also a regular for the University of Limerick football team in the Sigerson Cup.

Hegarty was a member of the St Patrick's Club and represented the outfit in all grades as a dual player. In October 2014, he played at full-forward when St Patrick's lost out to Ballylanders in the final of the Limerick Football Championship.

Hegarty first donned the Limerick jersey as part of the Limerick football squad, making his debut in a 3-15 to 0-8 Munster Championship defeat by Cork on March 19, 2014. He has won five All-Irelands, five Munster titles, and three National Leagues. He was voted Hurler of the Year in 2020, and has won three All Stars. He has been voted Man of the Match in two All-Ireland finals.

STEPHEN HINEY

(Height 6' 2", Weight 14 St)

Decade... 2000s/2010s

(Position... Wing-Back)

CHIEF CHARACTERISTIC... REMINDING US... THEY PLAY
A BIT OF HURLING IN DUBLIN TOO!

TOP ACCOMPLICES... GARY MAGUIRE, PETER KELLY,
PAUL SCHUTTE, LIAM RUSHE, MICHAEL CARTON, JOEY BOLAND

STEPHEN HINEY

*'I GOT IT CHECKED OUT AND IT WAS A DETACHMENT IN MY RETINA. I HAD A
BUCKLE INSERTED IN ONE OF MY EYES, A LITTLE PIECE OF PLASTIC TO TAKE
THE FLUID AWAY. IT'S FROM A TRAUMA TO THE HEAD, I HAD PICKED UP A BAD
KNOCK, AT SOME STAGE. I COULDN'T NARROW IT DOWN TO WHICH KNOCK...
BETWEEN HURLING AND FOOTBALL, THERE HAVE BEEN A FAIR FEW ALRIGHT!'*

– STEPHEN HINEY

THE Way of the Warrior...

Bushido, the way of the warrior, the code of the ancient warriors known as Samurai.

Based upon seven virtues or signs, Righteousness, Loyalty, Honor, Respect, Honesty, Courage and Consistency... they represented the strict philosophy that every true Samurai would live and die by. The essence of Bushido refers to not fearing death and dying with valour.

The life of a Samurai was a harsh, unforgiving one – a lonely road that demanded total and absolute sacrifice to a greater cause, a journey only the mightiest of warriors embarked upon.

Stephen Hiney knew a thing or two about the 'Way of the Warrior'. He had been introduced to the inter-county scene in 2001, and by 2008, at a time when Dublin had copper-fastened their irrelevance within the provincial and All-Ireland title races.

The Dublin hurling passport had been stamped

HARD
MAN
RATINGS
TOUGHEST:
9.2/10

MEANEST:
9.3/10

SCARIEST:
9.0/10

HARDEST:
19.4/20
☠

TOTAL
HARD MAN
46.9/50

with a second-class citizen tag. Perennially fire-fighting within your own borders made any sort of national gains an almost unassailable task. The behemoth of the capital's football team cast a long, disconcerting shadow over their landscape. Fighting a long, drawn-out war with the 'big ball' game for the cream of the city's talent was an uneven battle they were ill-equipped to fight.

The footballers had won 30 head-turning All-Irelands, which spoke a powerful language in terms of GAA recruitment drives.

Dublin was significantly behind hurling's big three of Kilkenny, Cork and Tipperary; their six titles did, however, place them fifth in the overall winner's list. Dublin also had won the Leinster Championship on 24 occasions (the second-highest total of any side).

That stat looked a bit flattering, with the last meaningful silverware arriving in the 1961 Leinster final win over Wexford. Most of the wins had been collected pre-50s.

Stephen Hiney's incredible journey of sacrifice began aged just 15 when he was informed that he was an insulin-dependent diabetic. When he was 22, he was told that he only had a 'slim chance' of ever playing hurling again after undergoing corrective eye surgery.

He recalled the alarming day when a casual visit to the doctor turned into a nightmare in 2005, as the doctor revealed a far more serious diagnosis than he had expected.

'The doctor said, "Well, actually, there is something a bit awry with it".

'I got it checked out and it was a detachment in my retina. It hadn't fully detached but it was close. I had a buckle inserted in one of my eyes, a little piece of plastic to take the fluid away from the back of the (left) eye.

'It's from a trauma to the head, I had picked up a bad knock, at some stage. I couldn't narrow it down to which knock. Between hurling and football, there have been a fair few alright!

'I've had some injuries that have kept me out of the game for a while, your hunger grows then. There's nothing you want to do except go out and play.'

Stephen Hiney was a true survivor.

He had been down and counted out on many occasions, but he always battled back, overcoming illness, injury, and incredible obstacles, to guide Dublin hurling to the promised land.

He had spent many years marooned in sky blue – courageously fighting against impossible odds. Dublin hurling was stuck in a rut for many years, with dismal outings in Leinster often a stable diet.

Cast adrift from the trophy-chasing pack, Hiney needed every single ounce of his soldier's creed, as he continued his lonely battle to make Dublin hurling relevant once again. Like all great warriors, he never retreated or took a backward footstep. He was Dublin's 'War Machine', often bloodied, seldom cowed, an omnipotent, rapacious, presence in the Dublin rearguard.

His unflinching adherence to the Warrior's Way would be rewarded when Clare legend Anthony Daly took the reins in the capital in 2008. Daly was a man that understood war in the trenches better than most.

The battles ahead would be bloody and brutal – needing proper soldiers to lead the charge.

Hiney was everything he had hoped to unearth in the capital.

Daly and Dublin were ready … It was time to release 'The Dogs of War'.

{ ESCAPING TO VICTORY }

DALY'S UNPARALLELED passion was infectious and re-energised the Dubs, infusing them with the Clarecastle native's Midas touch. They became a different animal and reached provincial deciders in 2009 and 2011 – both resulting in narrow reversals against Kilkenny.

As was the norm for his hurling career, nothing came easily for Stephen. The curse of the cruciate injury in 2011 set him back, as he sat out the capital outfits National League triumph that season, but he refused to bend, returning for Dublin's Leinster Championship winning season in 2013.

Daly loved the Ballyboden defender's combustible presence in the half-back division. Hiney was a ferociously driven hurler – a bone cruncher in the combat zone.

He was also an intelligent player, knowing when to hit hard and when to play. A hurler who possessed both the brains and balls required to survive at the highest level.

His form dipped in 2014, as he only managed one league outing that year against Galway.

'I only played the first game against Galway. I don't have fond memories of it. They gave us a lesson that day – we stayed on the bus.'

True to form, the ultimate warrior, Hiney, fought his way back the following season, as Dublin returned to a Leinster final against Kilkenny.

Hiney took everything life and hurling could throw at him. Serious injury, debilitating illness, and constantly swimming against the inevitable power of football in the nation's capital.

Stephen Hiney always knew only one way... The Warrior's Way!

THE
»——→ METROPOLITAN ←——«
MAN

STEPHEN HINEY was born on October 27, 1983. He hurled with Ballyboden St Enda's. The club is a famous dual-code outfit, and Stephen Hiney lined out in both hurling and football, as Ballyboden were perennial county title winners. He won six Dublin Senior Hurling Championships, and also bagged two senior football medals.

Ballyboden subsequently played their first-ever Leinster Club hurling tie against Wexford giants Oulart the Ballagh, and defeated the Slaneysiders. They qualified for the Leinster final, but found Offaly kingpins Birr a step too far.

At inter-county level, he was a tenacious and commanding presence for 13 seasons in the sky-blue of Dublin. He made his debut for the Metropolitans in 2001, but Dublin were always on the periphery of success as they rarely made the business end of the league and championship. When Antony Daly was appointed manager of the county team in 2008, he made an instant impact guiding Dublin to a Walsh Cup Shield win over Leinster rivals Offaly in Banagher. While the Dubs were trounced 6-12 to 0-12 in the Walsh Cup first round by All-Ireland champions Kilkenny in Parnell Park, Hiney would not have long to wait for major success. Dublin became transformed and won the National League in 2011 and added a Leinster Championship win in 2013.

PADRAIG HORAN

(Height 5' 11", Weight 14 St)

Decade... 1960s/1970s/1980s

(Position... Full-Forward)

CHIEF CHARACTERISTIC... FRONT OFFICE MANAGER
FAITHFUL COUNTY FORWARD DIVISION

TOP ACCOMPLICES... PADDY KIRWAN, BRENDAN BERMINGHAM, MARK
CORRIGAN, PAT CARROLL, JOHNNY FLAHERTY, PAT CLEARY

PADRAIG HORAN

*'I LOOKED UP AND SAW THE ROW GOING ON. I HEADED FOR THE GATE
AND, THE NEXT THING A CLARE CROWD CAME CHARGING TOWARDS
ME. THERE WAS AN AULD FELLA WITH AN UMBRELLA COMING FIRST
AND I PULLED, AND I HIT HIM ON THE FOREHEAD.'*

– PADRAIG HORAN

ON *October 14, 1912.*
   A former saloon keeper named John Flammang
Schrank attempted to shoot Theodore Roosevelt while he was
on the campaign trail in Milwaukee, Wisconsin. Schrank's bullet
penetrated Roosevelt's chest after cutting through his steel
eyeglass case and passing through a thick (50
pages) single-folded copy of the speech titled
'Progressive Cause Greater Than Any Individual'.

As shocked onlookers gasped, Elbert E.
Martin, an ex-football player, was the first to
react, leaping at Schrank, wrestling him to the
ground.

The former President Roosevelt staggered a little
after being hit, but straightened himself, and again
raised his hat, with a broad smile upon his face.

Theodore Roosevelt then continued on his way
to the venue where he was giving an election
speech, with blood seeping into his shirt. His

**HARD
MAN
RATINGS**

TOUGHEST:
9.6/10

MEANEST:
9.2/10

SCARIEST:
9.5/10

HARDEST:
19.7/20

**TOTAL
HARD MAN
48.0/50**

opening lines were as follows!

'Ladies and gentlemen, I don't know whether you fully understand that I have just been shot, but it takes more than that to kill a Bull Moose.'

Such was the location of the bullet, doctors concluded it would be safer to leave it inside the former American president's chest!

Offaly Captain Padraig Horan took his fair share of shrapnel for the Faithful cause. Like a certain American President, he may have staggered a few times, but he rarely hit the floor.

He was a leader who would inspire one of the greatest journeys in GAA history. A man who would willingly take a bullet in his chest for his beloved Offaly...

Offaly hurling was staring down a long dark tunnel. For the long-suffering Offaly hurling supporters, it had been 50 years since their last Leinster final.

In 1976, they lost to Westmeath, and later in the year they spluttered to a two-point win over Wicklow in the National League. The Liam MacCarthy Cup certainly wasn't in the conversation, and anyone foolhardy enough to be backing the Faithful for a first-ever Leinster title was a bit like a hopeful punter selecting a Grand-National 500-1 shot to land the spoils – strictly for old ladies to stick a pin in!

Still, as Oscar Wilde famously once perused... 'We are all in the gutter, but some of us are looking at the stars'.

Toward the end of those dastardly 70s, the Faithful began to build unity and a sense of togetherness, which had not always been the case with Offaly hurling.

Padraig Horan was a symbol of the new Offaly approach. He would have preferred a berth in the backline, but was willing to put himself about in the forward line to help the cause.

Horan was the proverbial 'tough bit of stuff,' a man who would die with his boots on for the county.

'I feel sorry when I hear people talking about hurling and not mentioning some of those hurlers that I recalled, because they were great bits of stuff.

'Mick (Rourke) was playing one day… we were playing Waterford and Mick was playing wing-back. I was centre back. Waterford were fierce dirty on the day and we were running out of subs.

'I turned around to O'Rourke and said, "It's about time we were levelling things up here now".

'The ball came in anyway and, as I'm up catching, O'Rourke pulled and made ***e out of my hand. I turned around to him and said, "I meant Waterford players!" You would think Offaly hurling was only invented in 1981, the way some people go on. We were almost there. If we had better coaching and more organisation, we might have won something earlier.

'Brother Denis brought a bit of shape to the thing in the 60s and 70s, and then Andy Gallagher took up the reins for a while before Diarmuid Healy came on board and those three men made huge changes in hurling in Offaly.

'There was no unity before that. Lads would go into the dressing-room, and we'd sit in the one corner and the Drumcullen lads would sit in the other corner. The management started introducing more social activities, meeting after games and having a cup of tea… and playing cards.

'That broke down the barriers and brought it all together.'

{ THE SWINGING SEVENTIES }

'We were involved in some rough tussles in those early years. I remember down in Tulla, in the late 70s, it was the making of us. We played Clare and a row broke out after the game...

Pat Carroll got hit and a ferocious row broke out. I wasn't involved in the row, for once. I was down the other end of the field.

'I was with Noel O'Donoghue, the referee, coming off the field and I looked up and saw the row going on. I headed for the gate and, the next thing a Clare crowd came charging towards me.

'There was an auld fella with an umbrella coming first and I pulled, and I hit him on the forehead. Who arrived beside me... only Willie Gorman. A couple of cousins got in beside me and I got in as far as the dressing-room. We were locked in the dressing-room for an hour... couldn't get out.'

When they did eventually get out, there was no stopping Horan and Offaly, as they won their First Leinster title in 1980, with Horan contributing a very impressive 4-5 (17 points), during the provincial campaign. The Faithful captain did even better the following season bagging a whopping 5-17 (32 points).

1981 was the red-letter year as the battling Padraig overcame injury to lift Liam MacCarthy as Diarmuid Healy's 'history boys' prevailed over Galway by three points. He collected another Celtic cross in 1985 as his inspirational point in the dying embers of the contest edged out a resurgent Galway.

In a career where he led from the front, he was wounded countless times on the battlefield,but he kept coming back. In the words of a certain American President... 'It takes more than that to kill a Bull Moose'.

THE CAPTAIN'S
» ———→ TALE ←——— «

PADRAIG HORAN was born on April 21, 1950. He spent close to three decades with the Faithful forward division. He played his club hurling with Offaly powerhouse St Rynagh's of Banagher. In an extraordinary period of dominance for the club, he won a staggering 11 Offaly titles, the last of his successes coming in 1987, after the Banagher side defeated Seir Kieran. At interprovincial level St Rynagh's also won three Leinster Club Championships.

He embarked on a coaching career after his retirement and became involved in team management and coaching. He led the Faithful to their only-ever National League win in 1991. He also managed St Rynagh's, and did a spell with the famous Birr club, leading them to a historic first All-Ireland Club Hurling Championship in 1995.

He also lent his expertise to the Laois senior inter-county team. Horan would make his first appearance for the Offaly senior side during the 1968-69 National League and was a totemic presence until his retirement after the 1986 championship. He bagged four Leinster Championship medals and a solitary All Stars award. He was also inducted to the GAA Hall of Fame.

JOHN HORGAN

(Height 5' 11", Weight 14.5 St)

Decade... 1960s/1970s/1980s

(Position... Corner-Back)

CHIEF CHARACTERISTIC... THE BLONDE BOMBSHELL DISPOSAL UNIT

TOP ACCOMPLICES... MARTIN COLEMAN, DENIS COUGHLAN, JOHNNY
CROWLEY, DERMOT MACCURTAIN, BRIAN MURPHY

JOHN HORGAN

'I'M AFTER HITTING THREE BALLS UP TO YOU, AND YOU'VE PUT THE THREE OF THEM WIDE. DON'T DO IT AGAIN.'

– JOHN HORGAN

And his ghost may be heard as you pass by that billabong
You'll come a-Waltzing Matilda, with me...

1971 Cork senior hurling final.

The sky might have cried a river before the throw-in, but little could dampen the enthusiasm of the faithful as they gathered for the latest instalment of the greatest club rivalry by the banks of the River Lee.

The 'Barrs and the 'Rockies were the only show in town and as complicated histories go, this match-up was up there with the best of them.

St Finbarr's and Blackrock had been rubbing each other up the wrong way for well over a century. Tracing the exact point when relations became fractured was not an exact science, but the fissure likely appeared because of the identity – or lack of identity – of the 1905 Cork Senior Championship winners.

St Finbarr's had won the 1904 final in a fashion

HARD MAN RATINGS

TOUGHEST:
9.4/10

MEANEST:
9.3/10

SCARIEST:
9.3/10

HARDEST:
19.2/20

☠

TOTAL HARD MAN

47.2/50

with their opponents, Castletownroche refusing to play in the decider – citing the choice of venue, the Cork Athletic Grounds, wasn't neutral.

When the 1905 Munster Championship finally got underway in May 1906, Blackrock were deemed Cork representatives in the Munster and All-Ireland Senior Championships.

This was determined on the basis of having been the last Cork club to have won a county final on the field of play, when they defeated the 'Barrs in the 1903 final.

St Finbarr's and Blackrock remained at loggerheads over who won what, and where and the bad blood simmered, before boiling over in a challenge match not long afterwards.

The fixture ironically in aid of the Mercy Hospital was abandoned after 50 minutes following, as newspapers reported, *an extraordinary exhibition of rowdyism*, involving both sets of players and supporters.

The furnace cooled over the decades with the last clash in a final as far back as 1926. When the two sides collided again in the 1976 Cork final, there was a massive attendance, for a contest that was sure to provide its share of fireworks.

Blackrock captained by a flowing blond-haired 21-year-old, were hoping to end a decade-long hiatus without the Seán Óg Murphy Cup. John Horgan represented the future for Blackrock – after a brilliant under-age shift for the Rebels littered with All-Ireland medals. The game turned into an ill-tempered affair with two players sent off and subsequently a number of suspensions, including Horgan.

The gamble on youth was well merited for the Rockies as, after a shaky opening quarter, they gradually wore down the St

Finbarr's resolve and had the legs to land the precious prize.

The young Horgan was unfazed by the physicality on show – as some of the more senior 'Barrs players tried to remind him of his place in the scheme of things. Being tangled up in Cork's biggest hurling rivalry was the perfect introduction to the Cork inter-county scene.

Tom O'Sullivan of Blackrock recalled the blond destroyer's impact on a seismic occasion.

'The tension was huge in that county final in 1971. Over 20,000 people there, everyone was aware of that history, but John kept everybody's feet on the ground. He was a great captain.

'And the game was dog-rough. Fellas needed to keep their heads, because there were fights all over the field, a couple of players were put off, and there were suspensions given out afterwards for other incidents.

'John was a rock that day. Absolutely fantastic.

'He really played a captain's role. That to me was his biggest test, and he really stood up for us.'

Both clubs were fined £30 for their indiscretions, and John would spend two months on the sideline. He returned in time to take part in a successful Munster campaign as the Rockies defeated Tipperary's Moyne-Templetuothy.

The Cork side rolled on to the All-Ireland club final against Rathnure, holding off a powerful late surge, allowing Horgan to raise The Tommy Moore Cup.

O'Sullivan continued, intimating that John was a true leader, quiet, but when he spoke everybody knew exactly what was required of them. 'If it had to be said, he'd say it. Fellas could be put in their box. One of his teammates said to me the day of his funeral, that at half-time in one county final Hoggy laid it on the line for him. "I'm after hitting three balls up to you," he said, "And you've put the three of them wide. Don't do it again".

'With that blond hair, he couldn't get away with anything on the field because everyone knew where he was at all times, but he was a very strong man physically, much like his father.'

John Horgan's legendary career had been written in the stars. He duly replicated his underage success at senior level – winning four All-Ireland medals, with his stirring exploits forever stitched in the fabric of GAA history.

Denis Coughlan who soldiered up ahead of Horgan on the half-line recalled the regard 'Hoggy' was held in by his peers.

'He fitted in very well with that Cork team, he was a shy man but got on well with everybody and was held in very high regard, not surprisingly with his record. As a club captain in particular he had a phenomenal record, and when we were going for four in-a-row in 1979, we were genuinely delighted for him because he was captain.'

The man who had a party piece few other corner-backs could ever claim – hitting 65s over the blackspot for fun – also had another, as Denis revealed.

'Something I always associated with him was the song, *And the Band Played Waltzing Matilda*. That was his party piece, and he sang that beautifully.'

The great man passed away on June 8, 2016, but the image would never fade of the iconic warrior with the blond flowing locks.

The magnificent 'Hoggy' will still hurl forever in our hearts.

And his ghost may be heard as you pass by that billabong
You'll come a-Waltzing Matilda, with me …

THE BLOND
»———→ FROM ←———«
BARRACK STREET

JOHN HORGAN was born on May 25, 1950 near Barrack Street on the south side of Cork city. His early hurling was at Horgan Sullivan's Quay CBS, and he was already making eye-catching progress at underage levels with the Passage club, before transferring to Blackrock in 1968.

Horgan had a successful career with the 'Rockies over the next decade. He became the only player to captain a team to three All-Ireland club titles. Blackrock won five Munster championships to supplement his five county senior championship medals.

Horgan began his inter-county career with the Cork minor panel. He appeared in three successive All-Ireland finals – winning once in 1967. He progressed onto the Cork under-21 team, where he continued in a winning vein when capturing back-to-back All-Ireland medals in 1970 and 1971.

He made his senior debut for Cork in the Grounds Tournament in 1969. He soon became a regular on the team during the 1969-70 National League. He collected his first Celtic Cross in 1970, before winning three championships on the bounce from 1976 to 1978. Horgan enjoyed spectacular success in the Munster Championship, winning an impressive six medals.

He won four National League medals also, and collected three All Star awards between 1974 and 1978. He was named Hurler of the Year in 1978. Horgan played his last game for Cork in June, 1981.

THE 50
TOUGHEST, MEANEST, SCARIEST
HARD-MEN
IN HURLING HISTORY

*Diarmuid 'The Rock' O'Sullivan lays down the law against Tipperary
in the 2004 championship*

Stephen Hiney breaks free out of defence, despite the presence of Kilkenny great Eoin Larkin, in the Leinster Championship in 2013

Michael 'Babs' Keating (back row, left) and the Tipperary team which claimed the All-Ireland title in 1971

Gearóid Hegarty and Limerick accomplices celebrate beating Clare in the 2023 Munster final

A disappointed Jim Greene during the 1983 Munster final, when Waterford fell to Cork

Johnny Pilkington played it laid-back, but played fiercely always for Offaly

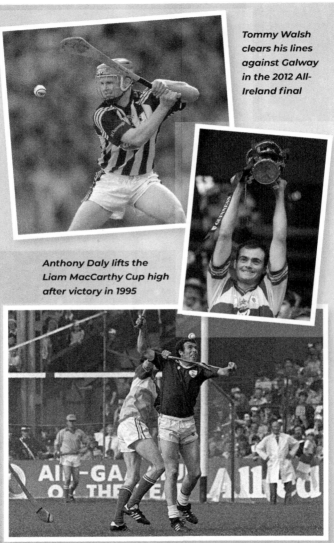

Tommy Walsh clears his lines against Galway in the 2012 All-Ireland final

Anthony Daly lifts the Liam MacCarthy Cup high after victory in 1995

John Connolly in action against Offaly in the 1981 All-Ireland final

*Ken McGrath is unstoppable in the Munster
Championship against Limerick in 2009*

The Kilkenny team which beat Cork in the 1982 All-Ireland final

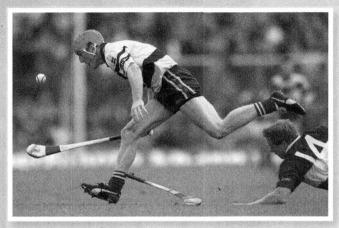

Brian Lohan stops another Tipperary attack in its tracks in 2001

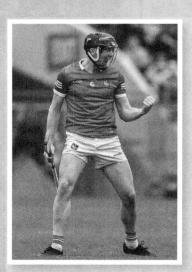

*Declan Hannon asks for more from Limerick during the 2022
Munster final win over Clare (left) and a bloodied Martin
Hanamy lifts the Liam MacCarthy Cup in 1994*

THE COUNTDOWN TO THE TOUGHEST MEANEST SCARIEST HARD-MAN IN HURLING HISTORY

SCORE OUT OF

50

50. Johnny Pilkington	46.4	29. Pádraic Maher	47.4
49. Olcan McFetridge	46.6	28. Sean Stack	47.4
48. PJ Cuddy	46.6	27. Kieran Carey	47.5
47. Ollie Baker	46.7	26. Pete Finnerty	47.5
46. Christy Heffernan	46.8	25. Jackie Tyrrell	47.5
45. Terence McNaughton	46.8	24. Tom Condon	47.6
44. Jim Greene	46.9	23. Tom Cheasty	47.6
43. Stephen Hiney	46.9	22. Johnny Crowley	47.6
42. Tommy Walsh	46.9	21. Nicky Rackard	47.6
41. Michael Duignan	47.0	20. Phil Bennis	47.7
40. Anthony Daly	47.1	19. Martin Hanamy	47.7
39. Michael Keating	47.1	18. John Connolly	47.8
38. Aaron Gillane	47.2	17. Michael Maher	47.8
37. Gearóid Hegarty	47.2	16. Seanie McMahon	47.8
36. John Horgan	47.2	15. Diarmuid O'Sullivan	47.9
35. Joe Rabbitte	47.2	14. Padraig Horan	48.0
34. Eoin Kelly	47.3	13. John Leahy	48.0
33. Ken McGrath	47.3	12. Tony Doran	48.1
32. Martin Quigley	47.3	11. Will O'Donoghue	48.1
31. Declan Hannon	47.4		
30. John Keane	47.4	AND...	

10. Ger Loughnane	48.2
9. JJ Delaney	48.3
8. Tony Keady	48.4
7. Sylvie Linnane	48.4
6. Frank Cummins	48.5
5. John Doyle	48.6
4. Brian Lohan	48.6
3. Mick Mackey	48.7
2. Christy Ring	48.8
1. Diarmaid Byrnes	49.0

John Leahy displays the spoils of war against Limerick in 1997 (above) and Ger Loughnane in action late in his career in 1981 (right)

Tom Condon races out of the Limerick defence in the dying minutes of the 2018 All-Ireland final, the ball safely in his fist

Aaron Gillane is fouled by a bamboozled Kilkenny defence in the 2023 All-Ireland final

Padraig Horan and Joachim Kelly savour Offaly's second All-Ireland win in 1985

Joe Rabbitte receives attention during the Connacht final against Roscommon in 1997

Ollie Baker 'lives' for the ball against Galway in 2002

Martin Quigley weighs up his options in 1983

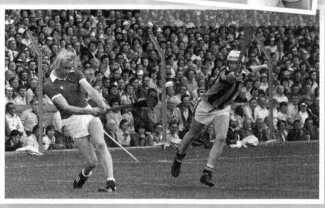

Cork legend John Horgan clears his lines against Cork in the 1978 All-Ireland final

*Peter Finnerty (second from left in the back row) and
Galway's All-Ireland winning team from 1987*

*Pádraic Maher enters the
battlefield one more time*

*A sure thing, Eoin
Kelly (above) quietly
celebrates another point
for Tipperary in 2012*

Seanie McMahon walks to the line after being sent off against Tipperary in the 2003 Munster Championship

JJ Delaney (left) clears his line once more in Croke Park

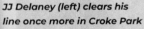

Johnny Crowley makes plain sailing of it against Kilkenny in the 1983 All-Ireland final

Michael Duignan celebrates the All-Ireland win in 1998

A fearful sight for any full-back line in the game, as Tony Doran takes a breather before wrecking more havoc

Imperious Tony Keady rules the Galway defence in the All-Ireland final against Tipperary in 1988

Sylvie Linnane holds solid in the Galway defence in the 1986 All-Ireland final

Will O'Donoghue was in control in every position on the field in 2023

Christy Heffernan wishes Dublin's John Twomey the best of luck before the 1991 Leinster final

Limerick's finest, Diarmaid Byrnes watches another long range point lift his county during the 2023 championship

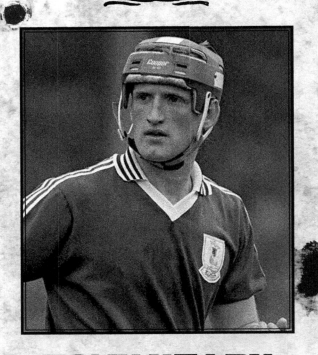

TONY KEADY
(Height 6' 1", Weight 14.5 St)

Decade... 1980s/1990s
(Position... Centre-Back)

CHIEF CHARACTERISTIC... GUARANTEEING AN INTER-COUNTY
FORWARD'S LIFE WAS A 'POINTLESS' EXISTENCE

TOP ACCOMPLICES... PETE FINNERTY, GERRY MCINERNEY, SYLVIE
LINNANE, STEVE MAHON, BRENDAN LYNSKEY, OLLIE KILKENNY

TONY KEADY

'MYSELF AND CROWLEY PULLED AROUND FOUR OR FIVE TIMES AND ALL YOU COULD HEAR WAS THE TWO HURLS CLASHING AND A BIG SPLASH GOING UP IN THE AIR EVERY TIME. THE BALL NEVER MOVED.'

– TONY KEADY

THE incessant rain paused fleetingly – before returning with a vengeance. The only items not teeming down from the Heavens appeared to be a few Jack Russells and the odd Cheshire Cat.

Croke Park fell silent for a moment, the mood music hushed as it dipped a few decibels. On the banks of the murky water, a seagull shook his wings and swooped upon a sodden chip.

The waves of sound from the 'Davin' rolled in again across the Royal Canal, a tribal call to arms of two warring factions.

Such was the soundtrack on All-Ireland semi-final Sundays. The bird took flight again, winging its way over the sparsely filled stadium, before disappearing gratefully into the half-light.

The Jones' Road acres appeared more likely to be hosting the Ploughing Championships than an All-Ireland 'semi'. Met Eireann's forecast for rain, and bucket loads of it, was strictly on the

HARD MAN RATINGS

TOUGHEST:
9.5/10

MEANEST:
9.4/10

SCARIEST:
9.8/10

HARDEST:
19.7/20

☠

TOTAL
HARD MAN

48.4/50

money. Croke Park looked aged and grey in the overcast shadows, half-day and half-night rolled into one.

The die-hards huddled together as best they could – with the majority shivering in the saturated stands. It was a day for overcoats and umbrellas, and the hot kick of a nourishing cup of Bovril.

The sliotar landed in a swell and distanced itself for a moment, almost disdainfully from the fray. Like a dog in heat, Cork's gnarled old warhorse, Tim Crowley arrived hungrily on the scene – but he was not alone. Keady broke into a hurried step just behind him. Flame-haired and fresh-faced, his eyes trained like a hawk firmly set on the prize. Alone they stood among the swaying multitudes, the old gunslinger and a young buck.

Crowley's pupils narrowed.

Croke Park was no one-horse town, and he had made a career out of teaching young upstarts never to rise above their stations.

Crowley drew first, and then they both went for it… bald-headed. Again and again, they pulled, with neither giving an inch. The ball never budged and neither did they. The staccato sound of well-honed ash whipped the crowd into a frenzy.

It was as impressive a cameo as any young man ever delivered on hurling's hallowed stage.

If Cork had any doubts about Tony Keady's place in the scheme of things, those flimsy notions were washed away in a swirling ball of Killimordaly fury.

Galway was different gravy now, no longer content to slink off into the night. The great man himself remembered the day he made his inter-county debut.

'I was at the beginning of my career and he was at the end of his. Myself and Crowley pulled around four or five times and all you could hear was the two hurls clashing and a big splash going up in the air every time. The ball never moved.

'So, I kind of said to myself, *I can compete with this lad.* That was progress as far as I was concerned.'

If you were to cut and paste a player's performance for use at a future date, rinse and repeat Keady's in 1985. The man wearing a white helmet was about to set the gold standard in inter-county defence.

Under the hood, Keady was a mesmerising mix of fire and ice and pulsated a raw unyielding power. His hurling was crisp and tidy, and he was imperious under the dropping ball.

He often effected breath-taking grabs of the interstellar variety, and when long-range free taking was in its infancy, he pioneered the fine art of pointing from another parish.

After his fairytale start to county life, some 'tough love' was lurking just down the road for Tony Keady. Offaly squeezed them out in the 1985 All-Ireland final, and the Rebels bit back in 1986. A defiant Galway rallied for a third bite at the cherry and in 1987 a six-point win over Kilkenny finally secured the Celtic Cross.

Galway's outstanding centre-back was in a reflective mood about those early reversals.

'Do you deserve to win one when you go straight in young? Maybe not. People will always say when they take over a team that they're building for three years, but if you win the first one you'll say thanks very much, I'll take it, but maybe you'll have to serve your time like anything else.'

When Galway followed up again in 1988, they appeared well set to seal a historic three in-a-row, but a trip to America was about to take all the wind out of Galway's sails.

'The Tony Keady Affair' would exile Galway's star defender for playing a club match illegally in New York. That ruled him out of the 1989 All-Ireland semi-final defeat to Tipperary, a decision that still rankles in Galway today.

'I was in America and did everything exactly to the book. Everything was signed and delivered, but apparently, there was a hiccup somewhere along the line that had nothing to do with me.'

Tony and Galway's star gradually dipped from there, but what a privilege it was to hitch a ride upon their magical carpet – filled with hurling wonder.

When Tony passed away suddenly in 2017, the game lost one of its most celebrated sons.

'Tony Keady was known as a dedicated family man and had a wonderfully generous disposition,' teammate Pearse Piggott revealed. 'But my greatest sporting memory is Tony thanking me after that 1988 All-Ireland final. I've never told anyone that before but that's how special Tony made me feel. Tony was a great hurler but he was blessed with buckets and buckets of good nature.'

His sense of humour was always legendary – as his response to RTÉ's Ger Canning's query on missing the Man of the Match presentation after the 1988 final revealed.

'Sure,' said Keady, 'didn't everyone already know that they gave it to me at half-time.'

When the thunder rolls from above... you can almost hear him there. Charging out of defence, all pomp and passion and dancing feet. Showing St Peter, and St Paul, and the good Lord himself... a clean pair of heels!

A TRIBAL WARRIOR'S LIFE

TONY KEADY was born on December 5, 1963. His league and championship career at senior level with the Galway lasted nine seasons from 1985 until 1993.

Born in Attymon, County Galway, he played his first competitive hurling at Athenry Vocational School. He was part of the 1980 Galway Vocational Schools team and went on to win back-to-back All-Ireland medals over the next two years.

He had a successful underage career with the local club Killimordaly, winning several minor and under-21 championship medals. He also won a county junior championship medal in 1983, and went on to win a county senior championship medal in 1986.

Keady made his inter-county bow at the age of 16 when he was selected for the Galway minor team, and was an All-Ireland runner-up in 1981. Having graduated from the minor ranks, he joined Galway's under-21 team - winning an All-Ireland medal in 1983.

Tony went on to make his senior debut during the 1984-85 National League and he won back-to-back All-Ireland medals in 1987 and 1988. He also added two National Hurling League medals. He was bestowed with the ultimate individual honour in 1988 when he was deservedly selected as Hurler of the Year.

Keady played his last game for Galway in April 1993, ending an amazing career in which he also won two All Star awards.

JOHN KEANE
(Height 6' 0", Weight 14 St)

Decade... 1930s/1940s/1950s
(Position... Corner-Back)

CHIEF CHARACTERISTIC... PROVOST HURLING'S
SCHOOL OF HARD KNOCKS

TOP ACCOMPLICES... JIM POWER, JIM CURRAN,
DAVY POWER, JIMMY GALVIN

JOHN KEANE

'I WELL REMEMBER THE OLD TIPPERARY MAN WHO PUSHED HIS WAY THROUGH THE THRONG OF ADMIRERS TO WHERE JOHN LAY AND, BENDING DOWN AND THRUSTING OUT HIS HAND, HE SAID THAT HE "WANTED TO SHAKE THE HAND OF JOHN KEANE... THE GREATEST MAN IN IRELAND".'

– PAT FANNING

THE Black Knight is a character who appears in a scene of the much-loved feature film, *Monty Python and the Holy Grail*. The knight is clad all in black and is based on the black knight of Arthurian Legends. His role in the movie is to guard a bridge over a small stream.

A supreme swordsman, the Black Knight is afflicted by a severe case of over-confidence and a staunch refusal never to give up. This leads to a hilarious encounter in the classic 70s comedy.

Despite losing various body parts in battle and having no arms or legs to continue, the armless, legless warrior, accuses his attacker of cowardice... for walking away.

John Keane was an integral part of Waterford's first All-Ireland win in 1948. Keane was a supremely skilled defender, who guarded the bridge for Waterford.

HARD MAN RATINGS

TOUGHEST:
9.5/10

MEANEST:
9.2/10

SCARIEST:
9.3/10

HARDEST:
19.4/20

TOTAL HARD MAN

47.4/50

John was a very personable and humble man – who certainly didn't suffer from the errant knight's unchecked sense of self-worth – but his staunch refusal to give up in battle was the stuff of legend.

The *Irish Independent* recounts that Keane suffered a workplace accident in 1943 which left him nursing a fractured ankle and damaged tendons. The medical advice was stark for Keane's ambitions of a quick return to action with his beloved Deise.

A timeline of four months minimum was set out for his recovery, but the spirit that was inherent within Keane had other ideas.

He made a remarkable recovery, which was likely aided and abetted by the prospect of lowering the reviled blue and gold clad Tipperary.

Games between Munster countries lend themselves to a parochial feel, as age-old rivalries and long-standing grudges tend to simmer just below the surface.

The pre-match handshakes are offered through gritted teeth as there is never any love lost between the Premier County and Waterford.

There was a general unease as John took to the field, and did not appear to be moving freely. The words 'failed a late fitness test' never applied to players like John Keane. There were times when he resembled the Black Knight. Battered, bloodied but totally unbowed.

At the end of the bruising contest, his ankle had swollen so badly that former GAA president and Mount Sion great Pat Fanning had to cut the boot off his foot, while his stricken comrade lay on the pitch.

A large and curious crowd gathered around the stricken Keane.

His towering display was not indicative of a man operating on one leg. He had given a defiant performance, operating at times from memory alone as he battled heroically through mind-numbing pain.

'I well remember,' recalled Fanning, 'the old Tipperary man who pushed his way through the throng of admirers to where John lay and, bending down and thrusting out his hand, he said that he "wanted to shake the hand of John Keane... the greatest man in Ireland".'

Those who were present on that most wonderful of days were inspired by Keane's incredible bravery, and left the ground feeling a little better about the world.

Heroic deeds remind us to reach higher and push that little harder. To seek inspiration – even in the darkest of moments.

In the stirring words of Frank Adler, 'The hero is one who kindles a great light in the world, who sets up blazing torches in the dark streets of life for men to see by'.

Even on the darkest of winter's evenings, heroes like John Keane warm our hearts and light the way.

{ONE LAST JOURNEY}

John was an instant success as a coach, training both club and county teams. He led Mount Sion to a record-equalling nine Waterford senior hurling titles in succession. In the 18 years between 1948 and 1965 the Mount Sion club won a staggering 15 county senior hurling titles and John was associated as player or coach with every success.

He lent his Midas touch to the county side as Waterford

annexed three Munster titles, one All-Ireland, one National League, and one Oireachtas title, on his watch.

After losing the Munster final in 1958, Keane's side wrestled back the chalice in 1959. That year they faced Kilkenny in the All-Ireland final again and, after a drawn game, Waterford prevailed with a thumping win in the replay to claim a second-ever All-Ireland title.

After being diagnosed with a terminal illness, John made a remarkable decision to tour the country, and visit many of his former hurling opponents. He knew deep down his time was limited, but as ever, he was determined to go out with a flourish.

He had made many friendships on the battlefield, and this gallant journey would, sadly, prove to be a bridge too far.

First, he travelled to Kilkenny to visit his great friend and Cats' legend Jim Langton. Despite being in acute distress, the following day he made the pilgrimage to Kinsale, where he met Jack Barrett, a former Munster Railway Cup comrade.

John's strength was failing fast, but he dug deep and ploughed on, to hook up with Jackie Power in Tralee. John Keane was inching towards Limerick when he died near Tarbert, Co Kerry, on October 1, 1975.

A fallen hero, John was only 58 years young, yet owing to his epic exploits, it felt he had been around forever.

His GAA life and extraordinary times were celebrated the following day, when thousands waited silently in the wind and the rain to say farewell, to not just one of Waterford's finest, but one of the greatest of all time.

The tears flowed as he was buried in the cemetery overlooking the sacred sands of Tramore. From his perch on high, he watches over his brethren. Waterford's warm embrace will forever cradle him close to its heart.

Great speeches, orations, and tributes flowed, but for all the fine-sounding words and scholarly tributes, the old Tipp man's cúpla focal, provided the most fitting of good-byes. If a picture paints a thousand words, then sometimes a few words evoke a thousand images.

'Farewell to The Greatest Man in Ireland.'

»——→ THE DÉISE DAYS ←——«

KEANE PLAYED his club hurling with Mount Sion in Waterford city. He was part of the first ever county title-winning side in 1938. He skippered the club to further county titles in 1939, 1940, 1943, 1945, 1948, 1949 and 1951. He made his senior debut in a National League game against fellow provincial rivals Cork, in 1935.

John established himself at centre-back, earning rave reviews in 1938 as Waterford defeated Cork to reach the Munster decider. History was secured as a narrow 3-5 to 2-5 victory gave Waterford their first-ever provincial crown, as they downed the 'Banner' county. Dublin denied Waterford a first-ever Liam MacCarthy as the Deise

succumbed in agonizing fashion, with the sky-blues prevailing with a 2-5 to 1-6 victory.

The defeat seemed to knock the stuffing out of John, and his fellow county men, and 10 long years passed before their next Munster crown in 1948. They then reached another All-Ireland final against Dublin.

They made a bright start, leading 2-5 to 0-2 at the interval, but Dublin rallied strongly in the second-half. John Keane, playing at centre-forward, had raised a green flag in the opening period, then plundered two more goals and led Waterford up the steps of the Hogan.

John Keane retired from inter-county hurling after the 1951 championship.

MICHAEL 'BABS' KEATING

(Height 5' 9", Weight 14 St)

Decade... 1960s/1970s

(Position... Wing-Forward)

CHIEF CHARACTERISTIC... TRAINING DONKEYS TO WIN DERBIES

TOP ACCOMPLICES... FRANCIS LOUGHNANE, DINNY RYAN, NOEL
O'DWYER, SEAMUS HOGAN, JOHN FLANAGAN, TOM RYAN

MICHAEL 'BABS' KEATING

'TAKING OFF THE BOOTS AND SOCKS, EVERYBODY SAYS IT WAS A GREAT THING TO DO, BUT REALLY IT WAS UTTER STUPIDITY. ESPECIALLY WHEN YOU CONSIDER THE FULL-BACK LINE THAT KILKENNY HAD... (PHIL) LARKIN, PA DILLON, AND (JAMES) TRACEY... THEY WEREN'T TOO WORRIED ABOUT WHERE THEY HIT YOU AT THE TIME.'

– BABS KEATING

WALTZING *through Kilkenny... it's bare-footed Michael Keating.*

The old broadsheet was yellowed and aged, like faded parchment. A closer inspection of the tattered newspaper would have revealed a barely discernible date of publication.

5th September 1971

The sepia image on the front page was of an imposing figure carrying a camán. His eyes are set with a steely gaze, his body readied at a fighting pitch, and prepared for war.

Of all the pictures, from all battles, in all the wars fought on Ireland's golden fields, perhaps this one is the most evocative – the most searingly and heroically valiant. The figure is bare-footed as the battle rages around him. He seems to care little

HARD
MAN
RATINGS
TOUGHEST:
9.2/10

MEANEST:
9.1/10

SCARIEST:
9.3/10

HARDEST:
19.5/20
☠

TOTAL
HARD MAN
47.1/50

for his personal safety, his glare is transfixed upon enemy lines. The story behind the timeless image was almost as incredible as the highly acclaimed incident itself.

A couple of years ago, Michael 'Babs' Keating was approached by a man who claimed he had witnessed the Premier legend playing barefoot in Cork. On the afternoon in question the man added he had picked the discarded boots up off the turf after the match at Páirc Uí Chaoimh. Over the years Babs has heard the shortest of stories, and the tallest of tales about the day he went barefoot in the park... Croke Park that is!

Tipperary and Kilkenny were renewing their age-old rivalry on All-Ireland day at a misty Jones' Road, when Tipp's prolific wing-forward, Micheal Keating could well have uttered one of the most famous lines ever delivered by astronaut Jim Lovell.

'Houston, we have had a problem!'

Ten minutes had elapsed in the second period when Babs felt a stab on the underside of his foot – and winced as a cobbler's nail had come up through the boot.

Babs had that sinking feeling and immediately discarded the offending footwear. Many would have questioned the Ardfinnan native's sanity at this juncture. Croke Park on All-Ireland final day tended to be the last place on planet Earth to attempt to tip-toe through the tulips!

It was also worth noting for historical purposes that the Premier County and the Cats tended to take a hands-on approach to any anatomical parts that are left exposed – particularly the ones that have legs attached to them! The fact that Babs was fully aware of the perils of All-Ireland day boot removal merely added to the mystique of the outlandish event.

'Taking off the boots and socks, everybody says it was a great thing to do, but really it was utter stupidity. Especially when you consider the full-back line that Kilkenny had... (Phil) Larkin, Pa Dillon, and (James) Tracey... they weren't too worried about where they hit you at the time.'

Keating had entered the final in fine fettle and his confidence was in no way impaired by discarding his footwear. He was coming off the back of a sensational scoring spree – his three goals against Limerick were decisive in the Munster final, while he registered an outlandish total of 2-12 in the All-Ireland semi-final win over Galway. Nothing appeared to faze Ardfinnan's finest and even when his gear bag was stolen before the final, he concluded the show must go on.

Following an intensive training session on the eve of the final, the Tipp players had dropped their bags inside the door of the local hotel. Keating, a columnist in the *Irish Sun*, recalled in the publication.

'I was working with Esso and earlier in the year I had been over in London at a conference.

When I was there, the one thing I really wanted to do was buy a new pair of boots.

'At the time in Ireland, you were limited really to just the Blackthorn boots. So, I got these lovely state-of-the-art Puma boots in London, and I was proud of them all that year.

'Luckily enough, on the night my gear bag went missing none of my hurleys were there. I had given them to Tommy Doyle; he was a specialist at repairing hurleys, and I'd asked him to make sure the bands were as tight as they could be for the game.

'But the boots were gone, and never to be seen again.'

With the clock ticking towards 'high noon', Babs decided to rummage through his bedroom and break out his old boots for one last throw of the dice. They definitely reflected the light of better days and were in need of some repair work, so he brought them to a shoemaker in Clonmel town. The first half of the final passed without any major drama for Babs and his ageing footwear.

Early in the second, the footwear gods called time on Michael Keating's venerable boots. What's rare is wonderful and what happened next, added another layer to the legend of Micheal 'Babs' Keating's already colourful life story...

{ THE BAREFOOTED WONDER }

'It happened so quickly and the game was still going on. Frank Murphy from Cork was the referee and he wasn't the kind of guy who was going to hold up the game to facilitate me.

'So, I just played on and when things started going well enough for you, then you didn't really think about changing, you just carried on.'

To the general amazement in GAA headquarters, Babs did exactly that.

'I was a free-taker and I remember one free I got at a very vital stage out under the old Cusack Stand, about 65 yards out and with a wet ball. Jesus didn't I kind of slip a bit, but luckily enough it just made it over the bar.'

Legendary commentator Michael O'Hehir's rousing summation described Keating as 'the bare-footed wonder' and the description has journeyed through the ages with the celebrated Premier assassin.

'At one stage I got a ball out under the Cusack and when I turned, I could see Dinny Ryan inside waiting. I put it in his pocket and he scored the last goal. Michael O'Hehir's description made a hero out of me.'

A Premier one… at that!

A HURLING AND FOOTBALL LIFE

BORN IN Ardfinnan, County Tipperary, Keating first played competitive gaelic games during his school days at CBS High School Clonmel. He was 16 when he first linked up with the Tipperary minor teams in hurling and football codes.

He was selected for the senior football panel during the 1960 championship and the senior hurling selectors came calling four years later. Keating excelled with hurl and ball, and became a regular member of both starting fifteens.

Hurling was the top dog in the Premier County, and it was no surprise that Babs won two All-Ireland medals, four Munster medals, and two National League medals. He was also an All-Ireland runner-up on two occasions.

The highly talented Keating was selected on both Munster inter-provincial teams. He won a combined total of three Railway Cup medals. At club level, he was a five-time football championship medallist with Tipperary specialists, Ardfinnan. Keating played his club hurling with the local side Ballybacon-Grange.

He was one of the finest hurlers of any generation and in 1971 he was named on the inaugural All Star team, and also collected the Texaco Hurler of the Year award.

Babs had an eventful term in management and coaching. He served as manager of the Galway, Offaly, and Laois senior teams, his most significant spell was with Tipperary, guiding them to two All-Ireland victories.

EOIN KELLY

(Height 5' 10", Weight 14 St)

Decade... 2000s/2010s

(Position... Corner-Forward)

CHIEF CHARACTERISTIC... KEEPING THE SCOREBOARD
TICKING OVER... AT A RATE OF KNOTS

TOP ACCOMPLICES... NOEL MCGRATH, PATRICK MAHER,
SEAMUS CALLANAN

EOIN KELLY

'I WAS TOLD, 'YOU'LL BE GOING IN NOW'. I NEARLY TURNED PALE, I WAS THINKING, 'OH NO BRENDAN, WILL YOU GET UP'

– EOIN KELLY

'**G**ERRY, is he right?'
    'Yeah, I'm just giving him an injection.'
'Don't mind that, stitch him.'

Nicky English was a worried man. His goalkeeper looked like he had been run over by a bus. Brendan Cummins was a long way from being right and marooned halfway between consciousness and a stopover at A&E in Nenagh General Hospital.

The Tipperary sub-goalkeeper watched the unfolding scene with increasing levels of anxiety. At some point in every sporting career, the present and the future collide. That's what you sign-up for, one of the hazards of the job.

Cummins then staggered to his feet and indicated his willingness to return to the scene of the crime. Eoin Kelly heaved a huge sigh of relief; as introductions to inter-county hurling go, replacing Cummins in an All-Ireland quarter-final was not one he had any intentions of adding

HARD MAN RATINGS

TOUGHEST:
9.3/10

MEANEST:
9.0/10

SCARIEST:
9.6/10

HARDEST:
19.4/20

☠

TOTAL HARD MAN

47.3/50

to his bucket list. Those were the joys of double-jobbing for the precocious young talent from the unheralded South Division club, Mullinahone. He had been held in reserve as cover for Cummins and the wily Tipperary boss, Nicky English had also retained him with a view to a possible slot in the forward line. The Premier boss knew that such was the young man's talent, he could have nailed down a job anywhere.

'I'd heard all about him. He was well heralded, he'd been with St Kieran's and he was physically very well developed. Lots of power and strength, a lower centre of gravity. He took less time to acclimatise to senior hurling.

'He took frees in his first year in senior hurling for Tipperary and that was it, on you go. That can interfere with general play, frees can become a burden for some, but never for him.'

When Kelly finally entered the fray in the final quarter, one of the greatest forwards in the history of the championship headed straight for the opposite end of the field… scoring a point in jig-time. The Premier lost, but Eoin's incredible Tipperary career was up and running. Kelly was a young man in a hurry and after joining the panel again in 2001, he copper-fastened his slot as Tipperary made it all the way to the league final. Clare provided the opposition, but the Premier without ever really impressing got the job done on a 1–19 to 0-17, final tally.

After that early addition to the trophy cabinet, Kelly added a Munster medal to his collection as Tipperary downed Limerick by 2–16 to 1–17. It got better for Eoin as he picked up his first All-Ireland medal, as two goals by Mark O'Leary provided the platform to withstand a late Galway rally.

Kelly was already delivering a serious down payment on his

undoubted potential. He was later honoured with his first All Star, while he was also named Vodafone Young Hurler of the Year. It came as no surprise to his old boss English, who had kept a watchful eye on the young stars development days. While he knew Eoin Kelly had all the attributes to become another Premier County legend, it was the sheer bustling physicality, and the ability to mix it with some of the meanest defenders in the modern game that really singled the Mullimahone hit-man out as something very special.

'The first day (against Clare in 2001) when those unbelievable two challenges came in from Baker (Ollie), and McMahon (Seanie)… they hit him with everything. They were seasoned, experienced, ultra-strong inter-county players. They hit him their best shots within 20 minutes of his debut… he won the ball, hit the ball and got up. Within a minute of that, he nailed a difficult free from the far side of the field.

'I just said, this was meant for him. The rest after that was never going to be an issue for him because he had everything else. There was no such thing as having to prepare him, he was ready. I could take no credit for producing Eoin Kelly except other than to pick him.'

Kelly appeared at times to breathe blue and gold, he lifted everybody around with his snarling, confrontational presence. Kelly was all things to Tipperary. It was as if he appeared to grow a few inches when he pulled the famous crest.

{KELLY'S EYE}

For the Premier he was the Rock of Cashel, Holycross Abbey,

and Roscrea Castle, rolled into one. Kelly just kept getting better, amassing huge totals, but worryingly for the Premier, there was little else to enthuse about. Eoin kept up his side of the bargain winning his second Young Hurler of the Year Award in-a-row, but it was a case of after the Lord Mayor's Show for Tipperary after the high of 2001.

English departed in 2002 after a chastening season, which saw them cough up both Munster and All-Ireland titles. The Premier had become remarkably fickle – the county that only did one in-a-row. Kelly then captained Tipperary to 2010 glory, sending the Kilkenny Drive-For-Five spinning off the road. His Championship career stats were astonishing – 21-368 looked like something pulled out of a telephone directory.

Tipperary's Brendan Maher had no doubt that he had been in the presence of absolute greatness, when paying a glorious tribute to his former teammate.

'I think if you put him in any position and gave him time there, he'd be able to master it. He's the best I've ever seen. I can't speak about the players of the past. Obviously, there are many great men that have played for Tipperary but definitely in my lifetime he's the best I've ever seen and I reckon he'll be the best we'll ever see.'

A penny for Eoin's thoughts on replacing Brenden Cummins?

He recalled his varying states of perplexity as his goal-keeping career went astray!

'I was told, "You'll be going in now". I turned pale. I was thinking, *Oh no Brendan, will you get up.* He got up and played on.'

Tipperary hurling owes legend Brendan Cummins, a debt of service... on two counts!

DIARY OF A PREMIER HIT-MAN

EOIN KELLY was born on January 6, 1982. The legendary right corner-forward first played competitive hurling whilst at school in St Kieran's College. He linked up with Tipperary minor team as a goalkeeper, before later joining the under-21 side. Kelly made his first senior appearance during the 2000 championship.

He hailed from a hurling background with his brother Paul, also lining out with the Premier. His cousins Niall and Ollie Moran both had distinguished careers with Munster rivals Limerick.

Kelly's total of 21 goals and 368 points ranks him as one of the highest-scoring forwards of all-time. He is also the Premier County's all-time top scorer. Throughout his career, Kelly made a total of 63 championship appearances, and he retired from the top level on December 1, 2014. He won two All-Irelands with Tipperary and a total of five Munster medals. Eoin also won two National League titles and was the recipient of six All Star Awards, equalling Nicky English's and Padraic Maher's total as the top Award winners for the Premier County.

He also represented Ireland at international level against Scotland in the compromise game. He won two Railway Cups and a senior County title with Mullinahone in 2002, when they upset hot-favourites, Thurles Sarsfields.

JOHN LEAHY

(Height 5' 9", Weight 14.5 St)

Decade... 1980s/1990s/2000s

(Position... Wing-Forward)

CHIEF CHARACTERISTIC... ENSURING FOR DEFENDERS THE DEVIL
WAS ALWAYS IN THE DETAIL

TOP ACCOMPLICES... MICHEAL CLEARY, COLM BONNAR, DECLAN
CARR, PAT FOX, CORMAC BONNAR

JOHN LEAHY

'HE WANTED TO BE THE PERSON TO TURN AROUND TIPP'S
FORTUNES, THEY HAD NICE HURLERS BUT NO DEVIL. AND HE WAS
A DEVIL. JOHN COULD GIVE IT TO YOU VERBALLY, PHYSICALLY,
OR HURL THE LIVING S***E OUT OF YOU.'

– PETE FINNERTY

ANGEL or Demon?

He was the darling of the Premier County, or was he the devil in disguise? The greatest trick the devil ever played was convincing the world he never existed.

The 1995 movie *The Usual Suspects* contains a memorable line spoken about the existence or non-existence of the Devil. It could well have been a tagline for Tipperary's terrific talisman – the mercurial John Leahy.

No hurler has divided opinion quite like the Mullinahone assassin. Loved and hated in equal measure, Leahy was a box of tricks and a powder keg of menace rolled into one combustible package. Some saw the Devil incarnate and others saw an artistic stickman, flawed in character, but utterly brilliant.

Love him or not, Leahy was all of the above

HARD MAN RATINGS

TOUGHEST:
9.3/10

MEANEST:
9.9/10

SCARIEST:
9.5/10

HARDEST:
19.3/20

TOTAL HARD MAN

48.0/50

and a few dollars more. Pete Finerty clashed swords with him on many occasions and had scars to prove it.

Leahy was a modern-day gunslinger with an itchy trigger finger.

When queried about life on the firing range, he boldly proclaimed… 'Jaysus, I loved it, yeah,' he affirmed. 'Genuinely! Give it to me and I'll f***ing give it back to you.'

He arrived from the junior side of Mullinahone. They had little or no hurling pedigree apart from Mikey Cahill, who had been the only Mullinahone man to wear the Tipperary shirt almost half a century earlier – for the minor team.

He played a starring role in Tipperary's march to the 1987 All- Ireland minor final where they lost to an exceptional Offaly selection. Mullinahone, a small parish, was enthralled by his exploits and a parade was organized in honour of their hero.

Leahy fondly recalled the astonishing scenes that unfolded in his native village.

'Twenty or 30 young lads sitting in the trailer and Mickey Hennessy, Lord rest him, playing *Slievenamon*. I remember they rang me. I was up at a friend's house.

'I said I wasn't coming down. The whole parish was out… "You have to come down". I was saying, "No… Please! No!" I don't want to do this!"

'They collected me outside my own house and here I was on the back of this trailer. Like, I didn't play for acclaim or that. It probably wasn't the wisest thing but I appreciated it and I think I handled it okay.

'Wally Scott singing on the trailer and a little bonfire at the GAA field. One of the greatest sentences ever said to me was a guy I worked with on the farm. He said to me… "I want to thank you for playing for Tipp. What I really want to thank you for is seeing Mullinahone on a senior Tipperary programme".

'That is what it meant to people. So, you had the backing of those people. That fed into it.'

John Leahy had burst onto the scene and he struck for glory – early and often. The bulk of Leahy's medal haul was garnered in his first three years at senior level, scooping two All-Irelands and an All Star. The future for Leahy and the Premier looked bright and all Blue and Gold, but soon events on foreign shores would, however, send his career into an irreversible tailspin.

He had developed a cocky on-field demeanour – which attracted a lot of unnecessary attention from opposition players and supporters alike.

Galway were in their pomp, and any Celtic Crosses that were to be mined would require extracting from one of the greatest half-back lines in the history of the game.

{ FOR PETE'S SAKE }

Tipperary's manager, the redoubtable Micheal 'Babs' Keating was heavy on the message to engage the famous trio, and seek to destroy, as Leahy revealed.

'Get in their face.' You were fighting for your county, like. And I think the game was more physical then. People went along to watch these individual battles. So, I was marking Pete.

And we f**king marked each other, like.

'And people went to see that.

'I didn't know Pete Finnerty. And I didn't really care who he was. I was aware of his reputation so my attitude was…*I am going to break you down. I am going to test you and see what is in you, like.'*

Leahy was young, but far from innocent and he followed 'Babs' instructions to the letter.

'I was asked to stop Pete hurling. I remember Bobby Ryan saying to me, "John, whatever f***ing happens, don't let Peter Finnerty put in that big clearance". Like, that moment in the 1989 semi-final; if it happened now, I probably would have been sent off. But I can always picture it. He ran past me with the ball and he put the ball out here like.

'And this thing rang through my mind. I can't let him clear this. Bobby will kill me! So I went for the ball but his hand was there, like. You got away with it then. And he gave it back to me.

'We gave it to each other – verbally, physically – nothing was off limits. You had two guys fighting for a cause. And you were allowed to do it.'

Sadly for Tipperary and John Leahy, it never got better than that. A brilliant league final display against Galway was a reminder of his prodigious ability. Injury, however, curtailed his run to another All-Ireland in 2001. Slowly his career petered out as he quietly exited the stage in 2003.

The star that had once burned so brightly fizzled underwhelmingly out.

Angel or Demon? The greatest trick the Devil ever played was convincing the world he never existed…

THE LIFE OF
LEAHY

LEAHY PLAYED his club hurling and football with Mullinahone. He won county medals in both codes at underage levels. Mullinahone's dramatic rise from junior level to senior was rubber-stamped when they were promoted to the senior grade in 2002.

John Leahy overcame a cruciate ligament injury to be appointed player-manager of the club's senior hurling side. In 2002, he sensationally orchestrated the club's rise to the top of the Tipperary senior ranks – when guiding them to their first-ever senior county title as they downed raging-hot favourites Thurles Sarsfields.

Leahy joined the Tipperary minor panel in 1987. That season he collected a Munster minor medal and joined the senior and under-21 Teams in 1988. In 1989 he won a Munster title with the under-21s and collected his first All-Ireland medal as the side ended the season as All-Ireland champions. In 1990 he won a second Munster under-21 medal, and he had the distinction of being the first player from his club to captain a Tipperary side to a Munster title.

He won three All-Ireland Senior Championships, 1989, 1991 and 2001. Leahy also collected five Munster Championships, 1988, 1989, 1991, 1993, and 2001. He also won a McGrath Cup medal for senior football and four National Hurling League titles during his time.

SYLVIE LINNANE
(Height 5' 7", Weight 13.5 St)

Decade... 1970s/1980s
(Position... Corner-Back)

CHIEF CHARACTERISTIC... ENSURING FORWARDS
REMAIN IN A HORIZONTAL POSITION

TOP ACCOMPLICES... TONY KEADY, STEVE MCMAHON, OLLIE
KILKENNY, CONOR HAYES, PETE FINNERTY

SYLVIE LINNANE

'THE MAN WHO DRIVES A JCB ON A MONDAY...
AND TURNS INTO ONE ON A SUNDAY.'

– MICHEÁL O'MUIRCHEARTAIGH

HE was the bilingual voice of GAA. Along with Micheal O'Hare, his exhilarating narratives, which were often offered as gaeilge, enthralled listeners from Newtownshandrum, to New York.

Micheál O'Muircheartaigh always seemed to nail the most evocative of lines during his epic commentaries on television and radio. He was Pablo Picasso, Michael Angelo and Ernest Hemingway... rolled into one!

He could paint a scene like an 'Old Master,' with vivid, sweeping brushstrokes, or pen an oration that would have made William Shakespeare weep!

Classic lines like... 'He grabs the sliothar, he's on the 50! He's on the 40! He's on the 30... he's on the ground!'

Whatever, wherever, or whenever, Micheál coined it. So, when he summarized a Galway hurling legend, Sylvie Linnane, thus, it was certainly hard to argue with.

HARD
MAN
RATINGS
TOUGHEST:
9.6/10

MEANEST:
9.4/10

SCARIEST:
9.9/10

HARDEST:
19.5/20

TOTAL
HARD MAN
48.4/50

'The man who drives a JCB on a Monday… and turns into one on a Sunday.'

Kilkenny great Liam Fennelly and Galway legend Conor Hayes both recall the legend of Sylvie Linnane – with Liam firing the opening salvo!

'It wouldn't be the first time Sylvie was pulling when he couldn't see the ball. I remember one day the whistle was blown, I think for an earlier free or something. He knew and I knew the whistle was gone, but the ball was still there… we both still pulled our living best.

'He left me with about eight inches of the handle of my hurl, that was it. It broke just below the hands. He went to do me… I went to do him. He was very strong in the pull.'

Sylvie certainly never spared the timber and invariably ended up needing a replacement, at some stage of the contest. A clash of the ash with Sylvie was a high voltage experience, as Hayes explained.

'He was actually a very skilful player, but you had to keep an eye on him all the time. He pulled one day, a wild kind of pull, and his hurley shattered… broke in two. Here he was running out towards the sideline with a piece of broken hurley in each hand, over his head, shouting for a new hurley… while at the same time, the ref was running in to sort out what had happened.

'Bad enough the wild pull, your man lying on the ground… it could even have been you, Liam! – the crowd behind the goal demanding for him to be sent off.'

With two pieces of ash in his hands, Sylvie was holding some rather incriminating evidence, which further incensed the crowd, who vociferously demanded a pound of Sylvie's flesh.

With cries of 'You tinker Linnane!' ringing in his ears, Conor Hayes decided it was time to pull rank. He knew Sylvie better than most, and his teammate's fetish for walking tight-ropes, with a greater frequency, than even the most seasoned funambulist.

'Here he was running out like a gladiator with the two bits of hurl over his head, shouting for a new hurl. I had to shout at him to stop and lower his arms.'

In September 1980, Galway were up in Dublin ahead of their second consecutive All-Ireland final. And he recalled a story himself.

The Tribesmen had missed out on the big prize the year before and were champing at the bit to take Liam MacCarthy back to the West. It appeared to be a case of the calm, before the storm.

Then as Sylvie and company were about to nod off, to a land where Liam MacCarthy was permanently bedecked in maroon and white ribbons, all hell let loose.

Sylvie was sharing a room with Steve Mahon at the time, and recalls that a couple became involved in a verbal attraction down on the street. All had been going swimmingly for the Galway contingent, until the verbals began to reach a crescendo, on ground zero.

Sylvie Linnane duly takes up the reins here.

'I ran into the bathroom, got the waste-paper basket, filled it with water and ran over to the window, and threw the water over the man. It did the trick, and he stopped, and the woman ran away.

'A happy ending, or so I thought until the man recovered from the shock and got really, really angry, and started to climb up the drainpipe to pay back the person who threw water on him.

'I didn't think the night before the All-Ireland was the best time to get involved in a brawl – especially as the guy looked like a pure psycho – and I decided discretion was the best part of valour. I turned off the light, so he wouldn't know where to find me.

'I went quietly back to bed and listened attentively to see what would happen. What I hadn't known at the time was that the light immediately below my room was on.

'The room belonged to another player who was not a man to mess with and, a few minutes later I heard him forcefully eject the intruder out of the window.'

Thankfully for Galway, despite their nocturnal adventures, they successfully raided the capital and absconded back over the border, with the precious silverware, safely in tow!

{ WHAT'S ANOTHER YEAR }

As well as being one of the toughest, yet most accomplished defenders in the annals of the game, Sylvie had a wicked sense of humour that often left bemused opponents, not knowing whether to laugh or cry.

In the dying embers of the 1988 All-Ireland final, Tipperary's Nicky English enquired of the referee, how long was remaining?

Sylvie happened to be in the vicinity as the Lattin-Cullen maestro was sizing up his limited options from the placed ball.

Linnane, mischievously, interjected, 'At least another year for you now, Nicky'.

The legendary 'Bard of Dingle,' the great Micheál O'Muircheartaigh would surely have approved!

»——→ INTO THE WEST ←——«

THE GORT native joined the inter-county scene at the age of 16, when he first linked up with the Galway minors. He made his senior debut in the 1976 championship, and soon became an indispensable part of a fearsome 'Tribe' backline. The future right corner-back on the Galway Hurling Team of the Millennium would go on to make 28 championship appearances during the mid-70s and late 80s, collecting three All Star Awards along the way.

In a star-studded Galway line-up, he shone brighter than most and he amassed two National League winners' medals, to complement his three Celtic Crosses.

He is one of a select band of maroon and white players to hold three All-Ireland senior medals.

In what was a bountiful era for the men from the West, he was also runner-up in three All-Ireland finals, as the Galway men emerged from the shadows under Cyril Farrell to become perennial title contenders.

He led his hometown club, Gort, to their first championship decider in over 30 years, defeating Kiltormer in 1981. After a year's hiatus, Gort, downed Castlegar with a 2-12 to 3-6 winning scoreline.

Linnane and Gort powered onward to the All-Ireland final against Ballyhale. The concession of a late goal to Dermot Fennelly would prove costly, as the Kilkenny side prevailed after a replay.

BRIAN LOHAN

(Height 6' 1", Weight 14.5 St)

Decade... 1990s/2000s

(Position... Full-Back)

CHIEF CHARACTERISTIC... HEAD OF SECURITY,
LIAM MACCARTHY'S ENTERPRISES

TOP ACCOMPLICES... ANTHONY DALY, COLIN LYNCH, FRANK LOHAN,
DAVY FITZGERALD, OLLIE BAKER, SEANIE MCMAHON

BRIAN LOHAN

THEY were the hurling rebels… who always had a cause. A rare breed of 'Banner' boys, who staunchly refused to tip their hats to time, or tradition. The one with the gruaig rua, the red-haired warrior – the one they made their blood-thirsty supremo, licked his lips more than most.

Ger Loughnane used to speak of the guilty pleasure he obtained from the distaste Brian Lohan held for any forward, who was sighted on his radar. The snapping, snarling, Shannonside native housed a healthy dislike for sniping assassins.

Ger Loughnane, a former defender himself by trade, was the voyeur, who peered through the keyhole as Lohan dispensed his own very personal brand of justice.

Lohan was the gamekeeper of the famous Clare side, managed by the Feakle Messiah, whose unique managerial message raised the 'Banner' from hurling's backwaters.

Loughnane took his frustrations of an

HARD MAN RATINGS

TOUGHEST:
9.7/10

MEANEST:
9.6/10

SCARIEST:
9.5/10

HARDEST:
19.8/20

☠

TOTAL HARD MAN

48.6/50

unfulfilled playing career and banished 'The curse of Biddy Early,' when Clare ended a staggering 81-year period of dormancy, towards the end of the second Millennium.

Brian Lohan was the tall and gangly rifleman, who patrolled and protected the Banner backline as if his life depended on it. The Shannon Cyclone could well have been the craziest of the Banner 'Crazy Gang'; Lohan seemed to unleash a sort of frenzied defensive 'Jihad,' as he protected the sacred Clare geansaí against incoming attackers, who were met with all the fire and fury, that bequeaths a practitioner of 'Holy War'.

He was a man of few words on the pitch and most forwards considered this to be a blessing of sorts as when he did become animated, it normally ended badly for those of an attack-minded disposition.

Mostly, Brian Lohan's hurling did the talking, as he seemed to glide around the backline, extinguishing fires and eliminating any potentially hazardous situations, before they developed. He had the perfect calibration for a modern-day defender. Supremely fit, and deceptively quick, he married enormous physical strength with a stealthy and silky finesse.

{ LOHAN GIVES LAZARUS A RUN FOR HIS MONEY }

Risk vs Reward?

The economics of the situation were not lost upon Ger Loughnane. The loss of Brian Lohan to a hamstring injury with 20 minutes remaining in the 1995 All-Ireland hurling final was the financial equivalent of the 'Wall Street Crash'.

Lohan represented the Banner's prime hurling stock, a blue-chip-investment. Loughnane, however, was also a pragmatic man and there was no room for sentiment here. No player could continue on one leg in the white heat of All-Ireland combat – no player, bar Brian Lohan, that is!

The maths for the iconic coach and schoolmaster, and its ensuing implementation, amounted to a very workable equation.

Lohan minus one leg = two of any other player.

The Clare physio signalled to Loughnane that Lohan had a torn hamstring and would have to depart the fray.

'Tell him he's not coming off!' was Loughnane's reply.

Lohan, who only ever departed unconscious or on a stretcher, didn't need much convincing, despite being in unimaginable discomfort. He duly galloped about 20 yards after a ball, a run which was certainly not for the faint of heart. The Banner faithful present winced, and peered through their fingertips, to see if their talisman still had any legs left. At which point a message advising viewer discretion from the national broadcaster – would have been greatly appreciated.

For the rest of the perplexed Clare fraternity, who were gathered around their homesteads, this was the moment to take refuge behind the couch.

To the naked eye, Lohan appeared to have consumed a few bottles of a well-known energy drink, and sprouted wings! It was an astonishing manoeuvre by any standards, the biblical standard bearer for miraculous recoveries, the great Lazarus himself would have been extremely proud of.

The great man himself nonchalantly trotted back, seemingly oblivious to all the fuss. At which point Brian Lohan entered a kind of mythical status – his 'street cred' going through the roof. Only an on-field amputation could have raised his soaring profile more. With Lohan purring like a '62 Chevy, the Banner kicked for home, ending a near century-long wait for an audience with Liam MacCarthy.

It was a day like no other. The crippled rose, the lame walked, and Brian Lohan raised his beloved Banner.

Brian continued his journey secure in the knowledge that 'The freedom of Clare' was safely bestowed upon him. On the road to iománaíochta immortality, he was unfortunate not to get another Celtic Cross in 1998, as Galway referee Jimmy Cooney's, premature blast of the whistle, ensured that the Banner would have to replay Offaly in the All-Ireland semi-final.

It was an extraordinary oversight by the official, which sparked a mass pitch invasion from outraged Offaly supporters.

Cooney recalled the infamous moments in the *Irish Independent*.

'Michael Bodkin, the nearest linesman to me at the time, came walking in, shaking his head,' he remembered. 'Then Aodán Mac Suibhne and one of my umpires arrived. All three of them were shaking their heads.

'I took a second look at the watch and I knew exactly what was after happening me. I had played a 30-minute half, instead of 35. At that stage, I wished to God the whole world could open up and take me away altogether.'

The notorious affair was later dubbed 'The day of the short whistle', and almost certainly changed the course of hurling history. It was a cruel blow for a county that had only ever won a handful of All-Ireland titles.

It was a bitter pill for Lohan as Clare had probably just about shaded the verdict on the day, and to add insult to injury, they lost out in the replay – with the Faithful going on gratefully to claim MacCarthy.

Litter however dimmed Brian Lohan's shining star, which shone brightest of all the Banner celestial bodies in their hurling universe. In the demented, and delicious reign of Ger Loughnane… Lohan proved to be the Banner's supreme soldier of war.

»——→ TO THE ←——«
BANNER BORN

BRIAN LOHAN was born November 14, 1971. He is the current manager of the Clare senior hurling team. Lohan began his hurling career at club level with the famed Wolfe Tones club.

He enjoyed a very successful underage stint and graduated to the club's senior team. A coveted county title soon followed, and he captained the club as they were crowned kings of the province, when they won the Munster Club Championship. Brian Lohan collected two Clare Championships during his career. Lohan lined out for Clare on the Under-21 team in May 1992, and he donned the Banners famous gold and blue for the first time aged 21, in 1993.

He won All-Ireland Championship medals in 1995 and 1997. Brian Lohan is one of only five Clare players to have made more than 50 championship appearances for his county.

During his gilt-edged career, he collected four All Stars, three Munster titles, and was honoured as Hurler of the Year. He was selected in the prestigious full-back position on the Munster Hurling Team of the Millennium.

He never lost a game for his province and ended his career with four Railway Cup medals, including as captain in 1996. After retiring, he started his coaching career at club level with Wolfe Tones and Patrickswell, before guiding the University of Limerick to the Fitzgibbon Cup title in 2015.

GER LOUGHNANE

(Height 5' 11", Weight 14 St)

Decade... 1970s/1980s
(Position... Wing-Back)

CHIEF CHARACTERISTIC... REMINDING CLARE PLAYERS
THAT MILK TURNED FASTER THAN THEM

TOP ACCOMPLICES... SEAN STACK, SEAMUS DURACK, JOHN
CALLINAN, SEAN HEHIR, JACKIE O'GORMAN, MICK MORONEY

GER
LOUGHNANE

'WHEN THE GAME WAS OVER, LOUGHNANE SLUMPED TO THE GROUND IN FRUSTRATION, AND AS HE THUMPED HIS HURLEY OFF THE TURF, ONE COULD IMAGINE HIS FEELINGS AND THOSE OF THE MANY OTHER CLARE PEOPLE IN THE GROUND. IT WAS A SAD SETBACK FOR A HOPEFUL TEAM AND ONE THAT MAY TAKE SOME TIME TO GET OVER'

– PADDY DOWNEY, *THE IRISH TIMES,* **JULY 31, 1978**

DON'T look back in anger…

Finest hours were never meant to end like this. The day that had promised so much would forever reign in Clare's infamy. Grown men would wake crying from their sleep – jolted by the haunting images of a graveyard called Tom Semple's Field.

They could have buried him alive there – if anyone had a spade handy.

He had lost the will to live in those torrid moments, when a shrill blast of the referee's whistle put the final nail in the Banner's coffin.

Deep down, he knew neither himself nor his fellow county men would ever conquer Munster. That particular aircraft had taken flight and they would be left eternally waiting in the departure lounge.

Ger Loughnane would go on to have an

HARD MAN RATINGS

TOUGHEST:
9.6/10

MEANEST:
9.5/10

SCARIEST:
10/10

HARDEST:
19.1/20

TOTAL HARD MAN

48.2/50

incredible career and was a shining light for the Banner, even on the darkest of days. There would be few darker than this as the Banner allowed Cork to prise the precious Munster crown from their grasp.

They saw 'What doesn't kill you makes you stronger' – whatever the merits of home psychology theories, Clare hurling would eventually see this fateful day of endings as a new beginning. Loughnane would bottle his hurt, and distil his sense of injustice, dispensing it by the crate-load to the devil's disciples, Cork, and Tipperary.

And then to the whole damn lot of them!

The man from Feakle was always going to be the catalyst. The curse of Biddy Early be damned…

Days like 1978 shaped one of the greatest managers in GAA history. Greatness should always be measured not by a man's successes, but by the hurdles and obstacles he has to overcome to get there.

Thurles was hopping on the fateful day of the Munster final. The Taoiseach, Jack Lynch and the President, Paddy Hillary were crammed in among the dignitaries. There to see if the Clare famine of 46 excruciatingly long years would finally be consigned to the history books.

The gates were padlocked an hour before the throw-in – with crowds of people still milling excitedly around the outside perimeters of the hurling cathedral.

The best Banner team in generations duly flopped – as the Rebels held them in a firm headlock from pillar to post. Ger Loughnane had the game of his life, but it mattered not a whit. Cork edged a turgid affair, doing what monarchs normally do, crushing even the slightest hint of rebellion.

The Banner seemed paralysed by fear. A bunch of shivering rabbits firmly caught in the glare of the headlights.

Loughnane tried manfully to stem the tide. Hooking, blocking, surging forward to ignite the Banner faithful. He fought and hurled until he could run no more. He died hissing and screaming, with his usual trademark defiance.

When it was over, he slumped to the turf.

The enormity of the reversal overwhelming his senses. He lay prostrate on the ground, an image and a headline that would be viewed in every corner of Ireland the following day. The fallen warrior Loughnane.

As well as Loughnane would hurl for the rest of his stellar career, the Banner never really hit the heights again as that damaging reversal hit them hard – exacting a terrible toll.

It left a chip on his shoulder which resembled a crater and when he was appointed manager of the Clare senior hurling squad in the middle of the 90s, the deep wounds had festered; there would be a number of old scores… that need to be settled!

{THE TRIP TO TIPP}

A bit like the famous Lord Kitchener World War One rallying cry, Loughnane boomed out the words.

'Your County needs you.'

Daly, Lohan, McMahon, and Fitzy answered the call – servicemen who would never be anchored by the conniving arm of history.

Loughnane's 'Love' for Tipperary was well documented. Cork,

Limerick, and Waterford were all on his hit list – but the preening Premier peacocks were his public enemy No. 1.

When he was once asked about Tipperary before a game he informed the startled reporter, 'Tipperary, if I had my way, I wouldn't tell them the time of the throw-in'.

Loughnane had a larger-than-life axe to grind with the Blue and Gold, who had a particular penchant for raining on the Banner parade and piling on the Provincial pain.

First up for the Feakle man was the small matter of breaking that losing Munster habit.

Loughnane's frenetic troops duly pole-axed Limerick in 1995, on their way to an unforgettable smash 'n' grab raid against Offaly, to finally locate that missing person – Liam MacCarthy.

In 1997, Clare and Loughnane were presented with an opportunity of a lifetime and a chance to wipe the slate clean with a dear old friend!

The Banner having feasted at the top table were ravenously hungry for more silverware. Loughnane's troops, like their manager, had a thing for Tipp. It was a hot and heavy affair, but it would be the Premier who would wilt under an unrelenting Páirc Uí Chaoimh sun.

It would get infinitely better for the Banner as Tipperary rallied through the back-door to reach the All-Ireland final. Lightning rarely strikes twice against the Premier, and when John Leahy broke through in the dying embers it looked like lights out in every house in Clare.

Leahy's stroke was batted away by Davy Fitzgerald and Loughnane had another pound of Premier flesh.

When Loughnane finally stepped away from the Banner hot

seat, Clare would no longer be the whipping boys of Munster.

Ger Loughnane, like all great fighters hauled himself off the canvas, to ensure that Clare hurling would never have to look back in anger… again.

THE
WARRIOR'S WAY

GER LOUGHNANE was born on January 27, 1953. He hailed from Feakle, County Clare, and first played competitive hurling for St Flannan's College. He represented the Banner at under-18 and under-21 level. Loughnane made his inter-county debut in the 1972-73 National League. The tigerish right-wing back was unfortunate to hurl in an era which saw the Banner struggle to make any in-roads in Munster or on the All-Ireland stage.

He was part of a cohort who lost five Munster finals and despite being a remarkably consistent presence, he would only add two league titles to his trophy collection during his magnificent Clare tenure.

His excellence ensured he was a regular member of the Munster Railway Cup selection - winning the competition on three occasions.

At club level, he was part of the Feakle side who lost their first championship decider in almost 30 years in 1987, but won notable success the following season, to give him his first county title.

He is, of course, best remembered for his managerial prowess as he guided the Banner to a couple of historic All-Ireland titles. During his six-year tenure as manager of the Clare hurlers, he guided the team to two All-Ireland and three Munster titles. He also had a two-year term in charge of Galway - which ended without success.

MICK MACKEY
(Height 6' 0", Weight 15 St)

Decade... 1920s/1930s/1940s
(Position... Centre-Forward)

CHIEF CHARACTERISTIC... HEAD OF GAA TICKET
SALES AND ENTERTAINMENT

TOP ACCOMPLICES... MICK CROSS, PADDY CLOHESSY, GARRETT
HOWARD, MICK RYAN, TIMMY RYAN, BOB MCCONKEY

MICK MACKEY

*'HE OFTEN SHOWED HIS BODY, ON SAY TUESDAY AFTER A GAME AND HE
WOULD BE BLACK AND BLUE. IT WAS A CASE OF STOP HIM AT ALL COSTS. YOU
WILL HEAR A LOT OF HURLING CRITICS CONFIRMING OTHER PLAYERS FOR
THEIR SCIENTIFIC PLAY, BUT MACKEY WAS SOMETHING SPECIAL, HE HAD
GREAT PHYSIQUE AS WELL AS SKILL AND MOBILITY, AND DARING SPIRIT.'*

– JACKIE POWER

INSIDE the mind of a killer…

Mackey surveyed the scene, and all the hell and carnage that went with it. Twenty-five yards to the goal and half of Galway waiting to scalp him. St Cronan's Park was situated at the far end of Roscrea. The town of 5,000 or so inhabitants has historically been an important market town. The settlement grew around an ancient church or monastery, founded by St Cronan in the latter part of the 6th century.

Roscrea is situated strategically in a gap in the hills on one of the legendary ancient roads of Ireland, the Slighe Dála. There was a buzz around the old trading town that day as excited locals were about to get a rare glimpse of the man who was the centre of the hurling universe.

Come throw-in time on the 15th of August 1936 the whole world and Delaney's dog had

HARD
MAN
RATINGS
TOUGHEST:
9.9/10

MEANEST:
9.0/10

SCARIEST:
9.9/10

HARDEST:
19.9/20
☠

TOTAL
HARD MAN
48.7/50

crammed in to see 'The Playboy of the Southern World,' strut his stuff. The road to Liam MacCarthy reached its penultimate stage, and ever the entertainer, Mackey was determined to bring a little piece of his sold-out Broadway spectacular to the North of Tipperary.

Such was the curious half-life of an inter-county hitman forever domiciled in a land of sporting schizophrenia – fugitive one moment, executioner the next.

He had a whiff of Western blood within his nostrils and the 'Assassin's Creed' demanded a swift execution. Galway was already close to flatlining; his heart rate quickened as he prepared his final judgment. It was time to put the lights out in the City of Tribes.

The route to the goal was treacherous, with six or seven angry Galway men barring his path. Mick Mackey in full flight, however, was a well-chiselled and extraordinarily powerful 15-stone and had the demolition capacity of a medium-sized wrecking ball.

Collecting a pass, he crashed through the 'wall of meat and bone', scattering the Galway defenders like a cluster of fairground skittles. He then pressed the nuclear button, unleashing a rasping, season-ending, kill shot.

After Mackey's barrelling run and nifty finish, all hell broke loose. Two rival gangs of Galway and Limerick supporters were taunting each other, baying for blood. They were separated only by a thin blue line of Gardai, who numbered…one!

The Limerick talisman had avoided full frontal charges, swinging ash, and a furious posse of Galway bounty hunters. It was another multi-dimensional and dazzling display of his prodigious talent. One of hurling's most cavalier performers committing another masterpiece to canvas.

Whatever the opposition, whatever the weather, and whatever the venue, Mick Mackey always ensured the Limerick bandwagon would keep rolling on. It was an era where solo runs should have carried a government health warning. Referees employed a simple operational manual as far as tackling was concerned... anything goes!

With third-man tackling 'a must-have defensive item', the only thing not levelled at attacking players appeared to be the kitchen sink!

None of those caveats troubled Mick Mackey's sense of derring-do. Into the tempest he raged – as wild and free as a marauding mustang.

The men from the West were aggrieved, claiming foul play in the build-up to the goal, and stormed off in protest. It was an emotional response that, in the end, mattered little. Mick's audacious manoeuvre had already secured the 'Treaty' passage to another decider.

It was another blockbusting performance from Mackey, who had also signed Tipperary's exit papers in the Munster final.

When Kilkenny were dismantled in the All-Ireland final, the genie was well and truly out of the bottle. It was full steam ahead for the Treaty Express, with Mick Mackey riding shotgun!

Mackey's career began in fairytale fashion when, with the 'Treaty' unable to field a team, he was summoned from the crowd for a league encounter with Kilkenny.

Despite the unusual selection criteria, Mick passed his unlikely audition with flying colours.

Hurling was in need of a 'poster boy', and Mackey delivered with a larger-than-life personality, allied to an electrifying skillset, which wowed the hurling public.

In an era before celluloid, there was very little, if any worthwhile footage of one of the ancient game's first real superstars. It added to the mystique and the legend – with eye witness accounts of his hurling sorcery passed down lovingly from generation to generation.

{ NO WHIPPING BOY }

He was tungsten tough and that was the minimum requirement in an era when hurling had many head-hunters, who fancied a piece of the Limerick and Ahane legend. With little protection afforded to 'special' players, Mackey was a marked man in more ways than one, as colleague, Jackie Power later reminisced.

'He often showed his body, on say Tuesday after a game and he would be black and blue. It was a case of stop him at all costs. You will hear a lot of hurling critics confirming other players for their scientific play, but Mackey was something special – he had great physique as well as skill and mobility, and daring spirit.'

Another member of the Limerick team, Dr Dick Stokes, alluded to Mick Mackey's incredible dynamism and hurling savvy as the elements that left his opponents chasing shadows.

'He was a very strong, well-built man… and could use it and could think as well as everything else. He was able to throw fellows out of his way in a very purposeful way. In other words, it was always where the ball was… it was always constructive. He was unique in that respect. He could go up the middle. He never had to go up the sideline or anything like that.'

And so it came to pass. The game of hurling had its first

bonafide superstar. You could almost envisage a Ringmaster excitedly belting out the inimitable Mackey's name minutes before throw-in. 'Roll-up – Roll-up – Roll-up. Witness the astonishing, gravity-defying, and electrifying, Mick Mackey.'

The Playboy of the Southern World is still a sold-out show!

THE MAKING OF MACKEY

IN 1931, Mackey was at his brilliant best as Ahane reached the final of the Limerick senior championship. A 5–5 to 1–4 hammering of Croom gave Ahane their first senior title and a first major honour for Mackey. It was the beginning of a decade of dominance as Ahane racked up an astonishing seven in-a-row, including four successive defeats of Croom, which brought Mackey's championship medal-winning tally to eight.

Mackey was a brilliant footballer, also starring with the Ahane senior football team. Five successive final victories between 1935 and 1939 brought his county title count up to 13 in both codes. He was not finished there, and racked up another magnificent seven county hurling titles, starting in 1942 to leave his hurling medals tally at an astronomical 15.

Mick Mackey made his inter-county debut with Limerick in the minor provincial championship in August 1929. Limerick were rising and Mackey was central to one of their best-ever periods of sustained success, winning five Munster titles, three All-Irelands, and five National Leagues.

Mackey received the ultimate accolade when during the GAA's centenary year in 1984, he was selected as centre-forward on the Hurling Team of the Century, and the Hurling Team of the Millennium in 2000.

The covered stand in the TUS Gaelic Grounds in Limerick was named the Mackey Stand in tribute to his memory.

MICHAEL MAHER

(Height 6' 0", Weight 14 St)

Decade... 1950s/1960s

(Position... Full-Back)

CHIEF CHARACTERISTIC... HEAD CHIEF CROKE PARK HOTEL

TOP ACCOMPLICES... TONY WALL, KIERAN CAREY, JOHN DOYLE,
JOHN O'DONOHUE, JIMMY DOYLE, DONIE NEALON

MICHAEL MAHER

*'DOYLE, WITH HIS TONGUE IN HIS CHEEK SAID, AND I HEARD HIM
SAYING IT MYSELF WHEN THE THREE OF THEM RETIRED FROM
HURLING, THAT THEY COULD CLOSE THE HOSPITAL IN NENAGH.'*
– MARTIN ÓG MORRISSEY

THE Maginot Line was a line of concrete fortifications, obstacles and weapon installations built by France in the 1930s to deter invasion by Germany. The line was impervious to most forms of attack, but crucially had one obvious flaw. Realising the strength of the fortifications, invasion forces opted to go around it instead!

Perhaps it might have helped if it was 'manned' by Kieran Carey, Michael Maher and John Doyle! Unlike the military's hi-tech fortification, the only way around the most infamous hurling line in history, 'Hell's Kitchen,' was through them.

The Premier three in-a-row was built around an unbreachable fortress of Messrs' Maher, Doyle and Carey. They were a raging tempest of cold, calculated, and pragmatic fury.

Waterford legend Martin Óg Morrissey once described what it was like spending time in 'Hell's Kitchen.'

'Doyle, with his tongue in his cheek said, and I

**HARD
MAN
RATINGS**

TOUGHEST:
9.5/10

MEANEST:
9.2/10

SCARIEST:
9.5/10

HARDEST:
19.6/20

☠

**TOTAL
HARD MAN**

47.8/50

heard him saying it myself when the three of them retired from hurling, that they could close the hospital in Nenagh. They were tough, no two ways about it They stood on ceremony for no one.

'If a clout could stop you scoring a goal, then you got a clout.'

They soldiered together from 1962 to 1966, forging a fierce, unbreakable line that set the 'gold standard' in defensive excellence. Michael Maher was at the heart of it all as he anchored the fearsome full-back line. The titles and accolades tumbled their way as they lured the unwitting and the unwilling into the searing defensive hurling inferno… of Hell's Kitchen.

Maher was the fulcrum of the suffocating spider's web; he was deft of touch and light of foot, similar to John Doyle, a hurling artist, who wore a velvet glove wrapped around a steel fist.

Where did the famous title come from? And how did this unflappable trio of hurling enforcers dispense their unique brand of justice?

One-third of that celebrated triumvirate was Michael Maher, who like John Doyle, hailed from Holycross, near hurling heartland Thurles. He revealed all to John Harrington in an interview on *GAA.ie*.

Harrington noted that the defensive behemoth Maher 'is quiet-spoken and unfailingly courteous, so it's hard to imagine him now as the defensive colossus who ruled the square in front of the Tipperary goal with utter ruthlessness.

'He was that man though, and he doesn't mind at all that history has painted himself and his two corner-backs as such a fearsome combination. Invoke the term 'Hell's Kitchen' in Maher's company and he chuckles at the good of it.

'John D Hickey put that name on us, fair dues to him,' Maher revealed. 'We never minded it at all either. There wasn't much said about it when we were playing, it was afterwards that people really started describing us as Hell's Kitchen.

'We were big and strong, I suppose, and protecting the goalkeeper was number one. We had no system as such, but we'd cover for each other when we could and get to the ball first if at all possible.

'Kieran Carey wasn't too spectacular in his hurling, but he was very strong. And Doyle was Doyle.

'At that time there was a big tendency to be too safe and play behind your man too much.

But the place to be playing, is to be out in front where you can get the ball and that's the way we played it.'

Michael Maher hailed from a family of hurling 'blue bloods.' He was a nephew of Michael Maher of famed Tubberadora, who captained Tipperary to three All-Ireland wins, and a cousin of 'Sonny' Maher, also, a three-time medal winner.

Their deeds and misdeeds were the stuff of legend and a forward's worst nightmare. Some stories that are part of the myth and mythology, sprouted arms and legs over the years. How could they not? Such was the power and the draw of the tempestuous trio, but there was one indisputable fact that was known for sure… inter-county forwards didn't need to be crazy to spend time in Hell's Kitchen, but it certainly helped!

Tony Wall one of the Premier's finest had the dubious privilege of crossing swords with his formidable colleagues in training, but had fonder memories than most, in his natural position at half-back. He had an eagle-eyed view of proceedings, as he manned the 'crow's nest' and remembers Mick Maher in particular, as a man you could bet your life upon.

'Maher was probably the toughest of them all. He was rock-solid in the middle and never moved off the square. Any forward really had to earn anything he got off him.'

John O'Donoghue was the netminder fortunate to be flanked by the terrible triplets, and he recalls in the same interview what it was like to have such able-bodied 'Bouncers' minding the Premier house.

'Well, they tell me I wouldn't have been any good if it wasn't for them,' says O'Donoghue with a laugh.

'It was certainly a great bonus for me though coming into the team as a 21-year-old to play behind a full-back like them. It wasn't just that they provided great protection, they also trusted me enough to let the ball through to me and let me deal with it while they held back their men which was a huge confidence booster for me."

'As hurlers, they were very much of their time. The rules of the day allowed defenders to be very physical and they were all extremely powerful men.

'Maher was the coolest head of the three. No matter what was happening he kept his composure and that's a great quality to have in a full-back.'

The hair-raising exploits of Michael Maher, Carey and Doyle echoed around firesides on long winter evenings. Wide-eyed infants and grizzled veterans marvelled at their notoriety, as they waited for the sod to thaw, and to herald the return of the sharp staccato burst of clashing ash.

Mick Maher always welcomed you to the battlefield, with a smile and hearty handshake.

…Welcome to Hell!

→ FROM FRYING PAN ←
TO HELL'S KITCHEN FIRE

MICHAEL MAHER (1930-2017), donned the blue and gold for 15 glorious seasons and was also a GAA administrator. Maher made his debut on the inter-county scene at the age of 16 as a member of the Tipperary minor team. The Holycross native was a permanent fixture for his beloved county from 1951 to 1966.

Maher played competitive hurling during his secondary education at Harty Cup specialists Thurles CBS. As part of the Holycross-Ballycahill team, he collected his first senior championship medal in 1948 at the tender age of 18. He added two more 'Dan Breens' to his championship collection in 1951 and 1954.

He enjoyed underage success with the minor team, grabbing a coveted All-Ireland medal in his debut season in 1947. Mick made his senior debut during the 1951-52 league, and it was the beginning of a period of unprecedented success in his native county.

He won a total of five All-Ireland medals, beginning with a solitary Celtic Cross in 1958, and four more in 1961, 1962, 1964 and 1965. He also won six Munster medals and eight National League titles. He pulled on the blue and gold for the last time in June 1966.

After being chosen on the Munster inter-provincial team for the first time in 1958, Maher was an automatic choice, and won four Railway Cup medals.

PÁDRAIC MAHER

(Height 6' 1", Weight 14 St)

Decade... 2000s/2010s/2020s

(Position... Wing-Back)

CHIEF CHARACTERISTIC... BIG GAME HUNTER

TOP ACCOMPLICES... CATHAL BARRETT, RONAN MAHER, BRENDAN
MAHER, SHANE MCGRATH, NOEL MCGRATH

PÁDRAIC MAHER

*'PAUDIE MAHER WOULD PROBABLY HAVE MADE ANY
TIPPERARY TEAM EVER. HE WAS SUCH A MONSTER AT WING-
BACK OR ANYWHERE ELSE HE LINED OUT. I CAN'T REMEMBER
HIM HAVING A BAD DAY AT THE OFFICE."*
– JAKE MORRIS

PÁDRAIC Maher was revered among Tipperary players and fans alike for his boundless courage and honesty of effort. In 13 championship seasons with the famed Blue and Gold, Maher was a constant omnipotent presence in the Tipperary rearguard.

Despite his relish for contact and an unquenchable lust for combat he almost appeared bulletproof at times. He simply refused to bend to an array of injuries that would have sidelined most mere mortals.

Somehow, someway, Maher always managed to stay in the fight. His remarkable durability allowed him to play 60 consecutive championship games. That's nearly four and a half thousand minutes of actual playing time.

It was an astonishing statistic by any standards, given the wear and tear associated with modern-day hurling. At times it appeared 'Paudie Maher'

HARD
MAN
RATINGS
TOUGHEST:
9.5/10

MEANEST:
9.0/10

SCARIEST:
9.2/10

HARDEST:
19.7/20
☠

TOTAL
HARD MAN
47.4/50

was indestructible. Cuts, bruises, sprains and tears, and even cracked bones, proved to be no more than minor irritants for the Thurles man. He was the 'jack of all defensive trades', and if any sector in the Premier defence was haemorrhaging, Maher was the man to stem the bleeding.

Successive Tipperary managers built their plans around him, safe in the knowledge that come Sunday, he would be there to anchor the Tipperary defence.

The sight of Maher raising the siege and galloping up the field stirred the Premier blood in the white heat of the championship battle. For all the fire and thunder associated with his name, he possessed a dazzling skillset. He was a superb reader of the game and delivered laser-like accuracy in his passing. His scoring average for a defender was truly impressive as he notched a half-century of points for Tipperary, which included a total of eight All-Ireland finals.

{THE SHOULDER ON JOE CANNING}

There were so many moments for the highlights reel, but current Tipperary starlet Jake Morris remembered the most high-profile of a stupendous career.

'I think the best memory I have of him is when we played the minor All-Ireland in 2016 and were sitting down in the Hogan Stand afterwards.

'And in the senior final, Pádraic Maher nailed Joe Canning a shoulder across the line out in front of us. I'll never forget the crunch of it, that shoulder that day.'

It was quite simply a 'where were you moment'. It was a

collision that shook Croke Park to its foundations. The stadium clock showed 23 minutes and at that moment Joe Canning's world stopped turning.

The Galway talisman had gathered possession of the ball on the Hogan Stand sideline.

Canning the hurling artist could wreak havoc in a phone box. Left with open space, he spelt danger with a capital 'D' for the 'Premier' county.

Canning gleefully weighed up the possibilities, as a stricken Tipperary scrambled desperately to shut the open door. Maher 'the hunter' was lurking in the vicinity, he had the scent of blood in his nostrils. His eyes narrowed as the Portumna legend started to cut loose. Maher moved into his slipstream, hungrily eyeing up his quarry. Like all good defenders, he loved the thrill of the chase.

For a moment they were suspended in time. The hunter and the hunted tethering on a high wire. Two giants of the modern game were about to collide; it was a collision that would not be for the faint-hearted.

Joe Canning had made a career out of leaving his pursuers chasing shadows. For Pádraic Maher, the hit was all about timing, as he closed ominously on Canning. Maher and Canning were big strapping lads and something had to give as the Thurles Titan thundered into Galway's finest… at full tilt.

Canning and Maher went flying out over the sideline as the bone-shuddering contact drew audible gasps from the crowd. Canning needed several minutes to recover and both men had to receive treatment for bloodied head wounds.

It was in many ways the perfect 'hit'. The outrageously well-timed shoulder would become the stuff of GAA legend, but Maher as ever preferred not to wallow in his opponent's misfortune or any injuries that he had accrued.

'It was the spur-of-the-moment thing, but thankfully we were both okay. The doctor said he had his work cut out to stitch it back up properly, he hadn't a lot to work with there, it's fine.'

The Galway man would return to the fray, but an injury sustained in an earlier tussle with Tipperary's Cathal Barrett had weakened him considerably. The tangle with Barrett turned out to be a down payment that Maher's ferociously timed hit cashed out on.

Joe was too badly shaken to have any further meaningful input in the contest. There were loud groans from the Galway faithful when their spiritual leader had to leave the fray some minutes later.

Paudie Maher carried on with a bloodied bandaged head and steered the Tipperary ship safely home. He had also made a last-ditch hook on Conor Cooney which denied the Tribesmen a near-certain goal towards the end of a pulsating first-half. As ever, he played down his role in yet another magnificent performance.

'It was everyone working hard and covering for one another and thankfully I got back just in time. There were 32 minutes on the clock at that stage and if that had gone in it would have been a sucker punch before half-time.'

Maher's two critical interventions tipped the balance, and ensured that Liam MacCarthy would winter in the heartlands around Slievenamon after a six-year hiatus.

Lar Corbett had soldiered with his fellow Thurles native for a large portion of his career, and upon the occasion of Pádraic's retirement, paid him the following glowing tribute.

'As a forward, you can get lucky on a particular day, as a defender you have to earn your stripes harder and you have to be more consistent over a longer period of time. He has done that far and above any Tipp player I have seen. He is the best in my lifetime.'

A LIFETIME IN BLUE
»———→ AND GOLD ←———«

HE BEGAN his Premier voyage as a minor in 2006. Later that year Tipperary faced Galway in the All-Ireland final. Pádraic gave notice of his undoubted potential with a calm assured display as the Blue and Gold were crowned champions.

He played a starring role as defensive anchor in the All-Ireland under-21 final against Galway in 2010, when the Premier young guns romped home on a 5-22 to 0-12.

He made his Munster Championship debut in 2009. Tipperary claimed provincial honours that year, with Pádraic relocating to full-back for the All-Ireland final against Kilkenny. The 'Cats' edged an attritional affair courtesy of a late and very contentious penalty award. Maher looked to the manor

born at senior level, however, earning a first-ever All Star award.

Tipperary qualified to play Kilkenny in a second successive final. Lar Corbett's hat-trick brought Kilkenny's 'Drive for Five' to a shuddering halt as Tipperary engineered a stunning eight-point victory.

With hometown club Thurles Sarsfields, he won seven county titles, the first in 2009 against Drom-Inch. He also won a coveted Munster Club title with 'The Blues' in 2012. His career was tragically cut short in 2022, on medical advice.

As the curtain lowered on the great man's career, he had 'filled his boots' with three All-Ireland medals, five Munster titles, and six All Star awards.

OLCAN McFETRIDGE

(Height 5' 7", Weight 13.5 St)

Decade... 1980s/1990s

(Position... Wing-Forward)

CHIEF CHARACTERISTIC... THE SMALL MAN WHO STOOD
TALLEST AGAINST THE HURLING GIANTS

TOP ACCOMPLICES... TERENCE MCNAUGHTON,
CIARAN BARR, PAUL MCKILLEN, BRIAN DONNELLY,
LEONARD MCKEEGAN, DESSIE DONNELLY

OLCAN McFETRIDGE

*'I JUST SORT OF GOT IT HALF-FIXED ABOUT 10 YEARS AGO,
HAD AN OPERATION WHERE THERE WAS BITS CUT OFF IT,
PLANED UP, SCREWED IN... IT'S MORE OR LESS JUST A CLUB
FOOT NOW, BUT SURE I'M NOT PLAYING ANYMORE ANYWAY.*

– OLCAN MCFETRIDGE

WOODY, Beaver, Hippy, Sambo, Pappy, Humpy, Cloot…

They love their nicknames in Antrim, and they love their hurling too. A quick glance at the names above sound more akin to an alternative list of the Seven Dwarfs than a hurling team.

Olcan 'Cloot' McFetridge on the other hand could well have made it into the 1938 picture book, which was written and illustrated by Wanda Gág, about the misadventures of those lovable fairytale legends.

Olcan McFetridge stood at varying diminishing heights, depending on what part of Antrim you were visiting. While five foot seven inches at a stretch was his maximum height, he was more likely in the five-foot-six category. Small was a term you could certainly associate his lack

HARD MAN RATINGS

TOUGHEST:
9.1/10

MEANEST:
9.1/10

SCARIEST:
9.2/10

HARDEST:
19.2/20
☠

TOTAL
HARD MAN

46.6/50

of inches with, but there was nothing small about the Armoy assassin's giant presence in one of the greatest Antrim sides of all time.

All-Ireland semi-final, August 6, 1989.

The Faithful had departed. Despite all the platitudes beforehand, the hurling public viewed Antrim 'as a nice wee team' – and one that would be exiting the race for Liam MacCarthy a little after the hour of three that afternoon.

The game was an appetiser for the main course which pitted age-old adversaries Tipperary and Galway in opposition, and more pertinently for sports fans the very real possibility of a contest breaking out.

What happened next was of the other-worldly variety as Antrim forgot their place in hurling society by failing to adhere to the time-honoured tradition which told them... the house always wins.

As the vanquished Faithful team very sportingly lined up for a guard of honour for their conquerors, the 64,000 assembled were having difficulty processing what had transpired during a wild 70 minutes.

The seismic shock had been predicated on a bedrock of brilliance provided by Brian and Dessie Donnelly. The relentless engine of Ciaran Barr had kept the Antrim Express firmly on track, and Terence 'Sambo' McNaughton was as ever a pillar of strength.

The dark-moustached and slightly portly Olcan McFetridge was the one, however, that did the most damage. He looked more like a member of a Mexican Mariachi band than an inter-county forward. You could have forgiven the Offaly players for feeling they had just been hit repeatedly over the head by a teddy bear, wielding a baseball bat, such was the paucity of the menace posed by Olcan's rather non-threatening demeanour.

The devil sadly for the Faithful, as ever, was in the detail. What McFetridge lacked in inches he ably made up for in mass. Olcan was built like a tank, of the Sherman variety!

He was made of serious stuff. Offaly began the process of softening up Olcan early in the contest, only to discover the Armoy club man's pain threshold went through the roof. He was a man that would have walked barefoot over red-hot coals for the Saffron cause.

Olcan was the ultimate trench warrior who could carry a pair of mules on his back, while carrying out a Blitzkrieg on the opposition backline.

Sambo McNaughton recalled ruefully that marking McFetridge was a task that even the mighty Cushendall wing-back struggled to find any traction in.

He also intimated that McFetridge was never one to spend hours honing his skills, that hurling was almost second nature to him.

'He was a talented wee bastard.

'I marked him at under-12, under-14... right up through. He could just do things with a ball... control-wise, touch, striking, catching over big men. In terms of physique, he would have been like a Maradona.

'Going to bed on a Saturday night, he's the one player you'd be worrying about the next day. He could make a **** out of you very quick and very easy.

'No matter how hard you hit him, you couldn't put him down – and I did try. He was like a rubber ball. Being aggressive with him was a waste of time because you couldn't intimidate him.

'Don't be thinking you're going up there to hear stories about how he spent 10,000 hours hitting the ball off the local church bell. Not a chance. Cloot just had it… and by f**k he had it in abundance.'

{ NO PAIN NO GAIN }

There were many stars that glittered on the greatest day in the history of Antrim hurling, but Olcan stole the show with a pair of golden goals that ensured a safe passage to just a second-ever All-Ireland senior final. He, as ever, took the day in his stride. McNaughton was well aware that his teammate wouldn't be staying awake that night dreaming about All-Ireland finals.

'If we lost, I wouldn't have come out of the house for a week, whereas if Cloot had phoned you up the day before an All-Ireland final and said, "I'm not going because I couldn't be bothered" you wouldn't have died of shock.'

For all the nonchalance, once he crossed the white lines, he was prepared to put his body on the *line*. He sustained a number of injuries early in his career which eventually came back to haunt him.

'I played my first game for Antrim against Laois in Portlaoise before Christmas, hurt my ankle again at the Oval and got back out in April or May 1989. Both times it was X-rayed it was just diagnosed as a bruised foot, but when I got it operated on they said there were two breaks in it.

'They weren't sure if I'd broken it twice at one time or two different times.

'I just sort of got it half fixed about 10 years ago, had an operation where there were bits cut off it, planed up, screwed in… it's more or less just a club foot now, but sure I'm not playing any more anyway.

'It's just for stopping on.'

His friend McNaughton coined him perfectly.

'He was our Georgie Best!'

Yes … wee Olcan was that good.

A LIFE IN
SAFFRON

OLCAN McFETRIDGE played his club hurling with his local club Glen Rovers GAC Armoy. The small Village had a population of just over 500 and suffered from a mass exodus of players due to the scourge of emigration. Eventually, they were unable to field a side in the championship and Olcan had to throw in his lot with the famous Antrim outfit Loughgiel. His career nearly never took off as he sustained a serious ankle ligament injury in 1987. He won one Ulster Club title, and was a prolific marksman in Loughgiel's march to the 1988 Ulster crown.

He was a dynamic presence during the late 80s and 90s. He made his inter-county debut in a league fixture against the O'Moore County, Laois, and first came to national prominence when playing a starring role in Antrim's Division Two National League campaign, as the Saffrons won a historic promotion to Division One.

Following in the footsteps of another Antrim forward, Olcan won a prestigious All Star Award in 1989, lining out in the exalted company of Galway's Joe Cooney, and a pair of Tipperary legends, Pat Fox and Nicky English. He had been preceded by O'Donovan Rossa's and Saffron legend, Ciaran Barr.

KEN McGRATH
(Height 6' 1", Weight 14.5 St)

Decade... 1990s/2000s/2010s
(Position... Centre-Back)

CHIEF CHARACTERISTIC... ENSURING OPPONENTS
FACED THEIR WATERLOO

TOP ACCOMPLICES... TONY BROWNE, DAVE BENNET, EOIN KELLY,
STEVEN BRENNER, EOIN MURPHY, DAN SHANAHAN

KEN McGRATH

'KEN IS ONE OF THE TRUE LEGENDS OF THE MODERN GAME.
SUPREMELY TALENTED AND LOYAL. AND INCREDIBLY
BRAVE BOTH ON AND OFF THE FIELD.'
– DAN SHANAHAN

2000? Would a new Millennium usher a brave new hurling world?

A band of raiders from the south-east, would pillage and plunder Munster hurling, usurping the old established order.

Their leader appeared to be 10-feet tall as he ruled the land and the sky. When the battle raged at its zenith, one man railed against tradition and turned the weight of history, firmly upon its head.

In the dying embers of the 2004 Munster hurling final, Waterford were clinging on to a slender, one-point advantage. It was breathless, demented fare. Forty scores and the width of a sweet-paper separating the sides.

Cork were pouring forward under a high dropping ball when Ken McGrath soared like an eagle, clasping the sliotar, and dispatching it skywards in the general direction of the Killinan End.

It was typical McGrath. When the furnace was

HARD MAN RATINGS

TOUGHEST:
9.5/10

MEANEST:
8.7/10

SCARIEST:
9.2/10

HARDEST:
19.9/20

☠

TOTAL HARD MAN

47.3/50

at its hottest you could always count on him to plunge his hand into the raging inferno.

Cork's legendary defender, Diarmuid 'The Rock' O'Sullivan, jogged past him as the ball disappeared into the shimmering Thurles skyline.

'Great catch', he conceded grudgingly, through gritted teeth. He knew, McGrath's timely intervention had sounded the death knell for that particular day. It was a sight that was all too familiar to many a side, who had floundered on Waterford's rock of relentless consistency.

McGrath was a majestic presence, who announced his arrival on the senior county stage in attack, before playing the majority of his senior days at centre-back for the Déise.

He garnered three All Star awards – in three different positions. He was selected at wing-forward in 2002, and followed that up with a midfield berth two years later. Finally, he nailed down the centre-back slot in 2007.

So many Déise days, and so many memories to treasure. McGrath was a talismanic figure in one of the most successful Waterford sides of any era. While the Déise, were unable to lift Liam MacCarthy during his reign, they thrilled their supporters with a wonderful brand of attacking hurling.

Ken was a dynamic and rugged presence at the heart of it all as Waterford duly announced themselves to a stunned hurling fraternity. They torpedoed the reigning All-Ireland champions, Tipperary as they ended a 39-year famine and became Munster champions in 2002. Ken's mixture of devilry, defiance, and daring, was the catalyst that overwhelmed the Premier, as Waterford claimed a long-overdue Munster SHC title.

Like a band of pillaging pirates, the Déise would usurp hurling's natural order, with the unnerving sight of a bloodthirsty McGrath leading the frenzied charge.

{ THE WARRIOR'S WORLD }

Looking back, he lamented how hurling had changed, how he missed going toe-to-toe with his direct opponent... *kill or be killed* and may the best man win.

As a raw 16-year-old, he joined the Mount Sion senior squad in 1994. The club was on the cusp of something special, but young Ken was about to discover that despite his tender years, the opposition would not be offering any exemption from the physical stuff, on the basis of age. It would lead to a harsh introduction to the adult game for the young corner-forward.

'I wouldn't have been physically up to standard either, senior hurling was a different game 25 years ago. A young lad like myself might get the better of a corner-back once, but if you did it twice, he'd let you know he was there, and you wouldn't try it again.'

The 'school of hard knocks' would be an invaluable introduction for the young McGrath and while the decade with Mount Sion flew past, the rules of engagement stayed the same. Fast forward to the 2004, Munster club final.

'Hurling was different in 2004 than to what it is now. Those games were real battles. There was no sweeper systems then. It was 15 on 15, and you went to war with them. I was up against Eoin Brislane, and I remember seeing the size of him. He must have been six foot four. He had a reputation for being a tough competitor, so I tore into him from the very start.'

McGrath's summary of the prelude to the final is a window to the warrior's world. The son of Mount Sion putting on the war paint, ready to quell whatever thunder Tipperary's champions, Toomevara, would reign down upon them.

Ken marked his territory, and whenever the good ships, Mount Sion and Waterford, were *shipping* water, he would move heaven and earth to keep his troops above the waterline.

For club and county, Ken won most of his battles, but a bigger one was looming down the tracks. In December 2013, he had his world turned upside down, when at the age of 36, he suffered a brain haemorrhage and ended up spending several months at Ardkeen Hospital in Waterford. Further complications awaited as tests revealed an abnormal valve and infection in his heart.

Facing the fight of his life, Ken displayed everything that made him great on a hurling field. Miraculously, he made a full and relatively speedy recovery from what was a complicated and extensive surgery. The man pulled no punches as he outlined his harrowing ordeal, in typical forthright fashion.

'For the first two days (post-operation) I can't remember a thing. Lads that got the operation done before me told me that when you wake up, you feel like you've been hit by a bus – that's the only way you can describe it.'

Ken's recovery came as little surprise to those that knew him best. The man who lit up our summers was never going quietly into the night. Images of the Déise super-trooper reaching for the stars still sends a shiver down our collective spines.

The motto of the Canadian Navy Seals captures mighty McGrath's career best.

DEEDS NOT WORDS...

THE DARLING
▶▶───▶ OF ◀───◀◀
THE DEISE

KEN McGRATH was born, on February 20, 1978. He joined the Waterford fold in 1996, and was a regular member of the starting fifteen until his retirement in 2011.

He is the son of former hurler, Pat McGrath and older brother of former player, Eoin.

Ken was 'Mr Consistency' for well over a decade - with his spectacular high fetching igniting crowds up and down the country. He has won four Munster winners' medals, as Waterford trumped traditional Munster heavyweights like Tipperary and Cork.

He was also part of the Waterford side that ended a 44-year drought when winning the National League. In the process they defeated a Kilkenny side at the peak of their powers in a 2007 decider at Semple Stadium.

At club level, in 1998, he won his first county club championship medal following a 3-19 to 0-10 annihilation of Ballyduff Upper. It was the first of a super six Waterford titles for Ken.

Mount Sion was a formidable outfit and won the Munster club title in 1982, with a hard-fought victory over Clare's Sixmilebrige. Two years later they were back in the decider, but lost out in a classic encounter to Toomevara.

SEANIE McMAHON
(Height 6' 2", Weight 14 St)

Decade... 1990s/2000s
(Position... Centre-Back)

CHIEF CHARACTERISTIC... ONE-ARMED BANDIT OPERATOR WHO
ENSURED FORWARDS NEVER CASHED OUT

TOP ACCOMPLICES... ANTHONY DALY, DAVY FITZGERALD, BRIAN
LOHAN, FRANK LOHAN, OLLIE BAKER, COLIN LYNCH, LIAM DOYLE

SEANIE McMAHON

*'IT WAS A VERY BAD CUT ON THE FOREFINGER AND THE BLOOD JUST
KEPT ON GUSHING. BY THE END, SEANIE'S BOOTS WERE SQUELCHING
WITH THE BLOOD THAT HAD SEEPED DOWN INTO THEM.'*
– CLARE PHYSIO, COLM FLYNN

THE greatest warrior in Spain sat silently upon his steed. His lifeless corpse was kitted out in full battle armour. The defence of Valencia had come at the ultimate price with the legendary fighter – whose nickname translates as 'Lord' – mortally wounded.

Even in death the 'Cid' would have the final say upon the blood-soaked fields. Such was the fear he generated – the terrifying sight of his resurrection scattered enemy forces. Their blood-curdling screams pierced the air as the defending forces emboldened by the sight of their leader's last stand, poured forth, savagely putting the invaders to the sword.

Rodrigo Díaz de Vivar was born into the Spanish nobility in 1043 and raised in the court of King Ferdinand the Great. He never lost a battle and was never beaten in combat. As in life, he proved insurmountable in death.

The Gaelic Grounds Limerick, 1995.

HARD MAN RATINGS

TOUGHEST:
9.7/10

MEANEST:
9.4/10

SCARIEST:
9.4/10

HARDEST:
19.3/20

☠

TOTAL HARD MAN

47.8/50

It was a sight to turn the Shannonsiders' blood cold. Limerick were losing the battle, but the 'Banner' had sustained heavy casualties, which ultimately looked like costing them the war.

Clare had run out of substitutes and their team-sheet certainly contained nobody by the name of Rodrigo Díaz de Vivar. They did, however, have a player who would turn out to be one of their greatest-ever warriors – but Seanie 'Mac' had been mortally wounded. The sight of a strapped-up Seanie, sporting a broken collarbone returning to the combat-zone likely had a similar effect as the mighty El Cid's famous last hurrah.

The telling moment of this particularly famous Munster final would be mined from a man operating with only three limbs. When McMahon gathered the strength to somehow force a turnover and from the ensuing line-ball, the Banner's winning ducks had fallen nicely in a row.

Fergal Tuohy's trusty sand-wedge swung the ball invitingly for Ollie Baker's coup-de-grace and the Banner's winning goal. The 'resurrection man' was back hurling four weeks later and the 'Ballad of Seanie Mac' was well and truly born.

The astonishing powers of recovery of the St Joseph's Doora-Barefield centre-back had been showcased a few weeks previously against Tipperary.

McMahon sustained a serious hand injury that bled profusely for the remainder of the contest. All attempts to stem the flow of crimson had stubbornly failed, yet McMahon soldiered doggedly onwards. Team doctor, Padraig Quinn furiously tried to staunch the flow of blood but could not turn back the ominous tide. McMahon's jersey was soon soaked in blood as team physio Colm Flynn recalled.

'It was a very bad cut on the forefinger and the blood just kept on gushing. By the end, Seanie's boots were squelching with the blood that had seeped down into them.'

It was a gruesome scene, more in keeping with a 'Slasher' movie than a Munster Championship game, but the blood-spattered McMahon never once looked like throwing in the towel.

That was the rub with Seanie Mac. If an on-field blood transfusion was required for his beloved Banner, he was willing to shed every last drop for the Clare cause.

Colm Flynn concurred with those sobering lines.

'Over the game, he lost about a litre. In fact, he lost so much, he started to feel a little woozy afterwards. It was suggested he go for a transfusion, but he wouldn't hear of it. That's Seanie… fierce tough in every sense."

His club coach, Louis Mucqueen had witnessed his selfless bravery time and time again, marvelling at the matrix of this incredible hurling man.

'If Seanie went, you could throw your hat at it. Take out McMahon and you open the front door. To be honest, if there was a transfer market in hurling, you couldn't afford to pay what McMahon would cost.

'I don't think you'll get a better hurler in Ireland or a better total package as a man. His presence on and off the field is simply awesome. He has such broad shoulders in every sense.'

{ WALKING THE WALK AND TALKING THE TALK }

Broad shoulders in every sense. McMahon was a born leader and hadn't been on the panel a wet day when he stunned his older teammates with an astonishing rallying cry as the Banner faced a judgment day with old foes Tipperary.

It was Sunday in the month of May 1994, and Clare hurlers had assembled in the Two Mile Inn outside of Limerick city. The Premier had done a number on Clare in the 1993 Munster final – an 18-point shellacking had well and truly burst the Banner bubble.

Less than 12 months had passed since the debacle and Len Gaynor, who knew more about Tipperary than most, opens the floor to any other speakers. Seanie McMahon is aged just 20 and he is about to make his first start as the team's centre-back.

As Vincent Hogan related in the *Irish Independent*, what happened next caught the more senior players totally by surprise. McMahon spoke passionately using phrases like 'payback' and it was time to 'man up'. Most of the assembled panel barely knew his name, but they would never forget that moment.

Hogan continues the story with Ger Loughnane turning to Gaynor, smiling and gasping, 'Jeez Len... after that, it's hard to see us getting beat'.

Two second-half goals duly downed the Premier, signalling the end of the line for Babs Keating's tenure as Tipp boss.

Winning Munster was Seanie's and Clare's greatest obsession, and after decades of seemingly never-ending heartache, they finally delivered in 1995.

'The dream in Clare was just to win the Munster final. I was at the 1981 Munster final, I was at the '86 Munster final... there in '93, played my first one in '94... and at that stage, all heartache for me.

'So, all we grew up with in Clare was heartache about Munster finals and going to Thurles and Limerick and these places with great expectation, and coming home heartbroken. I'd experienced that myself as well."

Munster titles, All-Irelands, All Star awards and immortality… The Ballad of Seanie Mac!

»——→A LEGENDARY LIFE←——«

SEANIE McMAHON played with his local club St Joseph's Doora-Barefield and donned the Clare colours from 1994 until 2006. He is the highest-scoring back in All-Ireland Championship history with 0-97 from 51 games. McMahon made his championship debut in 1994 against Tipperary and was an indispensable member of the Clare side that won the Munster Championship and All-Ireland titles in 1995.

Two years later, in 1997, the Banner ensure lightning would strike twice as they repeated the dose, with McMahon claiming his second Munster and All-Ireland medals.

Seanie scored the opening points for Clare in both the 1995 and 1997 All-Ireland finals. He also captained Clare to two successive losing All-Ireland semi-finals in 2005 and 2006.

With St Joseph's Doora-Barefield, he won an All-Ireland Senior Club Championship in 1999, and a Munster Senior Club Championship in 1998, 1999. He also won three Clare Club Championships.

At inter-county level, he added three Munster final successes to his All-Ireland Senior Championships in 1995, 1997. He won a host of individual awards including three All Stars, and Texaco Hurler of the Year 1995.

TERENCE 'SAMBO' McNAUGHTON

(Height 6' 1", Weight 14.5 St)

Decade... 1980s/1990s

(Position... Wing-Back)

CHIEF CHARACTERISTIC... MAKING FORWARDS THE MEAT IN THE SAMBO

TOP ACCOMPLICES... NIALL PATTERSON,
OLCAN MCFETRIDGE, CIARAN BARR, DOMINIC MCKINLEY,
LEONARD MCKEEGAN, PAUL MCKILLAN

TERENCE 'SAMBO' McNAUGHTON

*'YOU LEARNT VERY QUICKLY IN THAT CHANGING ROOM AND YOU HAD TO
STAND UP FOR YOURSELF. GOD REST, BRIAN THOMPSON (TRAINER), WHO
USED TO SAY, "I NEED DANGER MONEY TO TRAIN CUSHENDALL"... BECAUSE WE
WOULD HAVE FOUGHT WITH EACH OTHER EVERY OTHER NIGHT AT TRAINING.*

– TERENCE MCNAUGHTON

DURING the Persian Wars in 480 BCE, the Persian army attacked the Greeks at the narrow pass at Thermopylae, which controlled the only road between Thessaly and central Greece.

A courageous warrior, King Leonidas led 300 Spartans into battle against the Persian 'God-King' Xerxes and his invading army of more than 300,000 soldiers.

Leonidas and his band of 300 elite Spartans defended the gap to the last warrior against the mighty Persian force, although they knew they would die. Leonidas advised his men to eat a hearty breakfast, because they would have their next meal in the Underworld.

There were times during Terence 'Sambo' McNaughton's career he must have felt like the embattled Greeks at Thermopylae. Commanding

HARD MAN RATINGS

TOUGHEST:
9.3/10

MEANEST:
9.0/10

SCARIEST:
9.1/10

HARDEST:
19.4/20

☠

TOTAL HARD MAN

46.8/50

a bunch of heroic men with the odds heavily stacked against victory. The mighty forces of hurling's 'High Kings,' with their conveyor belt of talent and massive player resources, threatening to overpower and overwhelm a hurling outpost – manned by a tiny band of heroic warriors.

Yet, time and time again, Sambo sailed into that narrow gap, putting his body on the line in the face of insurmountable odds.

The story of Sambo and Antrim is in many ways the story of the fabled '300' Spartans, swimming against the merciless tide of hurling's aristocracy. He was the 'Saffrons' eternal, unwavering, indestructible warrior.

As a boy, Terence McNaughton used to puck a ball relentlessly against an old cottage wall. He had the remnants of half a hurley in his hand and, bit by bit, his unlikely destiny unfolded.

Entertainment was thin on the ground for young Sambo, so with necessity being the 'mother of invention,' McNaughton whiled the hours away, meticulously honing his craft.

'We'd no X-boxes back then and you didn't control the TV that had three stations. Your father controlled that. You couldn't watch TV so what do you do?

'It wasn't a conscious decision of, "I'm going to be a good hurler". You'd nothing else to do.'

It was far from plain sailing in his formative years as the naysayers were never far from his ears, wringing their heads in disapproval. He was the wrong shape, the wrong size, hurling was a high-velocity ballet – a precision game that had all fingers and no thumbs.

The doubters within his own club were convinced McNaughton's game would always be a square peg that was destined for a round hole. Conventional wisdom dictated that this boy was built like a bull, and bulls generally struggled with the demographics of a china shop.

'There are different things that stick out in my mind. I was told by a member of our club that I would never play senior hurling because I was overweight, a pudgy child.

'I can remember everything about that day. I can remember the smell of the cut grass, I could tell you what he was wearing. It was like putting a knife into me because I thought this was the only thing that I was half-decent at.'

The bull had thick skin though, and the cottage walls had served him well. He was a surgical striker of the ball with outstanding peripheral vision. His touch was gossamer-lined and he possessed a manic aggression, twinned with a hardy maturity that was eons ahead of his tender years.

He was just 16 when he played in his first county final for Cushendall. The 1981 decider was against old enemies, Ballycastle; such was McNaughton's stature within the group, he was detailed to mark the Ballycastle 'Libero' Peter Boyle, who was rated one of the Saffron county's finest wines.

McNaughton defended the Ruarí Óg Cushendall realm as if his life depended on it. Cushendall prevailed after a replay, with McNaughton having held Boyle to a point across the two games. It was a different environment back then, a harsh unyielding, manly world, but a young Terence settled quickly among adults.

'It was different back then. If somebody had deodorant they'd be classed as soft. We'd a lot of very strong characters – Danny McNaughton, John Delargy, Paddy McAteer – nobody worried about your feelings. You didn't have to think, "How do I say the negative and say the positive?"

'You got the negative and that's all you got.'

{ DIVINE INTERVENTION }

Sambo's stellar county final performance earned him a shot at the inter-county team, and divine intervention would propel him on the road to Antrim immortality as he later recalled.

'Like many GAA teams, going to Mass on the morning of a game was ritual. On this particular morning, prior to a league game with Kildare in Newbridge, one of the Antrim players didn't attend Mass and was duly dropped from the starting line-up.'

McNaughton, originally named on the bench, was promoted to the starting line-up.

'I remember Peter Boyle saying to me, "You're going to be here forever". That was in '81 and I quit in '97.

'You learnt very quickly in that changing room and you had to stand up for yourself. God rest, Brian Thompson (trainer), who used to say, "I need danger money to train Cushendall"… because we would have fought with each other every other night at training.'

For 16 years Sambo dealt with everything inter-county hurling could throw at him. He never took a backward step, carrying the Saffron flag proudly into battle. Manfully, he plugged the 'narrow pass' like the Spartans at Thermopylae, no more so than in the 1989 All-Ireland final against mighty Tipperary. One of Tipperary's finest, Nicky English was effusive in his praise of the Ruarí Óg warlord.

'Terence McNaughton was a really fair player. He was a great hurler as well, very skilful for a guy of his size. He was a hard player but he was a gentleman. In that 1989 All-Ireland final he carried the fight to Tipp.'

Throughout the ages, soldiers of war have carried the fight – often against overwhelming and impossible odds. These acts of random courage raise our hearts and let our spirits soar… all the way from Thermopylae to Cushendall.

» → A SAFFRON ← «
SOLDIERS SONG

HE WAS born in Cushendall, County Antrim. McNaughton first played competitive hurling for St Aloysius High School. He was introduced to the inter-county scene at the tender age of 16, when he first linked up with the Antrim senior team.

He made his senior debut during the 1981 'B' championship, as Antrim was crowned All-Ireland champions with a victory over London.

Antrim retained their All-Ireland title in 1982, with McNaughton collecting a second winners' medal following another narrow 2-16 to 2-14 defeat of London.

In 1989, the return of the Ulster Championship after a 45-year absence, saw Antrim take on Down in the decider, with McNaughton collecting his first provincial

medal following a 2-16 to 0-9 victory.

Antrim advanced to the All-Ireland quarter-final, where they accounted for Kildare. They then created one of the biggest shocks in championship history as a brace of Olcan McFetridge goals, and another brace from Aidan McCarry, floored raging hot favourites Offaly.

Despite suffering a heavy defeat to a Nicky English-inspired Tipperary in the All-Ireland final, it had been an unforgettable journey for one of hurling's minnows.

Terence won a total of eight Antrim titles with Ruarí Óg Cushendall, and seven Ulster Championships. He was also selected as an All Star in 1991, and 'Sambo' McNaughton also managed Antrim to a Walsh Cup trophy win in 2008.

WILL O'DONOGHUE
(Height 6' 5", Weight 15 St)

Decade... 2010s/2020s
(Position... Midfield)

CHIEF CHARACTERISTIC... THE TREATY'S WILLIAM OF ALL TRADES

TOP ACCOMPLICES... KYLE HAYES, DIARMUID BYRNES, CIAN LYNCH,
AARON GILLANE, BARRY NASH, TOM MORRISSEY

WILL O'DONOGHUE

'THE ONLY TIME I GET RECOGNISED IS...
IF SOMEONE THINKS I'M CIAN LYNCH'
– WILL O'DONOGHUE

WHEN the shadow of Declan Hannon's injury cast a cloud over Limerick's preparations for the 2023 All-Ireland final, John Kiely acted swiftly. The pivotal position of centre-back was a critical component of the Treaty's battle plans, and one which Adare's finest had manned majestically in Limerick's hour of need. It was here that Kiely demonstrated the clarity and decisiveness that all great leaders possess in wagonloads.

'We didn't want that indecision hanging over us,' he explained. 'If he was out, we needed to have a real live replacement. So, in order to give that player the headspace to really take on that mantle, the space needed to be completely cleared and no ambiguity about whether he was in or out.

'It was the right call, Declan wouldn't have been fit to play."

The man he chose for this most important of missions would likely have driven the team bus to Jones' Road as well and taking on the mantle was

HARD MAN
RATINGS
TOUGHEST:
9.7/10

MEANEST:
9.1/10

SCARIEST:
9.6/10

HARDEST:
19.7/20

☠

TOTAL
HARD MAN
48.1/50

something this ferocious warrior absolutely revelled in…

> *'The two most powerful warriors are patience and time.'*
> *– Leo Tolstoy*

The words could well have been inscribed on the gates of Páirc Uí Dromgúil, in Elm Drive.

Nothing had come easily for the fighter from Na Piarsaigh. He had always been one step from heaven only to be forever domiciled on hurling's Pathway to Purgatory. There he had wandered, cursed with washy platitudes and dammed with indifference. The big-time beckoning in the half-light only to be vanquished when he rose upon the dawn.

It seemed Will O'Donoghue had achieved a seemingly impossible feat. The fine art of hurling up a storm that only registered in a teacup. He was hiding in plain sight.

A man so modestly efficient he always seemed to hawk his wares at half-price.

Before Kiely's timely arrival, he seemed reconciled to hurling in a land beyond the inter-county bright lights. His legacy could well have been wrought in a couple of cold words.

N-E-A-R-L-Y M-A-N

Despite coming to prominence with Na Piarsaigh as part of a powerful 2013 county championship-winning side, O'Donoghue's ascension to midfield general of one of the small ball game's most omnipotent forces in history was distinctly of the slow-burning variety.

The towering centerfielder was on board for another Daly Cup triumph in 2015. He was swiftly promoted to club captaincy, with his bamboozling, all-guns blazing style of play – a perfect foil for the Caherdavin outfit's glittering array of stars.

Of all the pieces of the Limerick hurling puzzle, O'Donoghue appeared to be the perfect fit.

He was tall and athletic with a seriously advanced work ethic. Closing the attacking lanes was one of his fortes, and whenever a defensive line sprung a leak he always had the plumber's tape close to hand. The jack of all hurling trades was in essence, the perfect inter-county prototype – housing all the weapons required for the gladiatorial environments of modern-day hurling.

In his breakthrough season with the Limerick champions, it seemed just a matter of time before he crossed the club-county divide, but it would take almost five frustrating seasons before he would deliver on his undoubted style and substance.

His county career flickered in a halfway house – stuck infuriatingly between the low-level light of understated club excellence and the brash flashy persona of the intercounty big-city movers and shakers.

O'Donoghue was good – better than that, he was damm good – but nobody seemed to notice.

When John Kiely was handed the reins in the latter part of 2016, he cast his net far and wide in search of a different kind of Limerick hurler. Kiely's life in the teaching trade had thought him many things.

He was a student of Limerick hurling and having managed the county at intermediate level and being a selector at under-21, he was well aware that the Treaty's malaise did not stem from a lack of hurling nuance.

The old dogs had served Limerick well, but Kiely already knew it would be hard for them to digest new tricks. He decided to spin the wheel on the sword of youth – a ploy that was laced with peril and one that if he failed, he would surely perish upon.

He was also smart enough to know that there was still a place for older wiser heads on the 'Good Ship Kiely' and the journey to rarified heights would require a very particular type of player skillset.

William O'Donoghue was a wily operator at club level who always seemed to be just under the Treaty radar. Kiely recognised an abundance of gifts that, properly unleashed, would become the fulcrum of a new re-imagined Limerick hurling side.

When Will trotted on to Croke Park in the latter stages of the 2018 All-Ireland final, he went to work in his usual calm and understated fashion. The player who rarely sought the limelight or rarely shot the lights out, had finally come in from the cold.

When the team of all the talents knocked off a fourth All-Ireland on the bounce in 2023, he seamlessly slotted in at centre-back for their injured talisman, Declan Hannon. You would have been hard-pressed to notice any unusual deviations in the Limerick crankshaft as all defensive systems were purring smoothly.

Perhaps that is Will's greatest attribute – the ability to do every single task with supreme efficiency and a ruthless, stone-cold ferocity. While the Na Piarsaigh storm-trooper is always cast in the role of bridesmaid when it comes to garnering the headlines, he is happy to leave the plaudits to everyone else.

He often relates with a wry smile that even when surrounded by hordes of young fans after the battle, many say thanks to Cian, (Lynch) after he selflessly smiles and patiently signs autographs.

For all the modesty and the lack of bells and whistles, Limerick hurling fans need no counselling on the merits of the 'Quiet Man' of Treaty Hurling's understated values.

The ultimate teammate is also their ultimate warrior.

THE TALE OF
A TREATY TITAN

WILL O'DONOGHUE played in all grades at juvenile and underage levels for Limerick giants Na Piarsaigh. He had a very successful underage career in all grades including under-16, minor and under-21 competition.

He won his first county championship in October 2013, when he excelled at right wing-forward in a hard-fought tussle with Adare (0-14 to 0-12).

He showcased his versatility when he was deployed at midfield for the subsequent Munster Championship, as he claimed provincial honours when Na Piarsaigh defeated Sixmilebridge in the decider.

Na Piarsaigh and O'Donoghue went on to dominate the Treaty club scene, winning six titles, three Munster crowns and an All-Ireland club title.

At inter-county level, he made his first appearance for the Limerick senior hurling team in a 6-21 to 3-8 defeat of Kerry in the National League. Later, in August 2018, he was introduced as a 66th-minute substitute for Darragh O'Donovan as Limerick ended a 45-year hiatus to win the Liam MacCarthy Cup, defeating Galway.

In total, he has won five All-Ireland Senior Championships in 2018, 2020, 2021, 2022, 2023, and five Munster Championships.

In addition, he has won three National League titles, and was selected as an All Star in 2021.

DIARMUID 'THE ROCK' O'SULLIVAN

(Height 6' 2", Weight 14.5 St)

Decade... 1990s/2000s

(Position... Full-Back)

CHIEF CHARACTERISTIC... BOWLING THE OPPOSITION OVER

TOP ACCOMPLICES... BRIAN CORCORAN, JOHN GARDINER,
MARC LANDERS, WAYNE SHERLOCK, SEÁN ÓG Ó HAILPÍN

DIARMUID
'THE ROCK'
O'SULLIVAN

'I WAS OVERLOOKED... IT WAS A FAIR KICK. I WAS DISAPPOINTED.
I SUPPOSE WHEN YOU LOOK BACK THERE'S ALWAYS SOME BIT OF
POLITICS. SOMEBODY LOOKING AFTER THEIR OWN.'
– DIARMUID O'SULLIVAN

DWAYNE Johnson's larger-than-life presence was integral in the development of the then World Wrestling Federation (now known as WWE).

Johnson was an elite athlete at Freedom High School in Bethlehem Township, Pennsylvania, emerging as the outstanding performer on both the school's football and wrestling teams. His football prowess was such that he was ranked as one of the Top 10 defensive tackle high-school prospects in America.

His dream to be an NFL starter never fully materialised, as his role was mostly as a back-up to elite players. A superb wrestler, who was famous for his 'trash talking' in the ring as he taunted his beleaguered opponents. Dwayne Douglas Johnson is, of course, better known nowadays as 'The Rock,' and is one of the world's

HARD MAN RATINGS

TOUGHEST:
9.7/10

MEANEST:
9.0/10

SCARIEST:
9.3/10

HARDEST:
19.9/20

TOTAL HARD MAN
47.9/50

highest-grossing and highest-paid actors.

While we can't reliably ascertain if the Irish version of the 'Rock,' was a supreme exponent of trash-talking, Diarmuid O'Sullivan certainly shared his potent mixture of physical strength and athletic brilliance. He was the 'Rock,' that even the most celebrated of inter-county forwards, ultimately perished upon.

In sporting equations, bigger does not always translate to better, but Diarmuid O'Sullivan's beefy frame was also infused with a real hurling brain.

His career began in slow-burning fashion, as he was overlooked for a place on the Cork minor team in 1995. After a great year with the club, and a Harty Cup final success,he was clearly frustrated with his surprise omission and spoke passionately in its aftermath.

'I was overlooked… it was a fair kick. I was disappointed. I suppose when you look back there's always some bit of politics. Somebody looking after their own.'

It proved to be a minor bump along a golden road, as he was called into the minor fold, joining the panel the following year and making his only appearance on June 26, 1996 in a 0-16 to 1-9 defeat by Tipperary in the Munster Minor Championship.

The transition from the under-21 grade to senior level has proved to be a no-man's-land, for even the very best at the underage grade, but O'Sullivan made light of the potentially hazardous transition.

O'Sullivan was just 18 years old when he made his first appearance for the Cork senior team on March 23, 1997. He was selected at left corner-back for the 4-21 to 2-11 defeat of the Saffrons from Antrim in the National League.

He was later selected at left corner-back as Cork's Munster campaign ended in a championship defeat to Clare. At the end of a promising season, he was regarded as unlucky not to have been nominated for an All Star, but Rebel fans were clearly enthused by the birth of a bright and charismatic new star.

Diarmuid was appointed captain of the Cork senior team for the 1998 season. In mid- May 1998, he captained the team to the National League title following a 2-14 to 0-13 defeat of Waterford.

By 1999, he had made a large foot-print on the inter-county landscape and was switched to the full-back position for the championship. On July 4, he won his first Munster Championship medal after a 1-15 to 0-14 defeat of reigning champions Clare. In September, O'Sullivan was at full-back for the All-Ireland final against Kilkenny, where Cork edged The Cats on a rain-soaked sod at headquarters, winning by 0-12 to 0-11.

A stellar season was iced when he was voted Young Hurler Of The Year, and scooped a coveted first All Star Award.

Cork fans had fallen in love with the rampaging giant from Cloyne. O'Sullivan's all-action demeanour and swashbuckling style had electrified the team.

As O'Sullivan carried all before him, on his big, brave, broad shoulders, an incident in a Munster Championship game against Limerick would set him on a collision course with hurling immortality and set his legend in stone.

TG4 would rank an iconic O'Sullivan moment as No.3 on the list of the greatest hurling scores ever, and it would have been difficult to disagree with the innovative Irish television channel's assessment.

The 'Cloyne Colossus,' had developed a reputation for stampeding out with the ball and scattering the opposition like ninepins. as he raised the siege and sent laser-like deliveries behind enemy lines. The sight of the granite-jawed Diarmuid frowning ferociously as he prowled the periphery of the Cork square was not a particularly welcoming sight for opposition forwards.

As Cork was under the cosh against a fired-up 'Treaty' side, Ollie Moran delivered what appeared to be the perfect ball for a predatory inside forward. A large shadow stole over the sliotar as the big-game-hunter, O'Sullivan, gobbled up the ball.

At this point, it might be advisable to evoke the words of a *Stoke Sentinal* columnist describing Irish soccer international, Jonathon Walters.

THE HEART OF A LION
THE SKIN OF A RHINOCEROS
MAYBE NOT THE SPEED OF A CHEETAH!

The Rock set forth, spluttering through the low gears, building an increasing momentum. The unfortunate Jack Foley of Limerick was barring Diarmuid's escape hatch and was known to be a man who would take a bit of shifting. What happened next was the reason instant replays were invented.

The Rock delivered a perfectly fair shoulder-charge which flattened the bemused Foley. He cleared out the Limerick man, as he charged out like a train hitting top gear as the Rebel yell rose to a crescendo in the stands.

Onward he drove, before opening his massive shoulders and sending a shot that almost scorched towards the sun, before it obligingly dipped and arched over the bar.

It was the ultimate moment of defiance from the Cork talisman and although Limerick rallied to squeeze the Rebels out, it would be forever enshrined as one of the greatest scores in the history of the modern game.

Diarmuid 'The 'Rock' O'Sullivan, was the essence of true 'Corkness'. That lofty ideal of the unbroken soldier who battled to the bitter end. This was a Rebel who really had a cause.

►——→ REBEL WITH A CAUSE ←——◄

O'SULLIVAN BEGAN his hurling career at club level with Cloyne following in the footsteps of his father Jerry. He was a boy among men when breaking onto the club's adult team as a 16-year-old and his contribution led to a 1997 Cork Intermediate Championship title and ensured promotion.

He racked up almost 100 championship appearances for the club, and was a standout player, and was selected for the Imokilly divisional team which won the 1997 Cork Senior Championship.

He helped Cork to impressive back-to-back All-Ireland Championships in 1997 and 1998, at under-21 level, and entered the senior ranks with the Cork senior team in 1997.

He never looked back and was ever-present as a defender - making a combined total of 110 National League and Championship appearances.

O'Sullivan developed as a real leader for a star-studded 'Rebels' outfit, winning three All-Ireland Championships - in 1999, 2004, and 2005. O'Sullivan and Cork ruled the roost in the province, also securing five Munster Championships. Diarmuid is less well-known for his football exploits. He was one of a rare breed of dual players at the highest level, winning a Munster Championship with the Cork senior footballers in 2002.

He retired from inter-county hurling on May 12, 2009 and played rugby, where he had spells with Cork clubs, Highfield and Midleton.

JOHNNY PILKINGTON
(Height 6' 0", Weight 14 St)

Decade... 1980s/1990s/2000s
(Position... Midfield)

CHIEF CHARACTERISTIC... COURT JESTER WHO ENSURED WINNING
THE MIDFIELD BATTLE WAS A FOOL'S ERRAND

TOP ACCOMPLICES... MICHEAL DUIGNAN, BRIAN WHELEHAN, DECLAN
PILKINGTON, JOHNNY DOOLEY, JOHN TROY, DAITHÍ REGAN

JOHNNY PILKINGTON

*'THAT'S WHERE YE GET IT WRONG, YE HAVE ME DOWN AS HAPPY-GO-LUCKY. I
WOULD LIKE TO THINK THAT MY PERFORMANCES IN MY BEST YEARS WERE ONES
OF DETERMINATION AND THAT I NEVER GAVE UP, THAT'S WHERE I EXCELLED. I
NEVER GAVE UP, I TRIED ALL THE TIME, NO MATTER HOW BAD THINGS WERE.'*
– JOHNNY PILKINGTON

UIBH Fhaili, how I love you…

He had raged against the fading of the light for many a long day. The perception was he had never cared, but here was a man that cared more than anybody. Endless defeats had drained him and sapped his indomitable spirit.

Ghosts and shadows danced as he cast his mind back to the beginning. Sometimes a defeat defines your future success – more than any amount of hollow victories. O'Moore Park that day had left a scar, but the clouds of despair would herald a new dawn in hurling's world order. From that day forth, almost every cloud the Faithful saw would have a silver lining.

It was the light of better days. A day when two neighbouring tribes went to war…

It was clear after a few minutes that this was no ordinary day. This was a day that would cause a ripple in hurling's history of time.

HARD MAN RATINGS

TOUGHEST:
9.2/10

MEANEST:
8.8/10

SCARIEST:
9.0/10

HARDEST:
19.4/20

☠

TOTAL
HARD MAN

46.4/50

O'Moore Park was bursting at the seams as close cousins Tipperary and Offaly rolled up their sleeves for a bare-knuckle, whitewater ride in the All-Ireland under-21 final. While Offaly had triumphed when the sides clashed at minor level, it was Mick Minouge's

Tipperary charges who would claim the national bragging rights on this occasion. It had been a breathless encounter, oscillating wildly back and forth between those 'noisy neighbours'.

The Premier had all the pedigree at underage level, but this particular Offaly generation were no longer the whipping boys for hurlings 'Fancy Dans'.

It was an historic day for Offaly, who were appearing in their very first All-Ireland under-21 final. Seldom had an underage final thrown up such an embarrassing array of riches.

Tipperary had an all-star ensemble featuring John Leahy, Liam Sheedy, Declan Ryan, and Conal Bonnar. It would be the crowd next door, however, who would hog a large portion of the limelight for the following decade.

Offaly had signposted their quality when these sides had met at under-18 level, downing their lofty neighbours before a bemused Croke Park. This was a different breed of Offaly hurler, featuring the likes of Brian 'Sid' Whelehan, the brothers Pilkington, Declan and Johnny, Daithi Regan, and Johnny Dooley.

The narrow reversal at the hands of Tipperary only served to sharpen the Faithful swords, and one man in particular... was mad for the road ahead!

The Offaly train was about to leave the station with Johnny Pilkington manning the engine room. The Faithful and Tipperary having contested two underage All-Ireland finals in three years, passed each other like ships in the night at senior level.

The Premier's under-21 crew went on to win Liam MacCarthy that season, but it was Offaly who was arguably the one that left a bigger footprint on GAA history, winning Liam MacCarthy in 1994 and 1998.

Johnny Pilkington was clocking up the air miles at this stage, all over Ireland. He was a bundle of tireless energy as he drove the Faithful forward from midfield and manned the battlements when the opposition forces threatened to scale the walls.

He won his first Celtic Cross against Limerick in 1994. That prospect had seemed pretty remote with five minutes remaining. Then Seir Keiran's Johnny Dooley ignored instructions from the sideline and smashed a late free to the net, setting in motion one of the most unlikely comebacks on hurling's biggest stage.

When Pilkington entered hurling's colosseum he was a ravenous competitor, who strained every sinew for the cause. Those closest to him were never fooled by his happy-go-lucky demeanour, as behind the veil lurked one of Offaly's most tenacious warriors, as former Offaly boss Pat Fleury alluded to.

'Any day Johnny Pilkington went out on the field, he left everything he had in his body out there.'

Johnny's star was firmly in the ascendant, but the suspicion remained, however, that both he and his colleagues played hard – and partied harder.

{ DISPELLING THE MYTH }

By the end of his career, he had grown weary of the tag and the lazy caricature that had developed around Offaly hurling.

'Anyone that has played at inter-county level knows their hurling anyway, so you're not going to go out there as such if everything is a party lifestyle or anything like that. To play in the games we played in and to play as long as we did, you're just not going to do that with the supposed social life.'

For Johnny Pilkington, hurling for his beloved county was a business he took very seriously. While the wise-cracking Birr legend never 'looked' totally invested in the punishing life of an inter-county hurling star, nothing could have been further from the truth.

'That's where ye get it wrong, Ye have me down as happy-go-lucky. I would like to think that my performances in my best years were ones of determination and that I never gave up, that's where I excelled. I never gave up, I tried all the time, no matter how bad things were.'

After the 'Babs Keating affair' which ironically propelled Offaly to another All-Ireland in 1998, Johnny and Offaly began to run out of diesel – and eventually out of road.

They had one sting left in the tail for the hurling super-powers as they downed high-flying Cork in the 2000 All-Ireland semi-final. In a strange quirk of fate, Tipperary returned to win the 2001 title with Declan Ryan the only survivor from that historic day in Portlaoise. The young guns that lit up the O'Moore County's sod in 1989 would never meet in the championship again.

Whatever corner of the universe Offaly Gaels gather, the name Johnny Pilkington will be reverently whispered. It was the best of times, and when that much-loved Faithful legend finally departed, it was the worst of times.

Uibh Fhaili, how they loved him …

A FAITHFUL JOURNEY

HE PLAYED his club hurling with Faithful kingpins Birr during a period of unprecedented success for the town side. Birr were one of the greatest club sides of all time, winning All-Ireland titles in 1995, 1998, 2002 and 2003.

Alongside his brother, Declan and the Whelehan clan, they were masters of all they surveyed in Offaly, with Johnny winning eight county senior titles. At Leinster level, he also harvested half a dozen provincial titles.

He was part of an outstanding Offaly minor side that defeated a fancied Tipperary selection in the 1987 All-Ireland final, and he was part of the under-21 side that reached the 1989 All-Ireland final, losing to Tipperary in a classic, 4-10 to 3-11. He won a total of three Leinster under-21 medals, but just fell short of All-Ireland glory in the grade.

Johnny Pilkington made his first appearance for Offaly during the 1988–89 National League campaign, and became a permanent fixture on the matchday programme, until his retirement after the 2001 championship. Operating mainly around the middle of the field, he was a prolific scorer, notching up an impressive 6-56 in just over 40 appearances.

During his colourful tenure with the Faithful County, he won two All-Ireland medals, four Leinsters, one National Hurling League medal, and one All Star award.

MARTIN QUIGLEY
(Height 6' 1", Weight 15 St)

Decade... 1970s/1980s
(Position... Corner-Forward)

CHIEF CHARACTERISTIC... ACCIDENTALLY BUMPING INTO ANYBODY
WHO WASN'T WEARING A WEXFORD JERSEY

TOP ACCOMPLICES... TONY DORAN, JOHN QUIGLEY, NED BUGGY,
CHRISTY KEOGH, MICK JACOB, WILLIE MURPHY

MARTIN QUIGLEY

THE loneliest man in the World...

The mission to the Moon stopped the world below in its tracks, as people tried to process the enormity of what was unfolding, almost 238,855 miles away.

With 650 million watching transfixed around the globe – as Neil Armstrong stepped onto the surface – the loneliest man in the world began his journey. Michael Collins orbited the Moon alone in the command module, Columbia, for 21.5 hours.

During those hours of seemingly endless solitude, he was lost in the vast confines of space. The pilot silently and repeatedly executed 48 minutes cycles at a time – alone on the far side of the Moon. There was no radio contact with Planet Earth or his crew, all he could see was the vast, dark, and uninviting ball of rock.

The massive foreboding, barrier stood between him and anything that ever lived.

HARD MAN RATINGS

TOUGHEST:
9.6/10

MEANEST:
9.1/10

SCARIEST:
9.3/10

HARDEST:
19.3/20

☠

TOTAL HARD MAN

47.3/50

As Armstrong set foot on the cracked and fissured surface, he uttered the immortal words, 'One small step for man, one giant leap for mankind'.

Buzz Aldrin would also set foot on the barren lonely planet, but Collins – as per his mission brief – would travel hundreds of thousands of miles, get within 69, but never one step closer.

It seemed a cruel trick of fate in many ways, to journey so far and seemingly for so little reward. Collins is a mere annotation in one of mankind's greatest-ever achievements, a forgotten passenger on one of the greatest stories ever told…

As Martin Quigley gazed at the Liam MacCarthy Cup presentation, he felt like 'the loneliest Man' in the world. He journeyed many thousands of miles, but he would never get to climb the hallowed steps of the 'Hogan' and lift Liam MacCarthy. He would forever be the 'forgotten man' in one of the greatest sporting stories ever told. Quigley was a man that claimed he never actually retired, rather that Wexford had put him out to pasture! He mostly played in an era (the 70s), where the mantra of Love and Peace did not extend to intercounty hurling forwards.

Defenders rarely spared the timber, but Martin Quigley never flinched in the face of enemy fire, and always returned fire with some healthy salvos of his own.

Quigley was respected and admired all over the country for his bravery, honesty of effort and sheer bloody-mindedness in the trenches. Rarely has a man expended more in an ultimately vain pursuit of All Ireland glory, than the Rathnure colossus.

His haul of four All Star awards not only points to an astonishing level of performance, but also stands alone as Wexford's most decorated hero in the prestigious awards scheme.

To put his achievement in context, by the time he had amassed his fourth award in 1977, the legendary Tony Doran had only been selected once.

For Martin Quigley, individual awards were just a starter as he waited patiently for the main course of All-Ireland glory. Like a man lost in the desert, he had glimpsed the mirage of shining silver on countless occasions – or had he just imagined it?

For Quigley's valiant crew, Liam MacCarthy appeared to be an illusionist's cheap trick, forever lost in a hall of smoke and mirrors. It was becoming a quixotic quest – a pursuit of the unattainable by a bunch of well-intentioned sportsmen.

Every time Wexford appeared to have turned the corner, they merely arrived back in the same place again. Provincial finals came and went, and always with the same demoralising outcome. The 1976 Leinster final was the seventh in-a-row between Wexford and Kilkenny. 'The Cats' had the patent on the 'Bob O'Keefe' and were going for a provincial six in-a-row, and the small matter of an All-Ireland three in-a-row.

The Model men duly ripped up the script and shocked the reigning champions by 2–20 to 1-6. It was a result nobody had seen coming… least of all the Wexford supporters!

{ TRIBAL WARFARE }

With the unexpected gift of a second Leinster medal in his back-pocket, Martin and Wexford faced a considerable hurdle on the road to Liam in the form of a dangerous-looking Galway outfit. The Tribe was the original version of a GAA problem child. On their day they posed a serious threat to your ambitions and the mood-music early on indicated Wexford had just poked the bear.

With both sides in the single-digit column of All-Irelands, they roared into battle and the early exchanges hinted at a high-scoring classic. The tea leaves were duly vindicated as the scoreboard operator nearly ran out of numbers. The game ended in a 5–14 to 2–23 classic, and it was back to the drawing board at the newly opened Páirc Uí Chaoimh in Cork.

The second game was a bit cagier, but no less dramatic, however, as a single goal separated the protagonists. Wexford were relieved to emerge victorious by 3–14 to 2–14.

Their opponents in the All-Ireland final were a familiar foe, and Cork was a team who appeared to have placed a large hex on the Model County's backs. Quigley's men got off to a flyer and led by 2–2 to no score after just six minutes; however, Cork settled into the contest with Pat Moylan leading the charge. The sides were dead-locked at the interval, and there was very little daylight between them as they entered the final furlong. Cork somehow maintained their magnetic hold over Wexford – winning by 2–21 to 4–11.

Wexford, game as a pebble, returned the following season to win Leinster again. It was another dose of 'Groundhog Day' in the All-Ireland final as Cork dogged it out to win by the width of a green flag.

As Martin Quigley stared at the presentation of the Liam MacCarthy Cup, the grim realisation dawned on him.

He would be forever cast in the role of the forgotten one who had journeyed thousands of miles, just to be a mere spectator at the main event.

He must have felt like the loneliest man in the world…

SON OF SLANEY

MARTIN QUIGLEY was born in 1951 in Rathnure, County Wexford and hurled with the local side - winning his first senior county title with the club in 1971. It was the beginning of a remarkable period of dominance for Rathnure in Wexford, and further titles followed in 1972, 1973, and 1974. The club also extended its campaigns further in two of those seasons, adding Leinster club titles in 1971 and 1973.

Martin Quigley enjoyed further county medals in 1977, 1979, and 1980. He also was part of the side that won both county and Leinster titles in 1986. Rathnure also reached a number of All-Ireland Club finals but were defeated in all of them.

Quigley was involved with the Wexford minor team in the mid-60s. He won a Leinster title in 1967, before losing to Cork in the All-Ireland final. He won his second Leinster minor medal in 1968, before lining out in a second All-Ireland final.

He was successful on this occasion as Wexford beat Cork.

In 1969 Quigley moved up to the under-21 grade. Cork presented themselves as Wexford's nemesis at that point in Quigley's career as they succumbed to three All-Ireland defeats in-a-row.

At senior level Quigley played and lost two All-Ireland finals, against Cork in 1976 and 1977. He won one National League title, and is the only Wexford player to have won four All Stars.

JOE RABBITTE

(Height 6' 4", Weight 15 St)

Decade... 1990s/2000s

(Position... Centre-Forward)

CHIEF CHARACTERISTIC... PSYCHOTIC BUNNY WHO
CHASED FOXES AROUND CROKE PARK

TOP ACCOMPLICES... EUGENE CLOONAN, ALAN KERINS, KEVIN
BRODERICK, MICHAEL 'HOPPER' MCGRATH

JOE RABBITTE

'THAT WAS BROKEN, THAT WAS BROKEN, THAT WAS MASHED AND MANGLED. THAT KNUCKLE IS GONE. BOTH THUMBS, THE TOP JOINTS WERE BROKEN.'

– JOE RABBITTE

ALL-IRELAND semi-finals, a halfway house between heaven and hell. One moment astride the 'Pearly Gates', the next staring at a one-way ticket to the depths of despair.

Somewhere in the midst of the raging bedlam, Galway's grizzled titan caught the sliotar around the '40'. It was another nail in the Tipperary coffin. Games turn on such innocuous moments. The final acts are rarely a thing of beauty, ugly ducklings that give birth to a gaggle of welcome geese. He had been relocated from the edge of the square, to quell any late whiff of rebellion from the Premier County. Rabbitte's huge frame had come to the rescue, bearing gifts that hinted at a possible reunion with the ancient's game's finest silver.

The gnarled warrior from the hurling fields of Athenry was becoming disorientated, pain has a way of wearing you down. Time had stood still for him, as he became trapped in an eternal passage of exhausting play, extending his telescopic-like arm, then clearing out the bodies... over and over again.

HARD MAN RATINGS

TOUGHEST:
9.9/10

MEANEST:
8.8/10

SCARIEST:
9.0/10

HARDEST:
19.5/20

☠

TOTAL HARD MAN

47.2/50

At times during a fiery, and suffocating contest, Joe Rabbitte had become so immersed in the battle he had lost track of the time; the game had extracted all the rhyme and reason from his exhausted spirit. A familiar face snapped his nightmarish reveries, and he realised he had found his way back into the light. He had reached the end game in the 1993 All-Ireland semi-final.

'The first person on the pitch after the final whistle was P.J. Molloy, a member of our own club, and it was only when I saw him that it sunk in, we'd won. I was concentrating too hard before that to realise how long was left in the game.'

For Galway hurling, it was the Age of the Agonies. The perpetual contenders for Liam MacCarthy's crown would perish at the hands of the eventual All-Ireland champions six years in succession.

Joe Rabbitte was on board for each and every heart-breaking instalment. His inter-county career was etched all over his broken body. Starting at the tips of his fingers, he could recount a horrific tale or two. A tour around Joe's battered frame was a bit like a trip to an Accident & Emergency ward. Was there a bone in his body left unbroken for the Galway cause?

He catalogued, once upon a time, a mind-boggling list of injuries that were sustained in a wretched run of ill fortune. Joe Rabbitte was a man who put his hands, where you wouldn't put your hurley – and how it showed.

{ STICKS AND STONES }

'That was broken, that was broken, that was mashed and mangled,' he sighed. 'That knuckle is gone. Both thumbs, the top joints were broken.'

At this point, some sort of reader discretion disclaimer should have been issued – as Joe was only getting started!

In 1992, he broke two ribs against Cork in a league game. The following season in another league game in Ballinasloe against Clare, he sustained a broken finger and didn't know it!

He then smashed another one at training in Pearse Stadium and spent the next three months strapping the fingers together. A month before the All-Ireland semi-final against Tipperary, he added a broken hand into the equation.

At this juncture, Joe was subjected to some rather dubious medical practices, as another double fracture was added to the mix. One included cutting a corner off a plastic lunch box and strapping it to the hand for protection. Joe recalls that one worked a treat!

In the 1994 Connacht final, a defender floored Joe and kicked him in the calf, bursting a muscle. 1995 was another accident and incident-packed season for Joe, who 'made pulp of one of the index fingers' against Cork at Pairc Ui Roinn.

'They put in a plate and, today, the finger is nearly an inch shorter than its twin. Sorest thing I ever had.' On painkillers, Joe lost a shocking two-and-a-half stone in weight but carried on playing regardless.

In 1996, he broke his elbow without realising, though he said the signs were there. His car had a central armrest and every time he made contact, it was like receiving an electric shock.

'Nearly crashed the car a few times with the pain.'

A month later, in the early stages of the All-Ireland semi-final with Wexford, a collision with George O'Connor broke his ankle. The indestructible Rabbitte duly hobbled off for an X-ray, and decided to include his arm in the scan.

'Do my elbow as well as the ankle,' he told the doctor.

'Want the good news or the bad news?' smiled the doctor later.

'I doubt there's any good news,' said Joe.

'You're right,' said the doc. 'We're going to have to operate on the elbow too.'

In 1997, disaster struck again in the Connacht final when Joe was hospitalised with a fractured skull. The medical advice was stark and to the point.

'Give it up altogether!' he was advised.

Joe's pursuit of a Celtic Cross came up agonisingly short, when despite a Man of the Match display against Kilkenny in 1993, they fell valiantly by five points. In 2001, Galway were within two points of Tipperary late on, with Joe baring down on goal. With only Brendan Cummings between the Athenry man and immortality, he had one shot at eternal salvation.

Just as he was about to pull the trigger, the referee made a 50-50 call and penalised Rabbitte. It was as close as he would ever come to claiming the Holy Grail.

His contribution to Galway hurling went above and beyond the call of duty. A man who shed every pint of blood, covered every blade of hay, for his beloved maroon and white.

Despite being wounded on the battlefield on countless occasions, he continued to fight on his back. If Purple Hearts were awarded for sporting courage, Joe Rabbitte would certainly have been one of hurling's most decorated soldiers.

NO ORDINARY JOE

JOE RABBITTE was a member of the Galway senior hurling team from 1990 until 2002.

He made his senior championship debut against the Premier County, Tipperary in an All-Ireland semi-final. In each of Joe Rabbitte's first six years of his inter-county life, Galway's championship campaign would end at the hands of the eventual All-Ireland champions.

He played club hurling with Athenry, where he won three All-Ireland Club titles and a total of eight county medals. He spent two decades hurling with the club, retiring in 2007.

Athenry controversially lost an All-Ireland semi-final to St Joseph's Doora-Barefield in 1999, with the Galway club infuriated that they had had a legitimate point disallowed. He became disillusioned with the game and retired initially, withdrawing from the panel after a National Hurling League match against Offaly, after appearing as a substitute. He would return to contest another All-Ireland final in 2001 against Tipperary, but another defeat edged him closer to retirement. In an eventful and colourful career, he also captured two National League titles for the Tribesmen.

Joe was forever immortalised by Micheal O Muircheartaigh's famous commentary.

'Pat Fox has it on his hurl and is motoring well now, but here comes Joe Rabbitte hot on his tail. I've seen it all now, a Rabbitte chasing a Fox around Croke Park!'

NICKY RACKARD

(Height 6' 3", Weight 14 St)

Decade... 1940s/1950s

(Position... Full-Forward)

CHIEF CHARACTERISTIC... A FORWARD WITH A
CLEARLY DEFINED SET OF GOALS!

TOP ACCOMPLICES... BOBBY RACKARD, PADGE KEHOE, NED
WHEELER, BILLY RACKARD, OLIVER 'HOPPER' MCGRATH, TIM FLOOD

NICKY RACKARD

'I WAS LUCKY ENOUGH TO BE ON A WEXFORD TEAM THAT HE WAS INVOLVED WITH... HE PUT HIS HAND ON MY SHOULDER AND THAT WAS LIKE THE HAND OF GOD TOUCHING YOU.'

– LIAM GRIFFIN

NICKY Rackard could well have been cast from the lines of the famous Dubliner's ballad, *Kelly the Boy from Killane.*

Penned by Patrick Joseph McCall to commemorate the centenary of the 1798 Rebellion, it celebrates the role of John Kelly, leader of the rebel victory at the Battle of Three Rocks in the Wexford Rebellion, which led to the liberation of Wexford town.

Tell me who is the giant with the gold curling hair
He who strides at the head of your band
Seven feet is his height with some inches to spare
And he looks like a king in command
Ah me boys that's the pride of the bold Shelmaliers
'Mongst our greatest of heroes a man
So fling your beavers aloft and give
three ringing cheers
For John Kelly, the boy from Killane

HARD MAN RATINGS

TOUGHEST:
9.4/10

MEANEST:
8.9/10

SCARIEST:
10/10

HARDEST:
19.3/20

☠

TOTAL HARD MAN

47.6/50

Tall and golden-haired, and a towering six foot three inches, the Rackard version of the Irish rebel warrior would ring many three-cheers from bold Shemaliers.

With Wexford hurling mired in the gutter, Rackard, who also hailed from Killane, would lead an uprising, one that would shake the hurling establishment to its very core.

Wexford hurling was limping along at a low ebb with their last All-Ireland win delivered in 1910, when they were known as the Wexford Shelmaliers.

The famous surname forever enshrined in Wexford means the 'powerful and brave'. It was a name that would resonate through the decades as a trio of dashing brothers would drag the 'Yellow Bellies' out of the doldrums.

Bobby, Billy and Nicky Rackard were just the tonic an ailing Wexford hurling scene desperately required.

Tony Doran had survived in the foxholes of inter-county hurling for nearly two decades. Some days you had to dig into the trenches and wait for the barrage of artillery to pass over. Other days you clamoured over the top, and met the incoming fire head-on.

He had soldiered with many brave men who wore the purple and gold sash into battle, but Nicky Rackard was a different breed.

In his autobiography, entitled *A Land of Men and Giants* Doran recalls the towering, golden-haired Wexford colossus, Rackard, that would leave him starry-eyed with wonder.

'Rackard?

'He was a big man… strong as a bull… and Rackard was the man to drive the team. When we were playing in the field across the road as kids we all pretended to be Nicky Rackard... nobody else. But the three Rackards were all big men.

'Nicky stood out for so many reasons... for taking frees... scoring goals and that was a big thing for us all... he was taking 21-yard frees and he was never going to tap the ball over the bar... he was going for goal every time.'

The road to salvation for Wexford would yield few instant returns, however, as both Nicky and his brothers toiled for over a decade, with little or no tangible reward.

When Nicky moved to Dublin in the 40s, he developed drinking problems as he revealed in a series of memoirs. 'There were spells of being on the dry and there were other spells of being on the bash. There were car crashes and wild binges.

'There were blackouts, which experts know are nearly always a certain sign of alcoholism.'

The years rolled past and it looked like the Wexford's talisman's career would be forever blighted by the bottle. Nicky and Wexford were running out of time in their pursuit of an elusive All-Ireland. The passing of a close friend in 1951 would set Nicky on the road to redemption, prompting almost six years of abstinence from alcohol. Within that period, he was at his brilliant best as he was finally liberated from his demons.

Having reached the decider in 1951, where they succumbed to Tipperary, they kept plugging away and in 1954 powered through to another All-Ireland final where they faced Cork.

Nicky had scored a mind-boggling 5-4 against Dublin in the Leinster final and followed up with 7-7 against a hapless Antrim in the semi-final.

In a nerve-shredding contest, Bobby Rackard's duel with the

great Christy Ring was one of the highlights of a hard-fought encounter, decided by a late goal by Johnny Clifford of Cork.

{ REACHING THE PROMISED LAND }

Despite the set-back, Wexford reached the All-Ireland final the following year against Galway. In front of 78,000 spectators, an early Nicky Rackard goal gave Wexford the perfect platform and they cruised to a 10-point victory.

Time was rapidly catching up on Nicky, but he was determined to finish his career with another audience with Liam MacCarthy. Wexford's incredible effort to deny Cork and Ring his ninth All-Ireland medal the following year, was one of Nicky's finest hours.

The decisive passage of play provided one of the most compelling storylines on All-Ireland Sunday. With Wexford up by two points, Ring bore down on goal with only Wexford net-minder Art Foley to beat.

Somehow, Foley saved and the play carried on – with RTE's Michael O'Hehir, commentating on Radio Éireann, describing it thus:

'Time ticking away now and English sends it away up the field.

'Wexford attacking again and the ball goes out on the wing to Tom Ryan… Tom Ryan and Vin Twomey going for it. Ryan trying to solo his way through. His way is blocked by Vin Twomey. 'He goes back for the ball, he hand-passes it across the centre. Out comes Nicky Rackard… 21 yards out, he can take a shot.

'He takes a shot… and it's a goal. It's A GOAL.

'It's a goal and you've never seen such excitement in all your life. Hats, coats… everything you can think of have gone into the air and

the whole of Croke Park has gone stark staring wild.'

Of all the stars that ever shone in Wexford hurling, none ascended higher or illuminated the hurling landscape more brightly than Nicky Rackard. The tall, blonde, goal-scoring machine, added a real A-List star quality to the pages of hurling history.

A dash of Hollywood… in the heart of Killane!

THE LIFE OF A LORD

NICHOLAS RACKARD was born on April 28, 1922. His championship career with the Wexford senior team spanned 17 years from 1940 to 1957. He is the hurling championship record goal-scorer of all time with 59 goals.

He was born in Killane, County Wexford. His father, who was an avid cricketer, introduced him to the game of hurling. An uncle of Nicky's, John Doran won an All-Ireland medal as a gaelic footballer with Wexford in 1918.

Rackard went to St Kieran's College in Kilkenny and won back-to-back Leinster medals in 1938 and 1939. He played for the local Rathnure St Anne's, winning a county Junior Championship medal in 1940, and four Senior Championship medals.

He was part of the Wexford minor panel and had just left the grade when he was selected for the Wexford senior team in 1940. Rackard was part of a number of talented Wexford sides, starting with the ground-breaking 1955 and 1956 All-Ireland winning sides.

He also won four Leinster medals, a solitary National League medal, and one Leinster football medal. He played his last game for Wexford in August 1957. He collected his only Railway Cup medal in 1956. Rackard retired in August 1957.

CHRISTY RING

(Height 5' 10", Weight 14 St)

Decade... 1940s/1950s/1960s

(Position... Centre-Forward)

CHIEF CHARACTERISTIC... PRINCIPAL CORKONIAN
SCHOOL OF HURLING WIZARDRY

TOP ACCOMPLICES... JACK LYNCH, WILLIE JOHN DALY, LIAM
DOWLING, PADDY BARRY, GERALD MURPHY

CHRISTY RING

'I'LL OPEN YOU THE NEXT TIME THE BALL COMES IN
HERE,' THREATENED ONE OPPONENT.
'IF YOU'RE STILL HERE!' REPLIED RING.

HE was a man that was all about timing…

When the movie *It's a Wonderful Life* flopped at the box office in 1946, it proved an age-old truism that timing is indeed everything. The movie directed by Frank Capra was aired again on TV in 1974 – as the result of a network clerical error – and went on to become a much-loved Christmas classic.

As the clock ticked to 30 minutes in the 1946 All-Ireland Final, the balding man hopped on his bike, departing from centrefield. He was a man that knew the route to goal – but on this occasion, he chose an unusual way to shake off his pursuers, by heading towards the corner of the field.

The nervously assembled Kilkenny back-six were by now in a small bit of a quandary with the words of the hit song by The Clash… *Should I Stay or Should I Go?* ringing ominously in their ears.

When he changed direction and headed straight for The Cats' goal he was still hopping

HARD MAN RATINGS

TOUGHEST:
9.9/10

MEANEST:
9.1/10

SCARIEST:
9.9/10

HARDEST:
19.9/20
☠

TOTAL
HARD MAN
48.8/50

the ball on his hurley without a care in the world.

At this juncture, the most-wanted man in Croke Park took on the appearance of a ghost as he waltzed past Kilkenny's captain, Mulcahy and sidestepped two more defenders. He then shot off the left-side and the ball whistled past a transfixed Jim Donegan in the Kilkenny net – for one of the greatest goals in All-Ireland final history. It was a critical score – at a critical juncture.

That's the thing about great players... for them, it's always about timing. Nicholas Christopher Michael Ring would go on to be celebrated in song and verse. His name would be whispered in hushed reverential tones. Wherever conversations were held regarding the hurling 'immortals,' Ring's name was always front and centre.

The Wizard of Cloyne will always hold the hurling world in the palm of his hand. The man in the 'cap' was also one of the toughest competitors and hardest men that ever crossed between hurling white lines...

When he wasn't stoking the fire on the field, Michael Maher of Tipperary was keeping a sharp eye on the usual suspects. Part of the famed 'Hell's Kitchen' defensive unit, the Holycross native was one of the guardians of the famous Tipperary 'Hell-fire Club'. After a lifetime of manning the Premier pumps, it was the usual suspects he remembered the most.

When queried on one occasion he rendered judgment on some of the ancient games most distinguished exponents, and reminded readers of the less well-known and the darker side of one gentleman in particular.

'The three best players I saw were Ring, Jimmy Doyle, and Eddie Keher... the three best consistent hurlers, though it helped they were from three top counties. I'm inclined to put Ring first among them. I found him okay to mark but he was inclined to get wild at times on the field.'

The nature of the beast back in the day was one of survival – and nobody had to locate it more than the most-marked-man-in hurling. The rules of the time encouraged physicality by the bucket-load!

Ring was blessed with both the stubbornness and the style to counteract the myriad of different ways opposition forces aligned themselves to counter the Rebel talisman's nuclear weaponry.

{ THE RING OF FIRE }

'It was a tough era of hurling,' recalled his teammate, John Lyons. 'People might have said that Ring was dirty but he wasn't. He was single-minded about winning the ball and getting a score and nothing in between was going to distract him.'

Lyons, like the rest of his Rebel colleagues, was mesmerised by the unrivalled sorcery of Ring.

In hurling terms, Ring was a 'genius', said Lyons. 'He was the best I ever saw. I never saw anyone do anything on the field that Ring couldn't do, and maybe better.

'In 1946, we were training and Ring put a '70' over the bar. The likes of Jack Lynch and Alan Lotty were slagging him, saying he couldn't do it off his left. He changed over and put another '70' over the bar.'

Incredible skill allied to the heart of a lion.

Ring was also as strong as a bull and whatever it took to get the Rebels over the line, he was more than willing to accommodate it.

'I would go through a stone wall to get a 50-50 ball. I would stop at nothing. My strength was largely hidden because I wasn't a big fellow. I never weighed less than 13 stone. I knew that travelling at speed, I could take on any player. I only used my strength when needed.

'All round physical strength was my best weapon. I never did weight-lifting or anything like that to develop this strength, I had it automatically and I'd say it was in the mind; 75 percent of everything is in the mind, and it's the mind that counts.'

Ring always found a way around the defensive 'heat' as teammate Willie John Daly remembers. With the Rebels trailing Limerick in the 1956 Munster final and the clock becoming a very alarming factor, he noticed Ring make a quick dash to the sideline.

Like any self-respecting magician, Christy knew it was time to delve a little deeper into his box of tricks.

'We were well behind,' recalled Willie. 'I remember him coming down to the sideline and wondering what he was at. He was changing his hurley.'

Ring had been well marshalled by Limerick all day and he headed back to the fray with a new hurley. The change worked the oracle as the 'Wiz' fired three goals in four minutes to sink the Treaty.

He was just as quick on the draw in the 'verbals' department and had a legendary reply for one particularly loud-mouthed defender.

'I'll open you the next time the ball comes in here,' threatened the defender.

'If you're still here!' replied Christy.

Christy Ring was always a man with a perfect sense of timing!

THE WAY
» ⟶ OF THE ⟵ «
WIZARD

CHRISTY RING was born on October 30, 1920. His league and championship career with Cork spanned 24 years from 1939 to 1963.

He made his senior debut during the 1939/40 league. Over the course of the next quarter of a century Ring amassed eight All-Ireland medals, including four championships in-a-row from 1941 to 1944. He won another All-Ireland in 1946, and three championships in-a-row from 1952 to 1954. He was the first man to hold Liam MacCarthy aloft three times as captain.

Ring won nine Munster crowns and four National League medals. He was named Hurler of the Year at the age of 38. He lined out for his last game for Cork in June 1963.

He set a host of championship records for his era, including career appearances (65), and scoring tally (33-208).

Ring joined the Munster inter-provincial team in 1941, and was an automatic choice on the starting fifteen for the following 22 years. He scored a staggering 42-105 and won a record 18 Railway Cup medals during his stint with the province. In the golden age of the competition, his prowess drew crowds of up to 50,000 to Croke Park for the final on St Patrick's Day. The decline in interest in subsequent championships was attributed to his retirement.

SEAN STACK

(Height 6' 0", Weight 14 St)

Decade... 1970s/1980s

(Position... Centre-Back)

CHIEF CHARACTERISTIC... ALWAYS THE
BANNER'S LAST MAN STANDING

TOP ACCOMPLICES... GER LOUGHNANE, SEAMUS DURACK, JOHN
CALLINAN, SEAN HEHIR, JACKIE O'GORMAN

SÉAN STACK

'THEY WERE MORE INTERESTED IN DESTRUCTION RATHER THAN CONSTRUCTION. BUT THAT CHANGED LATER ON. I CAME UP AGAINST THE LIKES OF MICHAEL RYAN, WHO WAS AWKWARD TO PLAY ON BUT HE WASN'T OUT TO BREAK EVERY BONE IN YOUR BODY. WHEREAS, IN THE EARLY TO MID-70S, EVERY CENTRE-FORWARD WAS DESIGNED TO NEARLY KILL YOU AND THAT WAS HIS CLAIM TO FAME.'

– SÉAN STACK

AT times during his career, Séan Stack must have felt like the Bob Dylan rendition of the classic Stealers hit *Stuck in the Middle with You.*

The Banner was stuck in that strange phenomenon known as the sporting middle, with a Munster title or Liam MacCarthy always agonisingly out of their reach.

Clare were not a particularly bad side, but the harsh sporting truth was they were not a particularly great one either. Undoubtedly, they had the potential to be a great team, but somehow, they always managed to deliver their mediocre version.

They had been close – so very close – on countless occasions. They had beaten every major county in Ireland on many occasions, just never

HARD MAN RATINGS

TOUGHEST:
9.5/10

MEANEST:
9.2/10

SCARIEST:
9.3/10

HARDEST:
19.4/20

☠

TOTAL HARD MAN

47.4/50

when it really mattered.

Séan Stack was haunted by so many near misses and so many gut-wrenching reversals. Yet, still, he forged on through the despair. Endlessly seeking, endlessly hoping for a glimpse of the promised lands of Munster or All-Ireland glory.

The province was shark-infested waters for the Banner's ambitions, with Limerick, Waterford, Tipp and Cork all lurking in the murky deep.

Séan Stack was from a GAA family… just not a hurling one! His father, Stephen was a Kerryman and played football with the Kingdom, before deciding to buy a farm in the neighbouring County Clare hurling stronghold of Sixmilebridge. Despite the football blood that coursed through the family's veins, young Séan was destined for a stellar career with the smaller ball.

Despite the DNA deficit, Séan would go on to become one of Sixmilebridge and the Banner County's greatest ever soldiers. He was a man any county would want in their corner. He led the line with a finely honed serrated edge, aggressive in the tackle, and possessed a razor-sharp hurling brain.

The Banner was locked-in to an endless cycle of self-sabotage. The Clare men were often their own worst enemies; feisty and ferocious in combat, they were also blessed with sublime skills. They almost ticked all the boxes but were always undone by the finest of margins – the space between your ears.

Stack alluded to this recurring theme which was often the bane of county's hurling fortunes, in the *Clare Game of My Life* series, as he recalled the 1978 Munster Final.

'We were marking men instead of going out and expressing ourselves.'

In his autobiography, John Callinan put his finger on it. 'Justin McCarthy was marvellous but his lead-up to the match was about how to stop Cork. We went out to stop Cork and we didn't go out and just play. We were every bit as good as them, if not better.'

'We could beat Kilkenny in Nowlan Park or in Tulla; we could beat Tipp or Limerick. We knew that the All-Ireland was there for us in 1978… if we could just get over the Cork hurdle. The most regrettable part for us was that we lost the match by two points, but we didn't play. We knew we had the handle of everybody.

'We just didn't perform. Every sportsperson would say that if you perform to your best and get beaten, you'll accept it in time. But when you know you didn't, you'll never accept it. We were down a point at half-time, having played against the breeze.

'We knew in our hearts that there was nobody else. There was nothing in Leinster that held any fear for us that time. The winners had Antrim in an All-Ireland semi- final. That was the galling thing about it. It finished up Cork vs Wexford in the final and there was a 12 or 15-point gap.

'Facing out for the second half, here was the 30 minutes that were going to define us as characters and as a team. We had come a long way in four years… and here we were. It just never took off.

'It has always been very hard to accept that… but a lot of us didn't perform. We have to put our hands up. Ger Loughnane and Seamus Durack performed, but an awful lot of us just didn't. I was terrible. Dreadful.

'From my time with Clare, it's the defeats that stick with me. I often meet some of the players from back in the day. They remember the good days… and I say that it's the bad days that always haunt me.'

{ LOCAL HERO }

Thankfully, for the long-suffering Stack, his club fortunes were a panacea for the soul.

Sixmilebridge were a formidable winning machine that yielded buckets of medals for the success-starved Listowel native. Seven county titles and a Munster club medal went a long way towards redressing the paucity of inter-county silverware.

The club that hadn't won a county title before Séan Stack joined the team, now had annexed titles in three different decades. Séan hurled senior with the club for over two decades, playing a starring role as the club emerged from the doldrums to be crowned kings of Banner County.

The club hurling scene in Clare was full of blood and thunder, and only the strongest survived as Séan revealed. 'Sixmilebridge had been senior before and had reached county finals in 1952 and 1962, but the 1977 success was our first.

'My last championship was in 1993 when we beat O'Callaghan's Mills. Then my wife convinced me that enough was *enough* and Sixmilebridge went out and won the All-Ireland a couple of years later. That'll tell you, I must have been more of a hindrance than a help!

'I played my first senior game when I was 17 against Clarecastle. The culture at that time was totally different. I think they bred these centre-forwards somewhere in the northern regions of Norway because they just came with a different agenda.

'Everybody knows the centre-forwards that played for Clarecastle, Newmarket and Brian Boru's! They were more interested in destruction rather than construction, were designed to nearly kill you and that was his claim to fame.'

It was a bounty very few players ever cashed in on…

» ⟶ STACK'S KINGDOM ⟵ «

SÉAN STACK was born in 1953 in Listowel, County Kerry. Stack first played in the famed hurling academy of St Flannan's College in Ennis. His prowess was evident from an early stage when he first linked up with the Clare minor team. He also featured with the under-21, junior, and intermediate sides.

He won seven county medals with Sixmilebridge and a Munster club title. Séan made his Muster Championship debut back in 1974 and soon became a permanent addition to the Banner ranks. He won two national titles in his Clare tenure in the form of National League medals. Despite many close calls, he never won a Munster senior title as he finished runner-up on five occasions.

He was a member of the Munster interprovincial team at varying stages and featured on the competition's winning side twice. He made a total of 28 championship appearances for Clare and announced his retirement following the conclusion of the 1987 season. He became involved in coaching and he was part of the Clare under-21 backroom team as a selector. At club level, Séan has managed a number of the biggest sides, including Sixmilebridge, Clonlara, Toomevara and Na Piarsaigh.

Despite Clare's lack of success during his playing career, he won an All-Star award and was voted on a special non-All-Ireland-winning Team of the Century in 1984.

JACKIE TYRRELL

(Height 6' 1", Weight 14.5 St

Decade... 2000s/2010s

(Position... Corner-Back)

CHIEF CHARACTERISTIC... MAKING LAR CORBETT
RESEMBLE THE INVISIBLE MAN

TOP ACCOMPLICES... TOMMY WALSH, JJ DELANEY, MICHAEL
KAVANAGH, PADRAIG WALSH, BRIAN HOGAN, NOEL HICKEY

JACKIE TYRRELL

'I REMEMBER SEEING JOHN MULLANE UP ON THE PODIUM WITHOUT HIS JERSEY. THAT WAS JUST CLASSIC MULLANE. WHEN I SAW HIM BARE-CHESTED IN 2007, I STORED THAT IMAGE IN MY HEAD FOR ANOTHER DAY. "THE NEXT TIME I RUN INTO MULLANE HE'LL HAVE HIS JERSEY OFF ALRIGHT," I SAID TO MYSELF. "BECAUSE BY THE TIME WE'RE FINISHED WITH WATERFORD, MULLANE WILL BE TOO EMBARRASSED TO BE WEARING THAT JERSEY".'

– JACKIE TYRRELL

'**O**N the right and left two seas enclose you, without your possessing even a single ship for escape. The river Po around you; the Alps behind hem you in. Her soldiers, where you have first met the enemy, you must conquer or die.'

They had journeyed to the gates of immortality only to find a familiar foe blocking their path.

The Kilkenny's 'Drive for Five' had encountered some stern resistance from the usual suspects, Tipperary.

When he addressed his troops at the dawn of the 2009 All-Ireland final, Brian Cody may not have used the great military general, Hannibal's famous call-to-arms, but as The Cats sharpened their claws… rest assured, he used something similar!

HARD MAN RATINGS

TOUGHEST:
9.2/10

MEANEST:
9.9/10

SCARIEST:
9.1/10

HARDEST:
19.3/20

TOTAL HARD MAN
47.5/50

When the battle commenced in Croke Park, Kilkenny was quickly hemmed in on all sides.

Wave after Blue and Gold wave, swamped their creaking defences as the Premier threatened to run riot.

Jackie Tyrrell peered coldly into the raging tempest, Tipperary's heavy artillery was bombarding the walls as the Kilkenny fortress looked set to be breached.

'Where you have first met the enemy, you must conquer or die.'

It was the early stages of the 2009 All-Ireland final. Tipperary's precocious young forward, Seamus Callanan was making serious tracks towards the Kilkenny goal. The Cats were alarmingly outflanked.

Callanan had a 'whiff' of a precious green flag in his nostrils. Cody's most trusted lieutenant took no pleasure in what he was about to do. The concession of an early goal in an All-Ireland final was not an option for Kilkenny.

He thundered into the Drom-Inch tyro like a rampaging bull. It was a sickening collision and Callanan crumpled to the ground... crisis averted.

Referee Diarmuid Kirwan stopped the play to allow attention to the stricken Tipperary forward and Tyrrell heaved a sigh of relief and jogged back to his station.

If anyone had any doubts about the defending champion's desire to retain their crown, Jackie Tyrrell had just provided a visceral statement of chilling intent.

Tyrrell would recall the controversial incident with a tinge of regret when speaking to former Offaly player, Brian Carroll on the 'A Hurler's Life' podcast.

'I hit Seamus Callanan a dirty dig, a lot of people remember it. I definitely regret that. I shouldn't have done it. If the referee picked up on it he possibly could have given me a red card back then.

'If you did it now, you'd definitely get a red card. It was something that I shouldn't have done, it was instinctive.'

That was the thing about front-line troopers like Jackie – their instinct left little room for mitigation. The warrior's spirit demands a certain degree of collateral damage. In the high stakes world of inter-county hurling, there will always be casualties. For Jackie, this was never personal... just business.

Franny Cantwell who kept goal for James Stephens during the 1990s and 2000s was ideally placed to make an early judgement on another iconic son of 'The Village'.

'I saw Jackie from the start,' Cantwell states. 'Some doubted, but I remember saying to fellas in work that we had this young lad who'd go to the very top of the game. You could just see the right stuff in him.'

His words would ring true as Tyrrell's rare combination of size, strength, and no little skill, would propel him to the very top of the inter-county game. Cantwell watched as Jackie often carried Kilkenny on his sturdy frame – no more so than when he rendered 'Hurler of the Year' Larry Corbett to a role as a spectator as Kilkenny defied the odds to reclaim Liam MacCarthy from their bitter foes in 2011.

He also felt Tyrrell never got the credit for his hurling prowess and the fact that his fearsome reputation often obscured it.

'I'd describe Jackie Tyrrell as the man who had everything – the man who gave everything, and the man who won everything. Jackie is a born winner. I don't think he ever got the credit in the media for how good he is hurling-wise. It was all about his physique, his toughness… There is far more to Jackie than his strength.'

{ ONLY THE LEAGUE? }

When Waterford inflicted a rare and unexpected defeat on Kilkenny in the 2007 National League final, their players and supporters celebrated the most unexpected of gifts.

The 'Deise' festivities were in full swing after the final whistle and seemed a tad over the top to an old war-horse like Jackie Tyrrell.

For Kilkenny's group of serial winners, defeat always ran deep. When John Mullane removed his jersey in a full-on celebratory pose, the Black and Amber sharpened the coldest of steel and readied it for delivery in late September 'I remember seeing John Mullane up on the podium without his jersey. That was just classic Mullane. When I saw him bare-chested in 2007, I stored that image in my head for another day.'

When the pair inevitably clashed later in the season with an All-Ireland title at stake, a flurry of jostling and wild pulling broke out.

Tyrrell and Kilkenny, however, were no shrinking violets and duly served up death by a thousand cuts in one of the most one-sided All-Ireland's in the modern era.

Tyrrell in his usual no-nonsense style delivered on his promise to a beleaguered John Mullane and Waterford.

Jackie stated on his retirement, 'I never settled for anything less than giving it my very best. I fought to the end, and I never gave up until the contest was over.'

Jackie Tyrrell represented all that was great about hurling aristocrats, Kilkenny. Timeless virtues like honour, sacrifice, and courage… The Warriors Code.

»——→ A CAT'S LIFE ←——«

HIS CAREER with the Kilkenny senior team spanned 14 seasons from 2003 to 2016. Tyrrell's family was steeped in hurling tradition. His father, Dermot Tyrrell played for the O'Loughlin Gaels club and was an All-Ireland Minor winner in 1973.

Jackie also represented St Kieran's College – where he won back-to-back Leinster medals, before claiming an All-Ireland in 2000. Jackie also represented the James Stephens club at juvenile and underage levels before progressing to the senior ranks in 1999.

Along with an All-Ireland winners' medal in 2005, he also won two Leinster club medals. Tyrrell made his debut on the inter-county scene at the age of 17.

At under-21 level, he had the honour of captaining his side to an All-Ireland title in 2003.

Over the course of the next 14 seasons, he garnered nine All-Ireland medals, the first as a non-playing substitute in 2003. He was an integral member of a record-equalling four championships in-a-row side from 2006 to 2009, and four championships in five seasons between 2011 and 2015. He was an All-Ireland-winning captain in 2006. He also won 11 Leinster medals and six National League medals.

TOMMY WALSH

(Height 5' 7", Weight 14 St)

Decade... 2000s/2010s

(Position... Wing-Back)

CHIEF CHARACTERISTIC... CROKE PARK HIGH-JUMP RECORD HOLDER

TOP ACCOMPLICES... JJ DELANEY, JACKIE TYRRELL,
MICHAEL KAVANAGH, PAUL MURPHY, BRIAN HOGAN, EOIN MURPHY

TOMMY WALSH

*'THE FOLLOWING MORNING, TOMMY WAS UP AT 8AM. HE GOT ONE OF THE
LADS WHO WAS ON THE STAG, BUT WHO WASN'T DRINKING, TO DRIVE HIM
OUT TO THE BEACH IN WEXFORD. HE WAS STILL DRUNK WHEN HE JUMPED
INTO THE FREEZING IRISH SEA. "TONY KELLY ISN'T TRAINING IN THE SEA IN
THE MIDDLE OF NOVEMBER," HE WAS ROARING.'*

– JACKIE TYRRELL

IF you pause for a moment, you can almost hear it whispering through its 200-year-old stately walls. The motto for St Kieran's College is 'Hiems Transit', which is Latin for 'The winter has passed'.

If you linger a little longer until the school bell tolls, you will encounter a rare sight, that is a compelling reminder of what this iconic college is all about. This is a hurling place. The evidence is unashamedly strewn around every nook and cranny.

Scores of discarded hurleys and helmets briefly abandoned, lay proudly against the grainy hallowed walls. Each and every one of them has a story ready to be told. For you cannot walk a single step here without feeling hurling seeping into your bones.

The unfettered ash tree grows to be one of the tallest trees in the forest, up to 30-40m

HARD MAN RATINGS

TOUGHEST:
9.5/10

MEANEST:
8.9/10

SCARIEST:
9.0/10

HARDEST:
19.5/20
☠

TOTAL HARD MAN

46.9/50

(100/130ft). The excelsior component of its scientific name means 'higher' or 'loftier'.

Yet, there is nowhere in Ireland that the mighty ash stands taller than within the most famous hurling nursery on the island.

When the playing ends, academics resume again. The endless relentless cycle of sporting and academic brilliance, dancing through the decades.

St Kieran's College was founded in Kilkenny, in the diocese of Ossory in 1782, and named after St Ciarán of Saigir, Apostle of Osraige, one of the first-ever saints to be born in Ireland.

The college has many famous past pupils including actor Ralph Fiennes, who received two Academy Award nominations.

The place is synonymous with hurling and has enjoyed incredible success in all grades, winning 24 All-Ireland Senior Colleges finals and over 50 Leinster Senior Colleges titles.

Past pupils read like a 'who's who' of hurling's greatest ever players… Henry Shefflin, Eddie Keher, Eoin Kelly of Tipperary, and Nicky Rackard of Wexford. No list of the greatest ever sporting Illuminati in St Kieran's would be complete, however, without Tommy Walsh.

The Tullaroan Tornado was a raging sea of defiance in Brian Cody's brigade for well over a decade, ruling the battlefront by air and by sea.

'Overpower, Overtake, Overcome,' the mantra of tennis giant Serena Williams, summed up Tommy Walsh's unquantifiable talents. Not the biggest, not the strongest, not the quickest, but none of the above really mattered.

He had a huge heart and an unquenchable will. He was a ball of fury coated in the hardest enamel. At times it appeared he carried a step-ladder as he soared above lanky attackers, and extinguished any incoming aerial and ground bombardments.

His career began in sparkling fashion with the under-21 side and a surprise phone call, while he was pucking a ball around the back garden of his family home, made him an offer he couldn't refuse!

'There weren't any mobiles around then; well, I certainly didn't have one anyway,' Walsh explained. 'And the mother called me and said there was someone looking for me on the phone. It was Brian (Cody).

'He just asked me to be involved in a few training sessions, there wasn't any real invitation onto the panel. Luckily enough, I did okay and was kept on the panel for the rest of the year.'

Former past-pupil of St Kieran's and Offaly star, Brian Carroll has a theory on why someone so diminutive ruled the hurling skies as he detailed on *SportsJoe.ie* 'I remember this game we used to play and I'll tell you, this is why Tommy Walsh was so good in the air...

'So, one poor young lad would be asked to strike the ball, there could be 30 or 40 lads under it jumping up and trying to win it. It was all within the rules of the game alright, but Jesus, it was absolute blue murder and if you won the ball, you were the man, like.'

Tom Hogan has spent a lifetime in St Kieran's, as a student in the 70s and as a teacher. Managing the senior hurling team affords him many unique insights into the mindset of a hurling phenomenon, and he concurred with Carroll's observations.

'The very same thing still continues today. Usually, what happens is fellas leave their hurls down and go up and try to catch the ball. One fella hits the ball up among around 30 fellas, and the strongest survives you know!'

{ MARKED BY LARRY CORBETT }

In the 2012, All-Ireland semi-final viewers could well have been advised not to adjust their television sets. Tipperary's celebrated forward, Lar Corbett appeared to abandon his attacking role to mark Tommy Walsh.

It was a tactic Corbett had become acquainted with while in Australia, a vast sporting wasteland of a continent. Given both Tipperary's and Corbett's questionable applications of this rather strange methodology, it's not really hard to see Aussie's comparative lack of sporting successes per capita… on a world stage!

While Tommy was slightly curtailed and bewildered by the 'hurling heist of the century in reverse', the Premier's removal of their chief scoring threat proved a bridge too far, as a baffled Walsh revealed years later.

'I was marking Pa Bourke and I was obviously following him, and Lar was following myself trying to stop me hurling and it was just a massive mistake. I felt for Tipperary.

'He couldn't get on the ball with the tactics that Tipperary was employing so it was frustrating but there were no real verbals. The only verbals that were going on were between me and Jackie. He just kept telling me to look at the scoreboard and forget about it.

'They should have backed Lar Corbett that, whether it was Jackie Tyrrell marking, whether it was JJ (Delaney), whether it was Paul Murphy, he would bring them into the edge of the square, man-on-man, and took him on because Lar could destroy you in a second.'

Tommy Walsh played the game just like he did in the schoolyard. When his career ended, perhaps he laid his hurley against the hallowed walls of the college ready for the next man up in the never-ending cycle of St Kieran's... Royal Hurling Family.

A SAINT AND SCHOLAR'S
»———→ PILGRIMAGE ←———«

AT ST KIERAN'S College in Kilkenny, Walsh established himself as a key member of the senior hurling team. In 1999, he won his first Leinster medal following a 3-13 to 1-11 defeat of Dublin Colleges.

He collected a second Leinster medal in 2000 as Dublin Colleges were again defeated by 2-13 to 1-10. St Flannan's College of Ennis provided the opposition in the subsequent All-Ireland decider, and St Kieran's and Walsh were put to the pin of their collars before prevailing 1-10 to 0-9, earning Tommy a precious Croke Cup All-Ireland medal.

Tommy also played with University College Cork. In 2004, he was a left wing-back as UCC lost to Waterford Institute of Technology in the final of the Fitzgibbon Cup.

Walsh was a member of the Tullaroan minor team and under-21 sides that won county titles, before graduating to the senior ranks. He first played for Kilkenny at the turn of the century when he joined the minor side. He won his sole Leinster medal in 2001 beating Wexford. With the Kilkenny under-21 team, he won his first Leinster medal that year following a 0-12 to 1-4 defeat of Dublin, and an All-Ireland medal against Galway.

At senior level, he was part of the legendary Brian Cody side and mined 10 Leinster titles, nine All-Irelands, seven National Hurling Leagues, and a staggering nine All Star awards.

BIBLIOGRAPHY

Ollie Baker: Extracts from *Clare: Game of my Life* (Hero Books)

Tom Condon: Interview on *the42.ie*

John Connolly: Interviews with Anthony Daly *(Dalo's Podcast)* and *Irish Independent*

Johnny Crowley: Interview in *Cork: Game of my Life*

Anthony Daly: Column in the *Irish Examiner*

JJ Delaney: Interview on *SportsJoe.ie/GAA Hour Live*

Michael Duignan: Extract from *Life, Death and Hurling* by Michael Duignan

Pete Finnerty: Interview in the *Connacht Telegraph*

Jim Greene: Interview in *Waterford: Game of my Life*

Martin Hanamy: Interview in the *Irish Independent*

Declan Hannon: Interview in *The Irish Times*

Christy Heffernan: Interview on *Hoganstand.com*

Stephen Hiney: Interview in the *Irish Independent*

John Horgan: Interview in the *Irish Examiner*

Tony Keady: Interview on *GAA.ie*

Eoin Kelly: Interview in *the42.ie*

John Leahy: Interview in *The Irish Times*

Sylvie Linnane: Interviews from the *Irish Examiner/Blood, Sweat, Triumph and Tears: Tales from the GAA*, by John Scally

Brian Lohan: Interview in *Irish Independent*

Mick Mackey: Extract from *Hell for Leather – A Journey Through Hurling in 100 Games.*

Michael Maher: Interviews in *Waterford Game of my Life/GAA.ie*

Pádraic Maher: Interview in the *Irish Sun*

Olcan McFetridge: Interview in the *Irish News*

Terence McNaughton: Interview in the *Irish News*

Joe Rabbitte: Interview in *Irish Independent*

Nicky Rackard: Memoirs from *The Sunday Press*

Christy Ring: Interview in the *Irish Examiner*

Sean Stack: Interviews from *Clare: Game of my Life*/John Callinan autobiography *'To Play, To Live'*

Jackie Tyrrell: Extract from *The Warrior's Code: Jackie Tyrrell, An Autobiography'/A Hurler's Life* podcast

Tommy Walsh: Jackie Tyrrell autobiography *The Warrior's Code/* interview on *Sports.Joe.ie*/Interview on *Laochra Gael*